A Politics of Impossible Difference

D1568460

A Politics of Impossible Difference

The Later Work of Luce Irigaray

PENELOPE DEUTSCHER

CORNELL UNIVERSITY PRESS

ITHACA AND LONDON

First published 2002 by Cornell University Press

First printing Cornell Paperbacks, 2002.

Printed in the United States of America

Library of Congress Cataloging-in-Publication Data

Deutscher, Penelope
     A politics of impossible difference : the later work of Luce Irigaray
/ Penelope Deutscher.
        p.   cm.
Includes bibliographical references and index.
     ISBN 0-8014-3825-X (cloth : alk. paper) — ISBN 0-8014-8797-8 (pbk. :
alk. paper)
     1. Feminist theory.   2. Feminism.   3. Multiculturalism.   4. Equality.
5. Sex role.   6. Irigaray, Luce.   I. Title.
     HQ1190 .D4897   2002
     305.42'01—dc21

                                                              2002001599

Cornell University Press strives to use environmentally responsible suppliers
and materials to the fullest extent possible in the publishing of its books. Such
materials include vegetable-based, low-VOC inks and acid-free papers that are
recycled, totally chlorine-free, or partly composed of nonwood fibers. For
further information, visit our website at www.cornellpress.cornell.edu.

Cloth printing   10 9 8 7 6 5 4 3 2 1
Paperback printing   10 9 8 7 6 5 4 3 2 1

Contents

Acknowledgments

Thanks first to Eva Ziarek who gave me her time and ideas on early drafts of this book, to Kelly Oliver who first suggested the idea of writing it, and to an anonymous reader for Cornell University Press who made excellent suggestions for revision. I am very grateful for Elizabeth Grosz's classes on Irigaray in the 1980s and for the books and essays by Elizabeth Grosz, Margaret Whitford, Tina Chanter, and many others who have debated Irigaray's work. I have been lucky in the intellectual community of Jennifer Biddle, Victoria Barker, Rosalyn Diprose, Robyn Ferrell, Isabel Karpin, Elizabeth Wilson, Vicki Kirby, Linnell Secomb, Cathy Vasseleu, and Natalie Stoljar, in whose company at different times the ideas in this book developed. I am also grateful to the research students who worked with me on Irigaray—Joanne Faulkner, Evelyn Swinnerton, Fran Gray, and Joanne Purcell—and other graduate, honors, and undergraduate students at the Australian National University who were so often the best part of the working week. Paul Patton, Moira Gatens, Genevieve Lloyd, Elizabeth Grosz, Margaret Whitford, and Dorothea Olkowski took the time to support research grants leading to the finished book—thank you.

Thanks also to several institutions who hosted papers on Irigaray and provided me with debate about them. I thank Kelly Oliver and the Women Studies center at the University of Texas at Austin; Eva Ziarek and the Department of English at the University of Notre Dame; Ann Smock and the Department of French, University of California at Berkeley;

Michelle Boulous Walker and the students' society at the Department of Philosophy, University of Queensland; Hugh Silverman and the participants in the International Philosophy Seminar, Alto Adige, Italy (who generously welcomed me to the luxury of a two-week seminar on Irigaray); Laurent Milesi and the center for Critical and Cultural Theory, Cardiff University; Simon Critchley and the Department of Philosophy, University of Essex; and panel participants and organizers at many IAPLs and SPEPs. At Cornell University Press, my thanks to Catherine Rice and Susan Tarcov. Valerie Hazel's index was much appreciated.

Finally, my thanks to some institutions, friends, and family in whose company, offices, or homes parts of this were written: the Australian National University; the American Academy in Rome Northwestern University; Madeleine Fava; Irene von Moos; Sandi Buckley and Brian Massumi; Elizabeth Wilson; Pat Morton and John Dutton; Kelly Oliver; Don and Pat Jasper; Rosanne Kennedy; Lisabeth During and Ross Poole; Victoria Barker and Tim Burgess; my parents, Pauline Payne and Max Deutscher; my terrific sister Pepita Payne; and my dear partner Michael Jasper.

My thanks to the editors for their comments about and improvement of the following essays. While none have been incorporated in their original form, I have freely drawn on them.

"'The Only Diabolical Thing about Women': Luce Irigaray on Divinity," *Hypatia: A Journal of Feminist Philosophy* 9 (4) (1994): 88–111.

"Mourning the Other: Cultural Cannibalism and the Politics of Friendship (Jacques Derrida and Luce Irigaray)," *differences: a journal of feminist cultural studies* 10 (3) (1998): 159–84.

"French Feminist Philosophers on Law and Public Policy: Michèle Le Doeuff and Luce Irigaray," *Australian Journal of French Studies* 34 (1) (1997): 24–44.

"Luce Irigaray's Sexuate Rights and the Politics of Performativity," in *Transformations: Thinking through Feminism,* ed. Sara Ahmed, Jane Kilby, Celia Lury, Maureen McNeil, and Beverley Skeggs (London: Routledge, 2000), 92–108.

"Is This a Question of Can Saying Make It So? The Declaration of Irigarayan Sexuate Rights," in *Feminist Perspectives on Law and Theory,* ed. Janice Richardson and Ralph Sandland (London: Cavendish, 2000), 71–87.

"Irigaray Anxiety: Luce Irigaray and Her Ethics for Improper Selves," *Radical Philosophy* 80 (1996): 6–16.

"Love Discourses, Sexed Discourses? Luce Irigaray's *Être deux,*" *Continental Philosophy Review* 33 (2) (2000): 113–31.

I gratefully acknowledge the Australian Research Council for the award of a large A.R.C. grant, and the Australian National University for internal faculty grants supporting this project.

PENELOPE DEUTSCHER

A Politics of Impossible Difference

Introduction

In 1999, feminist political philosopher Susan Moller Okin asked a contro-versial question, "Is Multiculturalism Bad for Women?" In the same year, French feminist philosopher Luce Irigaray answered "no." Her 1999 work *Between East and West* argues that the politics of feminism and the politics of multiculturalism are intrinsically linked. Multicultural politics needs feminism, and feminism is never not about cultural difference.

The following chapters reconstruct Irigaray's theoretical approach to the question of feminism's relation to multiculturalism: a feminism em-phasizing sexual difference. Feminisms promoting equality and those promoting difference are often seen as opposed. Irigaray does not accept this opposition. In chapters 1 and 7, I will make reference to a formulation proposed by Joan Scott: perhaps equality is not the means to achieve equality, nor difference the means to achieve difference. As I shall argue in chapter 1, Irigaray does not think women's equality can be satisfactorily achieved with equality politics. She argues for the affirmation of sexual difference as an alternative basis for equality. However, she does not argue for a politics of recognition whose role would be to affirm a sexual difference taken to precede the time of that recognition. I shall consider the alternative proposed by Irigaray: a politics anticipating difference.

Throughout much of Irigaray's corpus, she has seemed to neglect issues of race and cultural difference in favor of sexual difference. Among her later work, *Between East and West* offers an Irigarayan approach to multi-culturalism. The fact that a feminist who affirms sexual difference also en-

1

dorses multicultural politics might confirm the worst suspicions of some critics about multiculturalism. In fact, Irigarayan and multicultural politics have long incurred very similar criticisms. It is said that embracing the language of cultural or sex specificity is naïve. It is a language on which those who would justify inequitable treatment have always drawn. This study of Irigarayan politics embarks from the controversy surrounding Susan Okin's concerns about the double standards of multiculturalism.

Concerns about a politics respectful of difference frequently target its inconsistent application in the hands of those who espouse it. Why did the French public demand "flexibility and respect for diversity" for the Magrébin girls who attended French schools in Muslim headscarves but remain indifferent to other issues such as the practice of polygamous marriage and clitoridectomy in France? asks Susan Okin (1999, 9). Michèle Le Doeuff has noted France's willingness to intervene in the affairs of other nations if there are economic or political benefits. This willingness must discredit its consistent lack of interest in the rights of immigrant women and foreign women in France, all the more because this lack of interest is given the political alibi of respect for cultural difference.

In addition to the charges of inconsistency and naiveté, I want now to consider some of the other main feminist criticisms of multicultural politics, before asking how Luce Irigaray may be situated in these debates. Okin (1999) has argued that group rights are potentially antifeminist, particularly where the male members of a group are "in a position to determine and articulate the group's beliefs, practices and interests" (12). She claims that the politics of difference tends to pay more attention to differences between groups. The result is a homogenizing account of the identity and culture of a group to which special rights might be ascribed. Groups contain diverse members and hierarchical power relations. Only a disingenuous politics of difference overlooks the differences within the group in the name of "respect for its difference." Moreover, most cultures have so consistently been patriarchal, she argues, that respect for cultural difference really amounts to respect for patriarchal culture. In fact, she asks whether it is not the very patriarchy of the culture in question that is indirectly perceived as meriting specific consideration in the name of the politics of difference. Respecting the patriarchy of nonwestern cultures is, she argues, no better than respecting the patriarchy of western cultures. Okin concludes that there is no reason to think that respect for multiculturalism will be good for women, and perhaps every reason to think it will be bad.

Okin uses the presence of women to remind us that a culture is not a univocal or self-identical entity. It contains its own hierarchies and exclusions, as well as being marginalized by other cultures. Emphasizing the diverse women at the heart of a culture that might merit respect or special legal consideration under the politics of multiculturalism is for Okin a means of undermining its apparent univocality.

A culture is never homogeneous. Notice, however, Okin's assumption that women are not "culture": they lie within a culture. A possibility not raised by Okin is briefly mentioned in James Tully's book *Strange Multiplicities*. What if women constituted cultural groups to whom the politics of multiculturalism might potentially apply (rather than just being considered parts of other cultural groups)? What should we say of cases where it seems that women "speak and act in their own ways" (Tully 1995, 178)? Tully offers the suggestion of Carol Gilligan that western women might tend toward a "care" rather than an abstract, principled approach to moral dilemmas. Will Kymlicka (1999, 33) asks if feminist arguments for "affirmative action, women-only classrooms, gender-specific prohibitions on pornography, gender-specific health programs and the like" are not in fact a form of group rights.

How might Okin respond? Perhaps with the view that considering women as a cultural group homogenizes them. The differences among women are suppressed in the name of the politics of difference. A multiculturalism that treated women as a cultural group would certainly be bad for some women, she might argue, most obviously those excluded from the beliefs, practices, and interests considered to pertain to women as a cultural group and revalued as such. Also, accommodating the special needs of different cultural groups of women might lead to a problem highlighted by Diana Fuss (1989, 104)—the fragmentation of identity into infinitesimal plural identities. Such fragmentation displaces, splinters, but does not correct the generalizing presuppositions of identity politics. Bonnie Honig (1999) points out that this problem extends to group rights. What happens when special rights are ascribed "to national minorities . . . immigrant groups and ethnic groups, but also to cultural and religious groups until virtually all of the population is covered in one way or another by some cultural exemption"? (35–36).

These are possible arguments. But Okin does not consider that the special rights for women mentioned by Kymlicka should be considered a form of cultural group rights. Interestingly, this is because she defines cultural group rights in terms of their disavowed internal hierarchies. In other words, she assumes that affirmative action, women-only classrooms, gender-specific prohibitions on pornography and gender-specific health programs do not introduce or reflect differential power relations among women: "The few special rights that women claim qua women do not give more powerful women the right to control less powerful women. In contrast, cultural group rights do often (in not-so-obvious ways) reinforce existing hierarchies" (Okin 1999, 131). One sees the argument go awry. The special rights claimed by women do not reflect hierarchies among women, so they represent women, but not women as a group. Women are not a group, because groups are hierarchical. But an argument more consistent with Okin's position might potentially question "women's rights" as vigorously as it questions "multicultural rights" the moment that it perceives the presence of differential power relations among women. It is easy enough to argue that the priorities of affirmative action, women-only classrooms, gender-specific prohibitions on pornography, and gender-specific health programs, do introduce and reflect hierarchies among women. Women of different classes, races, and cultural backgrounds assess and are situated by these rights very differently.

Okin does endorse a politics of recognition to the extent that she argues that women of all ages (and presumably of other kinds of diversities) should contribute to debates about group rights. Nor does she deny that social institutional structures crucially recognize individual subjects in their negotiation of identity. But she argues for "a form of multiculturalism that gives the issues of gender and other intragroup inequalities their due—that is to say, a multiculturalism that effectively treats all persons as each other's moral equals" (131). To the extent that both assume that cultural groups have specific customs and histories that are betrayed by a blanket legal treatment, Okin and Tully share an understanding of the status of recognition. In chapter 2, I ask what role French feminist Luce Irigaray might have in these discussions of women's possible cultural specificity. Reflection on the work of Irigaray clarifies something shared by Okin and Tully: the supposition that the culture entitled to "special *group* rights or privileges" (Okin 1999, 11) must exist before that legal or institutional recognition in order to have any kind of legitimate claim.

Okin's argument that multiculturalism might be bad for women has been widely criticized by respondents. Among the critics, Honig (1999, 37, 38) points out that Okin renders patriarchy a univocal force despite her own argument against the homogenization of "culture" and also that she seems to assume western liberal regimes are less patriarchal than other cultures. Azizah Y. al-Hibri (1999, 41, 44), Sander Gilman (1999, 54–55), and Homi Bhabha (1999, 80–82) have added concerns that she stereotypes the practices of a foreign other deemed barbaric as well as condescending to nonwestern women.

Agreeing with these criticisms, I draw attention to a noteworthy supposition of Okin's argument. She resists concepts of multiculturalism governed by the idea that conservation of tradition is an intrinsic good. Doesn't her argument provoke this question: What would it mean to support a multicultural politics that affirmed the specific needs and rights of cultures to whose articulation girls and women of different generations actively contributed? Any group's beliefs, practices, and interests are, as Okin argues, internally contested. Multiculturalist politics needs to respect rights and identities that are newly constituted and recreated and those that are to be determined in the future. It cannot affirm only tradition and history. A culture's right to transform its tradition and history must also be affirmed without this transformation becoming a further excuse for disenfranchisement and inequality. Yael Tamir (1999, 48) draws attention to the western romance about multiculturalism, which depicts indigenous and immigrant cultures as authentic and natural, in need of cultural preservation. Many declarations of indigenous group rights affirm the right to transformation as much as the right to conservation. To the right to traditional "languages, histories, stories, oral traditions," law ("the right to our own law, customs and traditions"), and culture ("the right to our unique cultural traditions and customs"), Australian Aboriginal activist Patrick Dodson (2000) adds the right to self-determination: "Aboriginal peoples have the right to self-determination; a right to negotiate our political status and to pursue economic, social and cultural development" (271). The right to cultural change complements the right to cultural conservation, and many Australian indigenous activists have emphasized this strongly in the articulation of the right to self-determination. In the words of Jeremy Webber (2000), "[I]ndigenous societies cannot be wished back into the past" (88). It is often a western cultural romance that—ambivalently—performs that wishing.

This raises the question of what kind of legal or public institutionalization could be given to a culture's right to transform and contest those identities for which legal recognition is also sought. Can the legal protection of rights be justified in terms of its recognition of possible future identities the law can only imagine? Can the law anticipate possible future identities without attributing fixity or unity to them? This book considers Luce Irigaray's argument for legal rights recognizing the anticipated transformation of identity. Susan Okin asks us to imagine the renegotiation of what we name a "culture" by the diverse women at its heart. This suggestion of Okin's is more radical than her own text seems to appreciate. According to what kind of philosophical basis might one understand such transformation and the possible rights associated with it?

I look at Irigaray's concept of the legal recognition of possible special rights and privileges of identities not legitimated by tradition or history. Such identities are not affirmed arbitrarily. Instead, Irigaray's politics is based in a notion of impossible difference. What concepts of identity and difference have most repeatedly been excluded—rendered most impossible—in a given culture, context, or history? Against what possible alternative identities have hegemonic forces most concentrated? Proposing a methodology for the interpretation of overdetermined, repeatedly consolidated exclusion of certain kinds of alternative possible identities, Irigaray reinterprets this pattern of exclusion as a kind of anticipation. She imagines the possibility of legal protection of the possible identities and traditions anticipated by diverse groups within a legal or institutional system. Tradition is one of the few means we have of affirming difference and its right to special legal and institutional treatment. But multiculturalism can involve not only a respect for traditional identities but also respect for identities newly negotiated and contested by diverse intracultural groups.

This book asks what philosophical basis might be given to the rights associated with an institutional openness to that reinvention. In relation to the politics of recognition, this book is about another difference, anticipatory difference. An indication of alternative possible identities can usefully be located within the exclusions and constituted impossibilities of tradition and history. Irigaray offers this kind of methodology in her discussion of sexual difference. In chapter 10, I discuss the use of an Irigarayan methodology for the analysis of impossible difference in relation to her treatment of multiculturalism. However, I shall argue that it is not in Irigaray's own recent comments about multiculturalism that we find the best resources for a contribution to this question. For this reason, I interpret her approach to multiculturalism in the light of conceptualizations of the impossibility of difference that she has offered throughout her career, not only in the most recent work.

This book reads Irigaray from the optic of many of her colleagues, French and American. I read her from the perspective of Michèle Le Doeuff, Drucilla Cornell, Judith Butler, and Gayatri Spivak. I situate Irigaray's work in the context of contemporary debates about the politics of performativity, recognition, multiculturalism, pro-diversity, and identity politics. I propose dialogues between her work and contemporary American feminist, political, legal, poststructuralist, and postcolonial theory. I also read her from the perspective of Jacques Derrida's later work. More than Lyotard, Deleuze, and most Anglo-American and French feminist theorists, Derrida has been an important interlocutor for Irigaray. Throughout her work, and up until her most recent publications, she has repudiated what she takes to be the negativity of deconstruction. Several chapters interrogate further this relationship in a debate whose possibility Irigaray herself has raised on many occasions. I think Irigaray's work, if not Irigaray herself, is fundamentally sympathetic to such a reflection. Irigaray affirms the "impossible" status of new, non-self-identical identities to come, and of the rights associated with them.

1

Sexual Difference as a Basis of Equality

An Introduction to Irigarayan Politics

> How can the double demand—for both equality and difference—
> be articulated?
>
> Luce Irigaray, *This Sex Which Is Not One*

In 1949 when Simone de Beauvoir's *The Second Sex* was first published, there was no radical feminist movement in France.[1] Elaine Marks and Isabelle de Courtivron (1981, 35) have described how this changed only in the late sixties.[2] Beauvoir depicts the 1940s as a period of great hostility to feminist ideas, despite the fact that women had just won the vote in 1944. Albert Camus, she recounts in an interview with Alice Schwartzer, "bellowed, 'you have made a laughing stock of the French male!'" She recalls, "[S]ome professors threw the book across their offices because they couldn't bear to read it. . . . Even the Communists tore me to shreds. They accused me of being a 'petite bourgeoise,' and told me, 'You see, what you are saying really doesn't mean a thing to working-class women in Billancourt'" (Schwartzer 1984, 72).

Despite the accusations that her writing was irrelevant, Simone de Beauvoir's feminism was directly concerned with the social, historical, and economic circumstances of women and practical affairs affecting French women of the period. Two decades later, Beauvoir came to be involved in a feminist movement that focused on abortion rights, marriage and divorce laws, the restriction of women to low-grade jobs, and other persistent inequalities between men and women.[3] But as Beauvoir's feminism became increasingly practical, many French feminist intellectuals in the 1970s were turning to new modes of literary production. The "new French feminisms"[4] have often been seen as removed from practical matters. Far more than the work of Beauvoir, the earliest work of Hélène

7

Cixous, Julia Kristeva, and Luce Irigaray could easily have incurred the charge of irrelevance. As Margaret Whitford (1991a, 11) points out, Luce Irigaray's work has been seen as inaccessible and elitist. Similar charges have been leveled at the two other main theorists with whom Irigaray's work has been associated, Cixous and Kristeva.

It is true that the work of each of these writers, particularly early in their careers, is often difficult to access. It has a technical and literary style that seems to restrict its readership. The references of all three theorists can be specialist, ranging from the history of philosophy to Lacanian psycho-analysis. In 1949, Beauvoir considered that the status of women would improve with a change in their economic and social circumstances and with their recognition as equals. The concern of some contemporary French feminist theorists has been to modify signifying spaces and sym-bolic structures. Voicing the concerns of certain readers, Claire Duchen (1987, 12) notes that French feminism has often been seen as "preoccupied with questions of psychoanalysis and language to the exclusion of practi-cally everything else." Whereas Beauvoir fought for equality between men and women, some contemporary French feminists have broken with the ideal of equality in favor of affirming sexual difference. Many others have been resistant to this development. Christine Delphy and Michèle Le Doeuff have been consistently wary of so-called feminism of difference. For Le Doeuff (1991), it is no better than a neofemininity, "based on the idea that women's true femininity is suppressed" (224).

Beauvoir herself was suspicious of the promotion of sexual difference by some contemporary feminists. In her view, this was a return to the old idealization of the eternal feminine. She protested, "[W]e shouldn't go to the other extreme and say that a woman has a particular closeness with the earth, that she feels the rhythm of the moon, the ebb and flow of the tides. . . . Or that she has more soul or is less destructive by nature etc. No! If there is a grain of truth in that, it is not because of our nature, but is rather the result of our conditions of existence" (Schwartzer 1984, 78). Beauvoir was disturbed to see some feminists apparently return to tradi-tional reifications of difference that long provided the alibi for prohibi-tions on women's full participation in public life. Such a feminism seemed to undermine women's basic concerns: equal rights and pay, abortion and reproductive rights, adequate childcare, representation at senior levels of employment, government, and the public sphere.

Michèle Le Doeuff (1991) has argued for more attention to the contexts in which arguments for difference are strategically deployed, particularly in public policy contexts. Sometimes legislators "forbid," sometimes they "authorize," "without necessarily 'making the connection'" (301, transla-tion modified). For example, very limited public funds are made available to support the lives of immigrant women in France. State indifference is often justified with a language of respect for difference. Le Doeuff asks whether the governmental avoidance of the issue of clitoridectomy in France is anything better than a concern to protect trade relations with Central and West Africa (298). In this case, the government seems to "authorize" difference. This glosses over the frequency with which it "forbids" difference. For example, there is little evidence of respect for cultural difference when pressure is exerted on "developing" countries to conform with the economic precepts of the World Bank.

Le Doeuff thinks that respect for cultural and sexual difference is regularly selective, opportunist, and cynical. But arguments for equality, no less than arguments for difference, can be used selectively and opportunistically. The obvious example is the use of policies of "equal treatment" to maintain social inequality. Arguments against affirmative action are often justified by reference to the politics of fair and equal treatment for all. Neither the language of equality nor that of difference is specially secure from rerouting to cynical purposes.

This does not answer the question of why some feminist intellectuals have come to favor the language of difference in particular. Reflecting on the work of Luce Irigaray is a means of understanding this turn. Why and how did Irigaray attempt to transform a philosophy emphasizing sexual difference into the basis for pro-feminist social and institutional reform? Why did she and some other French feminist intellectuals turn away from the language of equal rights self-evident to the feminisms of most earlier historical periods? Why does Luce Irigaray speak with only muted support for the "struggle for equal wages and social rights, against discrimination in employment and education, and so forth" (Irigaray 1985c, 165–66)?

In an early text, *This Sex Which Is Not One,* Irigaray questions the language of equality although she rarely questions the worth of its practical gains. Some might consider it impossible to challenge the language without undermining the gains. But Irigaray thinks we can endorse political equality while maintaining concerns about its terms. When Irigaray makes statements such as "[W]omen merely 'equal' to men would be 'like them,' therefore not women" (Irigaray 1985c, 166), she thinks we should be concerned about the conceptual paucity of equality. What language do we have in which to theorize social change? she asks. Is that language optimally adequate to imagining new and diverse possibilities of human and sexual existence? If we do not attend to new concepts for human existence, will our utopias be limited in their vision? Would new and more diverse possibilities open up from utopias theorized with a broader basis of invention? Could such inventions play an important role in our approach to legal and other practical reform?

Since Beauvoir's feminism aimed for equality between the sexes,[5] one can understand her wariness of alternative models of feminism. She thought a politics of difference would be bound to reify the traditional connotations of femininity, such as the emotional, the natural, the empathic, the passive, the bodily, the irrational. But Irigaray (2002) explains that she has no wish to reify sexual difference in traditional terms: "I am not referring here to a bad use of sexual difference, which leaves woman the guardian of the pole 'nature' in a unity of which man secures the pole 'culture'" (136, translation modified). Irigaray thinks a feminist politics of difference could contribute to new understandings of both equality and difference. For this reason she rejects, to some extent, the choice between these apparently opposed politics. She argues for an equality based in the affirmation of difference.

Joan Scott (1996) has described "the apparent need to choose sameness *or* difference (which can never be satisfied by either alternative)" as symptomatic of the problems faced by feminism in relation to its conceptual heritage. Feminism must both draw on and challenge this heritage (173–74). As I shall argue in chapter 7, Irigaray thinks that sameness can be satisfied only by difference. Interestingly, she also argues that difference can be satisfied only by sameness. Both difference and sameness need to be reconceived to make sense of this proposal. Her project rejects the conceptual paucity arising from the stark alternative between the ideals of equality and difference.

Irigaray's view is that one can pursue political and social equality while enriching the conceptual language with which such an equality is formulated. Equality need not be pursued with the language of equality. To fairly appraise her resistance to the latter, one should place it in the context of her commitment to equal rights and social freedoms for women:

> Simone de Beauvoir and Jean-Paul Sartre were always wary of psychoanalysis. I am trained as a psychoanalyst and that's important . . . for theorizing identity as sexual. I also have a background in philosophy. . . . [B]eing educated in both of these fields has meant that my thought on women's liberation has gone beyond simply a quest for equality between the sexes. That doesn't stop me from joining and promoting public demonstrations for women to gain this or that right: the right to contraception, abortion, legal aid in cases of public or domestic violence, the right to freedom of expression—etc., demonstrations generally supported by feminists. (Irigaray 1993b, 11)[6]

Irigaray goes on to explain that these rights signify in her mind not a right to equality but a right to sexual difference. This presupposes that po-

litical programs for social change must be concerned with ingrained signifying and symbolic structures for sexed identity and the problem of their
transformation. To understand her work, it is important to understand
this presupposition.

Like Beauvoir, Irigaray asks how women and femininity have been represented throughout western history. Where Beauvoir focuses more on
economic and literary history, Irigaray focuses on the history of philosophy. Both feminists argue that women have been the other throughout
western history. Women have been considered the exception or supple-
ment, not the norm, in discussions of the human. Also, women have been
associated with the privation of masculine qualities and capacities such as
reason and discipline. Women have been the other insofar as they have
been represented as "not-men." In this sense, Irigaray suggests women
have served as negative mirrors sustaining masculine identity. Cultural
and historical understandings of masculine identity have contrasted it to
traditional representations of femininity, with femininity understood as
an atrophy or lack of masculine qualities. The rationality of man has been
opposed to the emotionality of woman.

Irigaray's conclusion is that this long history inflects the terms in which
women are able to take up positions in the public sphere. They exchange
their role as not-men for that of like-men. We need an increased sensitivity
to the conceptual terms in which women's participation in the public
sphere is implicitly understood:

> In concrete terms, that means that women must of course continue to
> struggle for equal wages and social rights, against discrimination in em-
> ployment and education, and so forth. But that is not enough: women
> merely "equal" to men would be "like them," therefore not women. Once
> more, the difference between the sexes would be in that way cancelled out,
> ignored, papered over. So it is essential for women amongst themselves to
> invent new modes of organization, new forms of struggle, new challenges.
> (Irigaray 1985c, 165–66)

Are women's politics satisfactory when the language and ideals of traditionally male spheres are adopted? "When [women's] movements aim
simply for a change in the distribution of power, leaving intact the power
structure itself, then they are resubjecting themselves, deliberately or not,
to a phallocratic order. This latter gesture must of course be denounced,
and with determination, since it may constitute a more subtly concealed
exploitation of women" (Irigaray 1985c, 81). Irigaray concludes that this
"explains certain difficulties encountered by the liberation movements. If
women allow themselves to be caught in the trap of power, in the game of

authority, if they allow themselves to be contaminated by the 'paranoid' operations of masculine politics, they have nothing more to say or do *as women"* (166).

Such passages are widely interpreted as indicating Irigaray's view that games of power, authority, and rationality are inherently masculine and should be spurned by women. I do not consider this to be her position. It is uncontroversial that power, authority, and rationality have historically been associated with masculinity. Eschewing a pursuit of anything that has historically been associated with male authority would be untenable for women, and hardly a coherent political position. But it would also be naïve to think that women's exercising of varying degrees of power, authority, and rationality is immune from their historical associations with masculinity. In this sense, women are taking up a position of symbolic "equivalence" to masculinity.

The second concept that calls for preliminary comment is Irigaray's reference to women's having nothing to say or do *"as women."* This conveys the same idea again: women may be engaging as political agents, but they are doing so as male equivalents. Much of her philosophical work has relied on a complex understanding of the expression *"as women."* Does it indicate Irigaray's view that there is an essential or appropriate way that we could easily identify or retrieve for women to act or speak as women? No. Irigaray argues that we can give no content to the idea of women acting as women. She does not credit historical views of femininity as opposite or complement (emotional, empathizing, compassionate, maternal or indeed unstable, excitable, unreliable . . .). What then does Irigaray mean by the assertion that women cannot speak or act as women? Not that this idea has content but that it does not. There is no "as women" (except in the traditional sense to which Irigaray gives no credence) in terms of which women can speak or act. Once one accepts that there is no "as women" embodied in women's historical options of male equivalent, opposite, or complement, it is clear that acting or speaking as a woman is an impossible gesture.[7] Irigaray's reference to our inability to speak or act "as women" does not reflect any lack of sympathy for suspicions voiced (for example) by Hazel Barnes (2000) about beliefs in "innate differences between male and female; this, after all, was the assumption supporting women's oppression" (35). Irigaray (2002) explains, "I am thinking of a relation between the sexes in which woman and man each have a different subjectivity, based notably on both a relational identity of their own and a relation to language of their own" (136–37). This does not mean that she thinks women and men have different subjectivities. Rather, her concern is that we have made it impossible that they could.

Are feminist aspirations legible only in terms of equality with men? She explains, "[T]o demand equality as women is, it seems to me, a mistaken expression of a real objective. The demand to be equal presupposes a point of comparison. To whom or to what do women want to be equalized? To men? To a salary? To a public office? To what standard? Why not to themselves?" (Irigaray 1993b, 12). It is clear in such passages that she interrogates the conceptual terms according to which women enter the public sphere and men remain in it. If the rights many women won in the twentieth century allowed them to take on men's skins (1994, 79), the formulation of those rights has not sufficiently fostered new identity formations for women and men.

There are also practical concerns arising from the fact that women had not contributed to the formation and development of the public institutions they entered in the twentieth century (Irigaray 1993b, 54). Irigaray comments about "having equal numbers of men and women in all sectors of social activity in order to get them to progress. Of course on one level this is a totally desirable solution. But it's not enough . . . because the current social order, and that includes the order defining occupations, is not neutral when viewed in terms of the difference of the sexes. Working conditions and production techniques are not equally designed nor equally applied with respect to sexual difference. The targets and modes of work are not equally defined by, nor for, women and men. At best, therefore, equality is achieved on pay" (84, translation modified).

The apparent achievement of equality can sometimes disguise an actual undermining of women. Irigaray gives several examples. The entry of women into a sphere from which they have been excluded can occur at the expense of other, less privileged women. The successes of some women in certain fields should not blind one to concern for the status of women more widely. Even the success of women in certain spheres is often double-edged. If it is as the symbolic equivalent of men that women enter the spheres from which they were once excluded, this may not undercut simultaneous connotations of women as the other. A talented woman might be hired with alacrity, only to find her subsequent pregnancy the source of her colleagues' irritation. She feels she should take care to avoid seeming impassioned in meetings, or finds herself readily perceived as manipulative. This phenomenon allows for a clarification of Irigaray's point that women can enter the public sphere only as male equivalents. One can criticize this argument for its overly static and passive notion of our relation to cultural norms. It is not possible to adopt those norms without also perverting and transforming them. Surely Irigaray is wrong to deemphasize such inevitable transformation. A woman acting as male equivalent in the public sphere is not the same as a man acting as a man in the public sphere. In adopting the position, surely the woman also transforms and destabilizes suppositions surrounding it? I think Irigaray's point is that the woman nonetheless pays the price for ambivalent and contradictory interpretations of her presence. Her transformation of the role she adopts may be destabilizing, and perhaps usefully so. But the highly ambivalent interpretations of her presence do speak to the fact that she is uncomfortably perceived as both a woman and the equivalent of a man. Loudly supportive of equal treatment, the workplace is nonetheless quick to assume in the most stereotyped terms that women are different. Meanwhile it incorporates women only insofar as they fit traditionally male work arrangements and workplace practices. The public sector assumes, uneasily, that women are both equal and different. Public policy has, in many countries, achieved equal pay for some and equality of some work conditions. But it has engaged only inadequately with the cultural change associated with women's entry into traditionally male spheres.

The frequent associations of French feminism with feminism of difference may give an impression that France has progressed beyond equality politics. But issues of equality have taken on increasing urgency in French feminist debate and in Luce Irigaray's own work. If she laments the impossibility of affirming sexual difference, that lament is inflected with her concern about the apparent failures to achieve equality. While the proportion of women in the French workforce is high, the proportion of women at the most influential and symbolic levels in France (law, politics, public advisory committees, senior positions in business and government) is low. A common misconception is that French women have achieved their rights. The perception that feminism is outdated is stronger in France than in many other western countries.[8] There has been little support for such policies as affirmative action that (for all their problems) have enjoyed a reasonable period of political currency elsewhere. Support has been sporadic and often directed by international and European pressure.[9] Sustaining the debate around equality is a real imperative in the recent French context, Irigaray agrees.

Far from there having been sufficient progress on women's rights in France, Le Doeuff (1991) has speculated that perhaps "the second sex . . . never makes any certain gains" (243). Apparent achievements of the late twentieth century have often been weakened by other factors. Women have independent salaries but may retain a highly vulnerable relationship to family, employer, or institutional pressures. Each gain seems undermined in some way. French abortion laws remain much more restrictive than those of countries such as England and the Netherlands.[10] When women gain economic independence or access to legal abortion, working-class or immigrant women do not (Le Doeuff 1979, 56). Le Doeuff and other French feminists have noted the widespread belief that abortion has been legalized in France. In fact, French women gained a unilateral "exemption" from the illegality of abortion. That exemption technically reconfirms the illegality of abortion under French law (Le Doeuff 1991, 247).[11] Equality is consistently inconsistent. Inevitably, the vaunted commitment by the French state to achieving an equal number of women politicians was accompanied by its indifference to the conditions of women within its borders in many critical ways.

Equal pay for equal work is far from being achieved, writes Irigaray. Unemployment percentages and full-time as opposed to part-time employment percentages differ between the sexes, as do redundancy levels and union protection. Women are concentrated in underpaid, devalued sectors of the workforce that require less qualification. Sectors of the workplace retain a masculine-centered cultural ambiance and codes of conduct (Irigaray 1993b, 143–53). She writes, "[T]heoretically, women enjoy certain rights that they did not previously have regarding the acquisition or ownership of property. But . . . to assert that men and women are now equal or well on the way to becoming so has served almost as the opiate of the people for some time now. Men and women are not equal. . . . Take the work context, for example, where an employer might hasten to claim that he doesn't want to employ women because they make for a less stable workforce. Then he will agree to take them on provided he can underpay them" (Irigaray 1993b, 77, translation modified).

"Of course," says Le Doeuff (1991) dryly, "we rejoice when careers in the judiciary, or administration, places at the *grandes écoles* or work as a sculptor open up to women" (243). Nevertheless, one needs to be circumspect about such successes. They cannot be incorporated into a simple narrative of continuous progress: "[W]e no longer see these advances as irreversible steps foreshadowing other, vaster mutations" (243). For any success that might encourage, it seems that there are innumerable small truths that simultaneously discourage: "[L]ike harbor pools governed by a complex systems of locks and sluices, particular social spaces open to us and then close off again" (243). Irigaray agrees. Women working in public institutions "are often restricted in how far they can go in their career. Very few women reach the highest posts and they pay dearly for it, in one way or another" (Irigaray 1993b, 53). Thus Le Doeuff's pessimistic diagnosis (1991) that "it is as though defense mechanisms quieter and more complex than brutal exclusion . . . gradually gained in effect" (243).

Le Doeuff has often compared attitudes toward equal opportunity in France unfavorably with attitudes in England and America. Until recently, France was particularly hostile to the affirmative action and quota systems for equal representation of women and men in public life. More than 90 percent of the Assemblée générale has been male (Le Doeuff 1993a, 178). Sexual harassment is not a topic of concern in French universities as it is elsewhere. Le Doeuff (1992) notes that "in Great Britain, the Royal Society itself campaigns against sexism in textbooks. . . . [A]nglophones and the Quebecois are surprised at how behind the times we [French] are" (34n). France has resisted the adoption of nonsexist language modification longer than England, America, and Australia. This resistance prompted an acid essay by Le Doeuff (1992) on the persistence of male-biased rhetoric at the Centre nationale de la rercherche scientifique (the national research body), e.g., *"les hommes au C.N.R.S.," "la fraternité des équipes," "l'exigence de ces hommes," "l'égalité des hommes," "les sciences de l'homme"* (21). In response, she protests against "the denial of mixity: the adoption of a language that symbolically ignores the existence of women where they work and exist" (Le Doeuff 1993b, 127). Similarly, Irigaray notes the frequent public and media erasure of women in professional spheres. They are described as "ancien secrétaire général . . . député européen" rather than as "ancienne secrétaire générale," "députée européenne," or "député européenne" (Irigaray 1994, 50, 52). As Le Doeuff (1992) comments, "[C]ertainly, a lexical modification is not enough to guarantee the inclusion of women within humanity. But the resistance to every attempt at language modification is an extremely bad sign" (6). This resistance has occurred in a country priding itself on its egalitarian traditions and its full integration of women into the public sphere.

In analyzing the logic of public institutions, Le Doeuff argues that the contradiction between the rhetoric of good intentions toward women and the real undermining of women's social conditions is often no accident. Our attention is deflected from the frequently regressive nature of public policy by the seemingly worthy intentions of the state (or the media, or the education board, and so on). Consider the surprising turnaround of the French government on parity (the enforcement of equal numbers of women and men politicians in municipal and state government), given its long-standing hostility to affirmative action policies.[12] Le Doeuff's criticism of the parity policy surprised many. But she pointed out that the policy was serving as a blind for the real issues—such as government neglect of immigrant women in France. In any case, women were particularly encouraged into the least popular area, municipal politics. And despite the governmental support for parity, explanations were soon to be heard from ministers that they supported "flexibility" in the application of the policy.[13]

Le Doeuff and Irigaray are two French feminists who have offered acute analyses of the limitations of women's equality in France, despite the social progress of the twentieth century. Most would assume that an ever more rigorous equality politics is the obvious solution to the defects. However, Irigaray's concerns led her to a different conclusion. She came to ask whether the language of equality really was the optimal strategy. What if the very philosophy of equality implicitly presupposes women's inequality and the inequality of other groups? Is a more extensive reconsideration of the basis for legal and social reform unthinkable?

Two hundred years of the postrevolutionary egalitarian political tradition in France grounds its historical resistance to politics affirming sexual or cultural difference.[14] Rather than simply affirming difference, Irigaray proposes that the long-standing oppositions between the discourses of equality and difference be challenged. She favors attempts to theorize differences anew as alternative conceptual frameworks for equality. Many critics consider that Irigaray's turn to the language of difference is not justified by the failures of equality politics. But it is useful to reflect on Irigaray's broader claim. One must interrogate the conceptual basis on which women and other historically marginalized groups enter spheres previously closed to them. As Moira Gatens (1996) has argued, the philosophical reshaping of the social imaginaries in terms of which women and men operate as citizens is crucial to a qualitative change in the "relations between the sexes that are governed by institutions, such as law" (xiii). The transformation of social and sexual imaginaries is a crucial aspect of public policy. Why, asks Irigaray, should admittance to historically excluded spheres occur only on the basis of likeness? How to undermine the dominance of the logic of the like, without essentializing women and other groups as inevitably different? This is the dilemma with which Irigaray's project engages. It has implications beyond a philosophy of sexual difference. What occurs when other groups who have been excluded from the public sphere eventually enter it? One sees a similar discomfited readiness to perceive unlikeness and a concurrent inability to accommodate unlikeness well.

Concerned that women's advances seemed to be double-edged, Irigaray came to believe that equality should be grounded in a different philosophical framework: respect for the possibility of difference. Respect for the possibility of differences is not reducible to respect for differences. How to agitate for equality in the name of possible difference is the overarching practical problem of her work. She offers little account of the day-to-day political interventions and initiatives to be endorsed in a philosophy of sexual difference. For example, she comments that feminist activity clusters around certain themes: "rape, abortion, the challenge to the prerogative of the father's name in the case of judicial decisions that determine 'to whom children belong,' the full-fledged participation of women in legislative decisions and actions . . . must never disguise the fact that it is in order to make their difference come to pass [*faire advenir*] that women are demanding their rights" (Irigaray 1985c, 166). But how are women to insist on equality as a means of bringing sexual difference to light? While she has not engaged in depth with the practicalities, she has offered a developed theoretical account of the conceptual basis and justification for such a project.

Irigaray's early work in *Speculum of the Other Woman* and *This Sex Which Is Not One* largely consisted in analyzing how various theoretical and historical texts—particularly those of philosophy and psychoanalysis—have generated sedimented conceptions of women, materiality, and femininity. If women's politics cannot be adequately formulated within inherited discourses, the latter must be substantially subverted as the forerunner to the articulation of a more appropriate politics. Irigaray's work in this regard was aimed not at concrete political actions but at an overall historical tradition of male-biased philosophical discourse whose blind spots, moments of fragility, and incoherence she hoped to dislodge. Her rereadings of the history of ideas were intended to give a new conceptual base to (and thus support) practical concerns. When Irigaray (1985c) decided that the best option was, in her oft-cited declaration, *"to have a fling with the philosophers"* (150) she hoped to develop a context through which equality could be pursued without undermining women's symbolic, conceptual, transformational, and day-to-day interests.

Irigaray (1985c) affirmed that women were "obviously not to be expected to renounce equality in the sphere of civil rights" (81). Clearly, she envisaged the combination or coordination of ideals of sexual equality and difference. But an ambiguity remained about the possible form of such a coordination. As she asked, "[H]ow can the double demand—for both equality and difference—be articulated?" (81). On the one hand, Irigaray argued that the language of equality was an immediate political necessity in women's struggles. On the other hand, she argued that women risked alienation in their engagement in political struggles organized in the name of equality. Yet she did not want to place the short-term pragmatic aims of equality and the long-term ideological aims of difference—or the claims of practical and theoretical feminisms—in opposition to each other.

Accordingly, her work began to change, originally as a result of an involvement with Italian feminist groups and at one point the Italian Communist Party. In this context she first produced a series of writings written in an everyday, rather flat style, translated in the collections *je, tu, nous* (1993b) and *Thinking the Difference* (1994). These writings attempt not just a greater accessibility to a general readership[15] but also a more direct engagement with practical political concerns. For example, Irigaray formulates a series of "equivalent rights" for which women should strive. These rights spell out Irigaray's approach to such issues as family allowances, media and advertising representation of women, and taxation laws.

Groups affiliated with the Italian Communist Party (PCI), having invited Irigaray to various symposia through the 1980s, are said to have incorporated proposals that reflect her concerns as part of its contemporary political agenda. In *Thinking the Difference* Irigaray explains that "[t]hrough its elected representatives, notably at its XVIII Congress, the PCI announced that it intends to change its platform, particularly on the issue of women's liberation and the culture of sexual difference" (Irigaray 1994, xiv). She claims that these modifications are grounded in a feminist theory of sexual difference with which she is sympathetic. Certainly there has been close involvement between the Italian Communist Party and Italian feminist groups, who in turn have had a close involvement with Irigaray and also, in some cases, with the French feminist group "psychanalyse et politique."[16] This nexus has led to a formulation of Irigarayan concepts in a political party of considerable influence, which must be extremely rare—it has certainly not occurred in the French Communist or other political parties.

Irigaray does not renounce her "preoccupation with psychoanalysis and language" in favor of a practical politics. Rather, she tries to integrate these domains. She imagines hypothetical transformations of the symbolic order. She states: "I am trained as a psychoanalyst and that's important . . . for theorizing identity as sexual" (Irigaray 1993b, 11). She imagines a reinvention of the status of sexual identity that draws on the potential power of language to differently "create" and shape reality (Bono and Kemp 1991, 14).[17] She associates this reinvention with possible reforms of cultural, social, and political institutions. Such reforms could affect the way in which the sexes are understood and understand themselves and the terms in which they are socially represented and recognized. The "symbolic," in Margaret Whitford's presentation (1991b), is "the order of discourse and meaning, the order into which all humans have to insert themselves and which therefore precedes and exceeds individual subjectivity." Insofar as women enter into a historically patriarchal culture, they enter into a social order in which, as Whitford continues, they are left without adequate representations, images, and institutions to serve as identificatory supports (90–91).[18] In this context, sexual difference is an ideal seeking symbolic support. This ideal guides Irigaray's understanding of political activity: transformation of identity at the level of social and legal institutions, the media, the economy, and political, religious, linguistic, and cultural representation (see Bono and Kemp 1991,

12–13, 340–68, and see Milan Women's Bookstore Collective 1990). Concern about the legal and political mechanisms contributing to social forms of identity is seen in the following passage:

> As a woman, I would like to suggest some changes that you—you politically aware women working alongside men—should demand of lawmakers in order to establish a civil identity for women. (Irigaray 1994, 60)
>
> To give women—and men *as men*, too, incidentally—a subjective chance again, we must re-examine the issue of the rights attributed to each sex, rights understood in the strict juridical sense. This does not exclude changes to symbolic systems but must necessarily accompany them. (Irigaray 1994, 58)

As Whitford (1991b, 92) points out, according to this account no substantial change could be effected in women's position without a change in the symbolic, such as the formation of a powerful female symbolic.

Many contemporary Italian feminist groups also take sexual difference to be the emblem of important social change. They similarly take the symbolic order to be the appropriate level at which to strive for such change For example, we see this in Maria Luisa Boccia's understanding of the conceptual framework for feminist activism. Like Irigaray, Boccia writes that the presence of equal numbers of women in civic life is insufficient. Identifying with the paradigm of the free, independent, sovereign (male) individual is a form of alienation for women. A woman becomes alienated in "that strange indefinite identity which is given her when she takes on masculine behavior in a woman's body" (Bono and Kemp 1991, 364). Instead, we need to make the possibility of sexual difference socially credible and legitimate. "The principle of difference . . . responds to social alienation by trying to offer female existence a way of remaining close to itself, bringing together processes of social and political identification which affect it with processes of subjective identification. It is not by chance that feminism combines political with psychoanalytic thought" (Bono and Kemp 1991, 365). According to a psychoanalytic account, structural recognition and social identification are critical to the formation of subjectivity. The social and political reforms favored by Irigaray aim for alternative modes of identity structures for the sexes.

In *je, tu, nous*, Irigaray presses for practical legal reform in these terms, asking how such reform might "define women's lives as citizens" (Irigaray 1993b, 79):

> All the following issues of women's lives ought to be made the concern of and written into civil law: temporary concessions on contraception and

abortion; partial and provisional protection from and penalties against public and domestic violence against women; the abuse of female bodies for the purpose of pornography or advertising; discrimination in the sexist definition and use of the body, of images, of language; rape, kidnapping, murder. . . . These are only a few examples of what has to be legally specified in order to define women's lives as citizens. (Irigaray 1993b, 78–79)

Law concerning many of these issues has often been formulated in negative terms. For example, a "hands-off" reform is envisaged when demeaning representations of women appear in advertising, media, and pornography; violence against women and prevention of women's access to contraception and abortion are opposed with demands to "keep your hands off our bodies."[19] Andrea Dworkin and Catharine MacKinnon's proposed legal amendment on pornography listed contexts and instances of pornography against which there should be injunctions (see Dworkin and MacKinnon 1988).[20] As an alternative, some other feminist legal theorists including Drucilla Cornell have argued that the law's role is also to ensure "access to symbolic forms sufficient to achieve linguistic skills permitting the differentiation of oneself from others" and "the protection of the imaginary domain itself" (Cornell 1995, 4). Thus Cornell writes, "[I]t is not enough for the state to refrain from actively blocking women's 'choice' to have abortions" (33). Along with ensuring the establishment of safe access to and conditions for abortion, the state must also concern itself with the nature of the "social and symbolic recognition" of women associated with such provisions (33).

Many agree with Irigaray's supposition that symbolic, legal, and subjective issues of recognition are interconnected. Irigaray is among those feminist theorists who think that the law should operate in positive, and not only in negative or prohibitive, capacities.[21] A debate taken up in chapter 4 is whether Irigaray places too much confidence in the socially transformative potential of legal reform. But certainly, in her view, the role of the law amounts to more than enjoining, restricting, prohibiting, or even redistributing.[22] The law can offer innovative representations of subjects of different sexes and cultures. It can contribute to the optimal conditions for the formation of new identities for women and men.

Legal reform supported by Irigaray would prohibit demeaning images of women in advertisements. But such reform is not to be understood only in prohibitive terms. Irigaray thinks it has the potential to contribute to a refigured social imaginary in which women may locate themselves more positively. This point has been strongly emphasized by Cornell also, particularly in *The Imaginary Domain* (1995), despite considerable disagreements Cornell has had with Irigaray's work. Cornell supports a legal regulation of pornography in addition to a "degradation prohibition" (see Cornell 1995, 98ff.). But given her view "that law can protect the imaginary domain" (Cornell 1995, 105), Cornell also favors legal reform that would protect women's attempts to make alternative forms of pornography under different economic and structural conditions, and to open it up to new, more innovative meanings. The proliferation of such meanings can contribute to richer discursive contexts out of which transformed sexuate identities will develop.

In this chapter, I have considered Irigaray's concern that the very philosophy of equality might be historically hard-wired with an implicit supposition of women's inequality.[23] The most obvious response would be to ask whether the language of sexual difference is not also hardwired with the historical supposition of women's inequality. Shouldn't Irigaray be equally wary of the language of difference? One can respond in turn that Irigaray does not really endorse the tradition of sexual difference. She supports a politics of transformation and (re)invention of sexual difference and has nothing but the usual skepticism about historical depictions of sexual difference. But the reader is likely to wonder why she has not favored a politics of transformation of equality instead. I think the point is that, at least in Irigaray's own work, these politics are not so very distinct, and this point will be taken up again in chapter 7. A transformed politics of difference is one that reconfigures equality, equivalence, and sameness. Irigaray means her feminism of difference to act as a useful transformation, not an abandonment, of equality politics. In chapter 7, we will see her argument for a concept of sameness that presupposes internal difference, and a concept of difference that presupposes a refiguring of understandings of sameness.

The chapters that follow ask how Irigaray has engaged with issues of public policy and legal and institutional reform. She is, along with Michèle Le Doeuff, one of France's few contemporary women philosophers to have engaged with these issues. In order to trace this development in her work, I turn next to Irigaray's earliest writing, *Le langage des déments*, so as to discuss the emergence of a philosophy of sexual difference after that early work.

2

Irigaray on Language

From the Speech of Dementia to the Problem of Sexual Indifference

> For some time now, sexual difference has not played a part in the
> *creation of culture*, except in a division of roles and functions that
> does not allow both sexes to be subjects. Thus we are confronted
> with a certain *subjective pathology* from both sides of sexual
> difference.
>
> Luce Irigaray, Sexes and Genealogies

In 1973, Irigaray published her first book, *Le langage des déments*. She
holds doctorates in philosophy, psychoanalysis, and linguistics, and the
first of her studies belongs to the latter discipline. It presents findings
from studies of the speech patterns of sufferers of dementia. While thorough and scientific, the work contains an important oversight. It is the
kind of oversight, she would later argue, that impairs the rigor of researchers (Irigaray 1985a, 11).

The overall rationale for the design of the tests is carefully explained in
Le langage des déments. They were intended to evaluate views held in existing literature: for example, that dementia is accompanied by lexical impoverishment, particularly of names and dates, and that there is a greater
use of generic terms such as "thing" to the detriment of naming specific objects and concepts. Dementia is associated with incoherent, disordered
statements, inertia of ideas, digressions, lack of control in expression, difficulties in reception and interpretation, and impoverishment of categorical
thought (Irigaray 1973, 7–10). Among her concerns, Irigaray wanted to distinguish the linguistic specificity of subjects suffering from dementia from
that of sufferers of disorders such as aphasia and Alzheimer's disease.

She explains that her tests investigated the linguistic structure at work
in the verbal statements of dementia sufferers, so as to understand how
syntactic and grammatical rules are manipulated by them. Where there is

linguistic disorganization, she tries to analyze the level at which it occurs: syntax or semantics, for example. Are subjects' linguistic schemas disrupted only at the level of the linguistic pool at their disposal? Is there also disruption of the structure of communication, in the relations between subject, object, and interlocutor? According to what formations of language should we understand subjects suffering from dementia as "speaking subjects"? Irigaray (1973) defines a speaking subject as "a network of operations that must be conceptualized through the complexity of their interrelations" (12). She analyzes the relation of subjects suffering dementia to their own enunciations, to their interlocutors, and to the world. She interrogates the conditions and possibilities of their linguistic communication. Every response of each subject in each test is scrupulously reproduced in the work, which contains a large component of tables of test results.

In 1985, Irigaray would come to mock the scientism to which such work aspired (Irigaray 1985a, 7). But the conclusions of her 1973 work seem carefully considered and attentive to her data. She concludes that subjects suffering from dementia retain their phonological code while undergoing a relaxation of syntactic constraints. Some grammatical classes are impoverished more than others, and overall lexical stock does reduce. Words are attributed variable and inconstant meanings. Subjects are confused by semantic ambiguity or polysemia. They find it hard to generate and take responsibility for new messages. There is a loss of memory and attention, an inability to use language as a tool. The subject, Irigaray concludes, appears to be incapable of new relationships to the world, or at least of new verbalized relationships to the world (350). For example, a subject suffering from dementia can certainly react with opposition or resistance to new stimulations and unknown situations. But while one can react to a situation, "one cannot adapt to it, or name/articulate [*dire*] it" (350).

In this regard, Irigaray (1973) comes to a conclusion on which she would draw in later work. "The subject suffering from dementia," she argues, "is incapable of functioning as an enunciating subject. This subject is no more than an object of enunciations" (349).[1] No political or social significance is attributed to this situation. Irigaray draws no further conclusions from her findings, or any parallels with other subjects who might be considered objects rather than subjects of enunciation. However, this structure would later prove to be a recurrent interest in her work. At this early point, the same conclusion is also drawn in relation to schizophrenic subjects on whom she also conducted linguistic studies during the 1960s.[2] Later in her career, Irigaray would eventually come to ask whether women share some specificity in their relation to linguistic use. Do women tend toward a status as subjects or objects of enunciation?

Finally, Irigaray (1973) notes that those suffering dementia have difficulty in receiving, interpreting, and satisfying the questions of an interlocutor. They often manifest "attitudes of opposition and refusal addressed both to the object in question—a verbal test—and also to the observer" (349). "Frequently," she points out, "the interventions [of the observer] are tolerated very badly, particularly when they interrupt the automatic, uncontrollable 'monologue' of the subject" (349). This resistance does not indicate true dialogue or exchange between interlocutor and interlocutor. The subject interviewed is not necessarily responding to the interviewer as another subject. In this sense, communication is dysfunctional: "[O]ne could conclude that the addressee pole in dementia speech is dysfunctional. To do so might incur the objection that this discourse often appears to be an echoing repetition of the observer's enunciation, or the almost automatic follow-on, determined by the syntagmatic constraints of the discourse the observer has initiated. But in truth, we are not dealing with the addressee-as-a-you *[tu]*, but with the addressee's recall of the enunciation's context, which supported the already produced discourse" (349–50).

Notice Irigaray's concern with the subjective and interlocutive status of two speaking subjects. We seem to have before us an addressor and an addressee. But we must ask in what mode of subjectivity and recognition each speaks. Adequate communication requires at least two subjects, "I" and "you." A subject may seem to be speaking in dialogue but might not, in some respects, establish the "you" if speaking to the other only in the mode of recall, recollection, adherence to or rejection of a preestablished pattern. At this point, neurological and psychological disorder (dementia and, in other studies of the same period, schizophrenia) are the only instances considered of this phenomenon: "[I]t seems that, in the case of dementia, we are in the presence of a form of indifferentiation of the poles of enunciation. There is no longer an 'I' *[je]* and a you *[tu]*; an emitter and a recipient of messages. There is one unique pole of enunciation: language itself. This manifests itself as the very impossibility of any kind of 'communication'" (350).

Le langage des déments is particularly interesting to scholars of Irigaray's later work because she would later return to the discipline of linguistic analysis in addressing the problem of sexual difference. Such analysis has formed a substantial component of her most recent work. *Le langage des déments* is also of note because its methodological values would be repudiated by the author later in her career.

I have mentioned that the study scrupulously reproduces the responses of tested subjects. This allows the reader to compare differentiation and ambiguity in individual responses against the statistical data and conclusions drawn by Irigaray about them. In addition, we have seen that Irigaray is attentive to aspects of a candidate's response that resist the process of examination. For example, Irigaray takes pains to document responses such as hostility to questions, metacommentary on them, interrogation of their context, questions addressed in turn to the interviewer, silence, and failure or refusal to complete questions. Similarly, in her studies on schizophrenia, Irigaray again pays attention not just to the content and pattern of responses but also to the modes of response. These include such factors as whether the subject contests the question, whether the subject attempts to place it in a context, and the affective manner in which she or he responds (1973, 42). Although Irigaray does group, classify, and quantify the responses of the subjects in her study, differentiation among subjects is not entirely homogenized into commonalities and percentages of like responses. Small variations do not disappear from the presentation of the data in the interest of supporting statistical data and research conclusions. The listing of all speakers' responses allows the reader to consider instances of responses that might resist Irigaray's own conclusions.[3]

Since Irigaray devotes so much careful attention to the singularity of the subjects she examines in this 1973 study, it is striking that there is one potentially key aspect of the interviewees' specificity she does not discuss. This is their sex. Throughout, the tested individuals are referred to sex-neutrally as subjects. Because their attributed given names are abbreviated throughout the study (as "Steph," "Mar") and so on, the sex of individuals cannot be determined as we read their responses. The only indications that women have been included in the samples are the occasionally gendered nature of some of the responses and a table provided on one page of the work that includes the sex of the participants. In her other studies on schizophrenia, the question of differences between male and female respondents is not directly discussed. While individual test results are tabled, there is no identification of the sex of the participants (see 1985a, 35–53, 81–116, 189–221). This omission deemphasizes the possible importance of determining types of language use among sufferers of dementia and schizophrenia that might be more specific to women or men.

This is a phenomenon Irigaray would later term sexual indifference: a lack of interest in potential differentiation among men and women. Sexual indifference supposes from the outset the sexual neutrality of subjects with regard to language, habits, needs, responsibilities, embodiment, or experiences. Such working suppositions are not uncommon in scientific research, but Irigaray would eventually come to denounce them. No more of the neutral subject, she later declares in *Parler n'est jamais neutre* (1985a, 9). She criticizes the scientific values with which she aligned herself in her linguistic research up until 1973.

Published one year later in 1974, *Speculum of the Other Woman* might have been written by a different author. *Speculum* is concerned with the sexual indifference of the history of philosophy (Plato, Aristotle, Plotinus, Descartes, Kant, and Hegel) and—more surprisingly—of psychoanalysis (Lacan and Freud). Subsequent works would add Marx and the anthropologist Lévi-Strauss, in addition to further figures from the history of philosophy such as Spinoza, Nietzsche, Heidegger, Merleau-Ponty, Sartre, and Lévinas. Sexual indifference may be seen when philosophy, law, economics, or science supposes a sex-neutral subject. It may be seen in explicit indifference to questions of sex or gender difference or in failure to discriminate between men and women. But sexual indifference may also be at work in overt discussions of women and femininity. To take one example, in Freud's work girls are represented as "little men" (the equivalent of little boys), and women are represented as "desiring babies" (the complement to the male) or "desiring the phallus" (aspiring to be like men). Femininity is represented only in terms of a masculine reference point: as the same as, the opposite of, or the complement to the masculine. Although Freud takes himself to be interested in the problem of femininity and sexual difference, Irigaray (1985c) concludes that "Freud does not see *two sexes* whose differences are articulated in the act of intercourse and, more generally speaking, in the imaginary and symbolic processes that regulate the workings of a society and a culture. The 'feminine' is always described in terms of deficiency or atrophy, as the other side of the sex that alone holds a monopoly on value: the male sex" (69). Thus, sexual indifference may be present in the work of a philosopher who seems keenly interested in sexual difference.

Irigaray first became well-known as a philosopher for her close textual analyses of the phallocentrism of the history of philosophy and psychoanalytic theory.[4] *Speculum* analyzes a sequence of thinkers from Plato, Aristotle, and Plotinus through Descartes, Kant, and Hegel to Freud. The tenor of their references (or sometimes the lack thereof) to women, materiality, or femininity indicates that the feminine has been colonized as the other of masculinity. As Irigaray (1985b) declares, "[Y]ou men [are] speaking among yourselves about woman, who cannot be involved in hearing or producing a discourse that concerns the *riddle*, the logogriph she represents for you" (13). Woman is the other either where she constitutes "the *target*, the *object*, the *stake*, of a masculine discourse, of a debate among men" (13) or else where a sex-neutral subject is supposed in discussions of the human.

The mode of impartial neutrality adopted in Irigaray's earlier writing she now analyzes as inconsistent and self-contradictory.[5] Discourses, she now writes, are hardly ever truly sex-neutral (1985a, 11). Furthermore, texts that do pretend to represent femininity or women invariably depict variations on a male reference point. She locates many moments of self-contradiction or unstable logic in Freud's description of women: "The fact that Freud himself is enmeshed in a power structure and an ideology of the patriarchal type leads, moreover, to some internal contradictions in his theory" (1985c, 70). *Speculum* offers a long analysis of the fact that Freud both rejects and reinstates the representation of the opposition masculine/feminine by the opposition activity/passivity, for example.[6]

In focusing on the treatment of femininity by philosophers and psychoanalysts, Irigaray analyzes theoretical weaknesses in their work in an additional sense. She argues that there is a traditional reliance on the trope of woman as other in order to sustain an ideal representation of the masculine subject. Woman, says Irigaray, has represented an inverted or negative alter ego of the masculine. When contrasted with femininity as a negative other, masculine identity is all the more associated with positive qualities. Where women represent idle chatter, men represent serious rationality; where woman represents the minus, man represents the plus (1985b, 22). The othering of woman to represent the emotional and irrational, the weak and the irresponsible suggests the unacknowledged fragility of associations of the male with reason, strength, discipline, and civic responsibility. A degree of dependence on the othering of the feminine is the disavowed underbelly of philosophy.

Having analyzed how femininity and women have been represented, Irigaray attempts to go further. Can we define the ways in which they have *not* been represented? Women have not been represented in terms transcending relationality to a masculine reference point. Irigaray is not making a claim about what women are really like or how they have been misrepresented.[7] Instead she analyses how a given body of texts (such as those of Freud) do not represent women. Because similar patterns are seen in a series of thinkers throughout history, Irigaray thinks we can constitute an overall analysis of the sorts of representations of women that have been excluded throughout history. The philosophic logos has "reduce[d] all others in the economy of the Same" (translation modified). It has *"erad-icate[d] [l'effacement de] the difference between the sexes"* (1985c, 74). Irigaray then argues that these exclusions have been unstable or self-undermining.

To reduce feminine others to the economy of the Same implicitly recognizes the possibility that they could exceed the economy of the Same, she argues. To efface the possibility of sexual difference implicitly indicates the possibility of sexual difference. Irigaray plays with logic. If there is an exclusion, there must be something (even if it is no more than a mere possibility) to exclude. Irigaray does think that sexual difference (by which she means sexual difference not reducible to opposition, complementarity, or sameness) is culturally incoherent. She also thinks that throughout the history of ideas of western culture, male writers repeatedly deny that women are anything other than opposite, same, or complement. Some of her interpretations are extremely convincing on this point. Freud, as depicted in *Speculum*, is committed to this pattern. To describe him as actively excluding other possibilities for representing sexual difference seems only fair. This is the point from which Irigaray would profit. One need not be sure that "there is" sexual difference in order to be sure that Freud excludes it as a possibility.

When Irigaray concludes that the history of western culture has excluded sexual difference, notice how the ontological status of sexual difference is left entirely open. A writer could establish this diagnosis believing that there is no such thing as sexual difference. Another could draw the same diagnosis convinced that there is. Irigaray hoped to move the basis for critique away from claims about what there is or is not. She rejected the idea of asking "What is a woman?" (1985c, 122). She did not want her analyses of Freud and others reduced to such speculative and generalizing questions. One could achieve a good deal just by analyzing repetition in the patterns of representation of women in the history of western culture. One began to generate a sense of what that history has not wanted woman to be. It has not wanted women and femininity to be more than opposite, complement, or same as the male. The term "sexual difference" in her work is an open term, a pair of empty brackets. But the construction of these brackets nonetheless emphasizes that an active exclusion has taken place. As an Irigarayan concept, "sexual difference" represents something the history of western ideas has not wanted women and femininity to be: something more than opposite, complement, or same.

"Sexual difference" in Irigaray's work refers to an excluded possibility, some kind of femininity (open in content) that has never become culturally coherent or possible. Irigaray has continued to rely on this concept throughout her career. When she refers to the feminine, she does not refer to a buried or repressed truth. Nor does she envisage (by giving content to) a utopian new possibility of femininity. Sexual difference is not empirically known, except by its exclusion. Nor is it some unknowable outside of language and culture to which we could attribute identity or entity. It is "neither on the near side, the empirical realm that is opaque to all language, nor on the far side, the self-sufficient infinite" (1985c, 77).

Instead, it is a hypothetical possibility on the border of histories of representation of femininity. Not within them, because it has been excluded. Not entirely exterior to them, because insofar as it has been excluded it has been indicated as a possibility. For this reason the concepts of femininity and sexual difference generated by Irigaray have a paradoxical inside / outside, possible / impossible status. Hypothetically, the "recognition of a 'specific' female sexuality would challenge the monopoly on value held by the masculine sex alone" (1985c, 73). One can establish this point without asserting that there is a specific female sexuality or femininity. Irrespective of one's position on the latter, one can analyze and criticize theoretical contexts for their inability to tolerate such a possibility. Irigaray thought a good deal was revealed by Freud's repeated exclusion of such a possibility, for example. This exclusion must be considered the very emblem of phallocentrism.

In chapter 1 we saw the view of some feminists that affirming sexual difference is a mistake. The language of difference is too tainted to be any good to feminism. It can only consolidate conservative values. The objections of other feminists are less pragmatic. Some just dismiss the idea that women either are or might be importantly "different." This is an important debate, but it does distract from the question Irigaray wants to ask. Isn't something wrong when the very possibility of sexual difference is systematically disallowed by male thinkers? Shouldn't a culture that is deeply disturbed by the very possibility of such difference be questioned by feminists, whatever their own views about its ontological status or pragmatic politics? Commentary on Irigaray's work has been exercised by the question of whether or not there is sexual difference. But Irigaray reroutes this question. Her point is that western culture has rendered sexual difference impossible and that this should concern us, regardless.

I mentioned earlier that Irigaray's approach to difference need not be limited to issues of sex and gender, and with this in mind I will propose an analogy pertinent to Irigaray's 1999 work *Between East and West*. A colonized people is likely to have very different views about cultural difference. Burdened with representations of the savage, the tribal, and the irrational, some will counter by claiming equal or potentially equal rationality. Others might affirm alternative understandings and modes of rationality. Others might reject the values of western rationality altogether. Some might affirm a return to original cultural values. Others might affirm a reinvention or transformation of those cultural values. We should be wary of a colonizing culture's investment in excluding any of these possibilities. Its particular insistence that a colonized people should be same, different, opposite, or complement must be critically examined. The need for such critical examination holds, irrespective of whether difference, equivalence, reshaped difference, or reshaped equivalence is preferred by colonized peoples. Such choices should make us no less suspicious of a colonizing culture's apparent desire that a colonized people be the same, for example, or indeed that they be different. To return to the feminist debate about Irigaray's work, she is suspicious of a desire repeatedly manifest in western philosophy and psychoanalysis that women not be sexually different. We should be resistant to this desire, irrespective of our individual positions on the pragmatic and ontological status of sexual difference. Some critics, of course, would question Irigaray's diagnosis that western philosophers have excluded the possibility of sexual difference. But this is because western philosophy's love of models of complementarity and opposed otherness (representations of woman as nature and man as reason, of woman as empathy and man as dispassion, of woman as private and man as public, and so on) appears to express its love of sexual difference. Irigaray does not agree. We should not confuse difference with impoverished models governed by sameness, insofar as they subordinate women to a masculine reference point (complement or opposite to the male).

The recognition that the possibility of sexual difference has been excluded is disruptive, in Irigaray's view. Once we begin to muse on excluded conceptual possibilities, new ideas for how the feminine might be understood open up. Without making claims about the truth or reality of feminine sexuality, femininity, or women, Irigaray proposes to destabilize traditional representations of masculinity and femininity:

> [W]hat is important is to disconcert the staging of representation according to *exclusively* "masculine" parameters, that is, according to a phallocratic order . . . [to disrupt and modify] it, starting from an "outside" that is exempt [*soustrait*], in part, from phallocratic law. (1985c, 68)

Notice here that Irigaray describes the excluded feminine, using scare quotes, as "outside." It occupies the paradoxical border position that the excluded always holds. She says not that it is exempt from the phallocratic order but that it is exempt *in part*. In her later work, when Irigaray refers to women's identity, women's bodies, women's nature, or a feminine divine, sexual difference always retains this paradoxical status.

Speaking in the name of a feminine identity with this paradoxical inside/outside status, Irigaray was accused by critics of pretending to describe the truth of women. However, she had begun her career with statements deflecting that interpretation (Irigaray 1985c, 78). Instead, she proposed "repeating/interpreting the way in which, within discourse, the feminine finds itself defined as lack, deficiency, or as imitation and negative image of the subject, [so that women] should signify that with respect to this logic a *disruptive excess* is possible on the feminine side" (1985c, 78). In one of the most widely debated aspects of her work, she frequently mimics traditional representations of femininity so as to amplify them to a disruptive implosion.

Concepts of femininity exceeding the terms of man's other have traditionally been excluded from western discourse. As a disruptive strategy,
Irigaray wants to insert into philosophical texts, language, and culture a
concept of femininity she takes to be excluded. Because its possibility has
been excluded, there is no sexual difference. What resources remain for a
disruptive project? Irigaray sometimes reappropriates particularly traditional ideas about femininity, such as notions of the feminine as fluid, elu-
sive, or virginal, exaggerating them and reinserting them into the texts in
question. One example is Irigaray's depiction of women's "two lips" sexuality, another her suggestion that female virginity might form the basis
for legal reform.

Once she has exaggerated them, Irigaray sometimes theorizes such concepts of femininity as an "A/B" difference (which does not exclude other
possibilities: C, D, and E, for example), rather than as a relativity to the
masculine pole of the form "A/Not-A." This reworking is applied in a
number of domains: linguistic and legal reform, in addition to philosophical representation. It is first seen in *This Sex Which Is Not One*, published
in French in 1977. In the most well-known of the essays in this collection,
"This Sex Which Is Not One," Irigaray attempts a poetic evocation of the
ways in which women's sexuality is not represented. It is typically seen as
vaginal and/or clitoral. It is held to be the same or else the complement of
masculine sexuality, and subordinate to the requirements of reproduction.
Irigaray reappropriates and amplifies the association of women with sex.
However, she refigures that association in terms she thinks would be disruptive to the phallocentric representation of femininity as equivalent or
complement. Irigaray (1985c) asks why female sexuality should not be
seen in terms of self-caressing, a self-touching of two lips in continuous
contact, that which *"is neither one nor two"* (26), a plural sexuality, in which
one has *"sex organs [des sexes] more or less everywhere"* (28), an incompleteness of form, pleasures taken as much from touching as looking, and desire that might potentially "speak" a different "language" from that of a
man (25). As one of Irigaray's best commentators analyzes the project,
"the 'two lips' is not a truthful image of female anatomy but a new emblem" by which female sexuality can be positively, excessively, and sub-
versively represented (Grosz 1989, 116).

This Sex Which Is Not One was then followed by book-length studies of
Nietzsche (1991a), Heidegger (2000), and another broad-ranging study
that moved from Plato to Lévinas: *An Ethics of Sexual Difference* (1993a).[8]
Concurrently, Irigaray started to think increasingly about social reform
and structures of legal reform. We saw in chapter 1 that Irigaray is committed to ideals of equality but critical of the conceptual terms of equality.
Her concern is not just to generate poetically evocative concepts of

women's "two lips" sexuality. She is also concerned about women's legal and civic status, equal pay, and equal representation across all sectors of society. She has, particularly in her later work, engaged with issues of public policy, media and advertising representations, legal reform, and access to public institutions. The complexity of her philosophical analyses of the absence of sexual difference informs her approach to practical concerns and institutional reform.

Consider the application of an Irigarayan notion of sexual difference to institutional reform. Because of the historical evolution of a male workforce, public sphere, and electorate, women did not contribute to the shaping of their form, traditions, or discourse. Making this point, Irigaray claims not that women have a specific culture and identity to which the workplace or the public sphere is inappropriate. She does question the implicit supposition that women do not have a specific culture and identity to which the public sphere needs to make itself appropriate. As with her interpretations of Freud and the philosophers, Irigaray's point is not about the truth of women's identity or culture. She diagnoses implicit exclusion of a possibility from a given domain. This means we should exercise caution in the interpretation of passages such as: "There is still hardly any sort of work that enables a woman to earn her living as a male citizen does [*comme tout citoyen*] without alienating her identity in working conditions and contexts developed to suit men alone" (1993b, 85). If women pass from traditional exclusion from the workplace to simple inclusion, they are included as honorary men. And this, says Irigaray, should be seen as an alienation of them as women. However, it is not that women have an identity that is alienated. Rather, the very possibility that they could have such an identity is alienated from them. Irigaray (1994) asks: "For what do women's work and political affiliation mean if women have not got their own civil identity [*sans identité civile qui leur soit appropriée*]? Will they not be supporting and promoting a male tradition and society to which they remain alien, and which, to some extent, annihilates them as persons?" (41).

As suggested in chapter 1, Irigaray's concern is about the conceptual basis on which women are present in the public sphere. If women exchange a role as other for a role as equivalent to the masculine in order to be included in the public sphere, they remain symbolically "annihilated." Instead, Irigaray hypothesizes about a civil identity specific to women. Just as in her approach to the history of philosophy, she introduces a concept she takes to be absent from contemporary culture. Women's civil identity refers to an identity that does not exist. She tries to speak in the name of this impossible identity within the domain of institutional reform and reform of the civil code. Because she deems it impossible, reference to it is a deliberately paradoxical gesture on her part. The identity lacks specific content. For rhetorical purposes it must be either left empty, invented, or provisionally based on a disruptive exaggeration of traditional notions of femininity. "I shall then suggest some concrete legal changes that would give women a civil identity" (1994, 41). The content of that potential identity would be a matter of social and subjective transformation:

> Women's entry into the public world, the social relations they have among themselves and with men, have made cultural transformations . . . a necessity. (1993b, 67)
> It's important to understand and modify the instruments of society and culture that regulate subjective and objective rights. Social justice, and especially sexual justice, cannot be achieved without changing the laws of language and the conceptions of truths and values structuring the social order. (1993b, 22)

Irigaray (1993b, 85) argues that women are alienated by living as male citizens. Despite interpretation by critics to the contrary, she is not arguing that women have a specific identity that has been alienated by their role as a male citizen equivalent. Instead, Irigaray speaks in the name of a female civic identity that is impossible, since women have occupied cultural roles only as man's equal, complement, or other. She introduces into her analyses of the workplace, the law, and the public sphere the concept of impossibility developed in her readings of Plato, Hegel, Freud, and so on. "How can we govern [*gérer*] the world as women if we have not defined our identity, the rules concerning our genealogical relationships, our social, linguistic, and cultural order?" she asks (1993b, 56). The formulation does not suggest that women need to rediscover their identity. Rather, there needs to be a cultural reinvention or reconception of sexual difference through the reshaping of French public institutions. Thus we see her declare, "This political management requires the institution of a new civil code" (1994, 84). Calling, literally, for legal modifications to the civil code, she formulates a series of institutional proposals for a culture of sexual difference (1994, 60).

Her specific list of sexuate rights to be formalized at the level of the French civil code are printed in *je, tu, nous* (1993b, 86–89) and *Thinking the Difference* (1994, 60–62). Their broad headings include the right to human dignity, the right to human identity, the articulation of the mutual responsibilities between mothers and their children, women's right to defend their own lives and those of their children, certain financial rearrangements, equivalent systems of exchange for both women and men (including linguistic exchange), and equal representation in civil and religious contexts.

The rights seem to assert women's essential difference from men, a concept that most readers reject. It is here that we see the initial work Irigaray completed in relation to the history of philosophy informing the work on public policy. In her readings of the history of philosophy, Irigaray introduced a concept of woman not as she is, but as she cannot be. She thinks we can formulate women's rights similarly, in terms of excluded concepts rather than of given or existing identities. The French civil code should not just be reformed to better reflect the reality and needs of women's lives. It should also incorporate new concepts of sexed identity that might interrupt women's traditional role as other. The code requires a culturally inconceivable concept of women as different (not the opposite of, the same as, or the complement to a masculine reference point). In this sense, "we need laws that valorize differences" (1993b, 22, translation modified).

Her critics respond that a concept of sexual difference is far from inconceivable. It has a long tradition in writers such as Aquinas, Rousseau, Comte, Ruskin, and all those who have revered or deplored women as different: as nature, mother, muse, idol, or a certain absence of qualities. But Irigaray asks us whether what has been passed off under the banner of difference merits the name.

Irigaray (1993b, 11) argues for "equivalent sexed rights being written into the law" for women. She retains her commitment to equal rights, while trying to rethink their conceptual basis. Social institutions recognizing sexual difference would allow men and women to arrive at a more satisfactory state of equality. As she asserts, "[W]hat we do need . . . and it's essential, is for men and women to have equal subjective rights—equal obviously meaning different but of equal value, subjective implying equivalent rights in exchange systems" (1993b, 68). Although commentators have noted that "her own program for new values seems impoverished" and that "it is not clear . . . how one is supposed to implement the kinds of genealogies among women she advocates" (Lorraine 1999, 92), Irigaray (1993b) does spell out a political agenda. She calls for sexuate rights, and these are listed under seven categories:

1. The right to *human dignity* . . .
2. The right to *human identity* . . .
3. The mutual obligations of mothers-children shall be defined by civil law. . . . The respective obligations of the mother and the father will be defined separately.

4. Women shall have a right to defend their own and their children's lives . . . against all unilateral decisions emanating from male law (including in this respect armaments and pollution).

5. On a strictly financial level: . . . Celibacy shall not be penalized by the tax system. . . . Media broadcasts . . . shall be half of the time targeted towards women.

6. Systems of exchange, such as linguistic exchange, for example, shall be revised in order to guarantee a right to equivalent exchange for men and women.

7. Women shall be represented in equal numbers in all civil and religious decision-making bodies. (86–89)

Notwithstanding her view that the language of equality can subtly undermine women's interests, Irigaray's commitment to feminism of equality should not be underestimated. This commitment is seen in such items on the bill as number 7: the declaration that women must be represented in equal numbers in all decision-making bodies.[9] Focusing increasingly on public policy, institutional protection of equality between the sexes, law reform, and quotidian politics, Irigaray has carried over the methodology for a reconceptualization of difference developed in her analyses of the history of philosophy. Through her concern for issues of identity, she wishes to redress the predicament of equality politics: "[A]s for women themselves, they are caught in a dilemma: stuck between the minimum social rights they can obtain by going out to work, gaining economic independence, having a little social visibility, etc., and the psychological or physical price they pay, and make other women pay, for this minimum" (Irigaray 1993b, 85, translation modified). Reflecting on civic identity is, in her view, a means of addressing this psychological and physiological price.

However, throughout her work on the history of philosophy and subsequently legal and institutional reform, the author has not turned her back on linguistic analysis. Eventually, the analysis of sexual indifference would manifest itself in her approach to linguistics.

It is in *Parler n'est jamais neutre* (1985a) that Irigaray heaps scorn on the spirit of scientific earnestness and neutrality apparent in her earliest work. Considering her early project, she feels "first of all, an irritation and a laugh, faced with the postulates of scientific language. Scientific requirements, these norms and criteria of a procedure understood as rigorous, represent a reality for and against which I have measured myself for many years" (7). But Irigaray is too severe on her earliest writing. It is careful work, attentive to ambiguity and specificity in the responses of her interviewees. Barring its own "sexual indifference," many of the values guiding *Le langage des déments* are consistent with those manifest in the early works on the history of philosophy. Irigaray brings to the analysis of the history of philosophy, anthropology, and psychoanalysis the same attention to detail, singularity, silence, hostility, and resistance she demonstrated in her earliest linguistic work.

We have seen how an interest in the representation and possibilities for representation of women, femininity, and sexual difference took over as the overriding theme in Irigaray's work. Her poetic writing would attempt to evoke alternative, imagined possibilities for the identity of women and men. She would analyze representations of women and femininity in the history of philosophy, psychoanalysis, and anthropology. Her subsequent, more programmatic work would lay down proposals for social reform, including reform of law, language, the media, economics, and religion, which might open new possibilities for the identities of women and men. Yet throughout the twenty-five years of publication that were to follow, Irigaray's interest in linguistics would continue, while undergoing a transformation corresponding to the overall changes in her work. After her own initial indifference to the question, Irigaray would eventually subject difference between men and women to linguistic analysis. Having first constituted a grammar of dementia, Irigaray would later constitute a grammar of sexual difference. Its claims are strikingly consistent with the concerns of the earliest work, where Irigaray asked what the conditions of a sufficient situation of communication are. Is the addressee before us a "you"? Does the subject exist in an adequate I-you relationship with an interlocutor and in relation to others? Is the subject capable of functioning as a subject of enunciation? Or is she or he constituted as the object of enunciations? If, Irigaray (1973) argued, there are not two adequate "poles of enunciation," "I" and "you," the result will be "the very impossibility of any kind of 'communication'" (350).

Irigaray's work on the possible differences in language spoken by men and women first appeared in the 1986 paper "The Three Genders" (in Irigaray 1993c), in a collective anthology called *The Linguistic Sex* (Irigaray et al. 1987), and in a second anthology (Irigaray 1990). She concludes that women do not exist in an adequate I-you relation. "Gender," writes Irigaray (1993c), "stands for the unsubstitutable position of the *I* and the *you (le tu)* and of their modes of expression. Once the difference between *I* and *you* is gone, then asking, thanking, appealing, questioning . . . also disappear" (170). In other words, in gendered relations it is crucial that there be an adequate I and you. If not, relations between the sexes will be inadequate and monodiscursive. Irigaray's diatribe against the scientism of her early work includes a condemnation of scientific discourse in which the neutral language of the impersonal investigator excludes the possibility of

saying "I" or "you." There is no "I" or "you" or "we" in scientific language, she writes (1985a, 308). In the 1986 paper, Irigaray includes, along
with "the sciences, technological practices[, and] certain ways of regress-
ing into religiosity," "man today" as fitting this pattern of "no longer saying
I or *you* or *we*" (1993c, 170). She introduces a political and social-analytic
approach to linguistics that was not the concern of her studies of dementia
and schizophrenia. We should ask how particular linguistic meanings,
contents, and cultures have been authorized. And we should also ask how
language can "set up others"—in other words, other possible meanings,
contents, and cultures (1993c, 171). Irigaray introduces a new ethical dimension into her approach to linguistic analysis.

Her interest in dysfunctional linguistic usage carries over into the work
on sexual difference. Men and women suffer, not from dementia or schizophrenia, but from an absence of sexual difference: "For some time now,
sexual difference has not played a part in the *creation of culture*, except in a
division of roles and functions that does not allow both sexes to be subjects. Thus we are confronted with a certain *subjective pathology* from both
sides of sexual difference" (1993c, 172).

A key early paper dates from 1967, around the period when Irigaray
was working most with linguistic analyses of schizophrenia. In two papers concurrently published with these studies, Irigaray discussed the
language formations of hysterics and obsessional neurotics. The conclusions are reiterated in "The Three Genders" of 1986:

> It seems that patients labeled hysteric and those labeled obsessional do
> not use the same structures of discourse. Hysterics (or at least female hys-
> terics) generate utterances of the type: (I) ← Do you love me? → (you) or (I)
> ← like what you like → (you). Obviously this is not a simple example of
> what one immediately hears said.[10] This is a model sentence gained by ana-
> lyzing several bodies of recorded utterances and reducing them to kernel
> phrases. The obsessional patient, on the other hand, produces this type of
> discourse: (I) ← I tell myself that perhaps I am loved → (you) or (I) ← I
> wonder if I am loved → (you). (Irigaray 1993c, 174)

In 1967, Irigaray drew no particular attention to the sex difference of the
subjects analyzed. Hysteria tends to be clinically associated with women,
and obsessional neurosis more with men (although there are, of course,
male hysterics and female obsessional neurotics). This is a point strongly
emphasized by Irigaray in the 1986 paper, but barely mentioned two
decades earlier. Similarly, none of Irigaray's linguistic studies on schizophrenia through the sixties and early seventies analyzed potentially different relations to language of male and female schizophrenics. By con-

trast, in 1986, Irigaray notices that "female *schizophrenics* do not work out their own idiosyncratic codes in the same way as male schizophrenics" (1993c, 174).

At this point, Irigaray lays out a program for future study. She reconsiders the results of existing published studies and hazards the hypothesis that there is a general difference in the language use of men and women, not just within "certain so-called homogeneous groups" such as schizophrenics (1993c, 174). These differences pertain not just to content, she speculates, but also to syntactic and grammatical formulations. "This," she suggests, "can be interpreted as showing that the subject who generates the utterance is adopting a different position toward language, the object of discourse, the world, the other" (175). From this point on, Irigaray would pursue linguistic studies focusing on the subjective relationship to sexual difference manifested in both content and grammatical structure as a means of diagnosing the individual's relationship to the world and others. The pattern we have seen attributed to the hysteric and the obsessional neurotic in 1967 returns. Though from this point there would be few references to the early research, when Irigaray comes to offer a typology of fundamental differences between male and female discourse, she does so by repeating the formulation originally used in her discussion of hysterics and obsessional neurotics:

> The typical sentence produced by a male, once all modifications have been allowed for, is:
> *I wonder if I am loved* or: *I tell myself that perhaps I am loved.*
> The typical sentence produced by a woman is:
> *Do you love me?* (1993a, 134, translation modified)

The repetition of the linguistic formulations previously attributed to hysteria and obsessional neurosis consolidates the suggestion that men and women are suffering from the absence of adequate sexual difference. The modes deemed male and female are analyzed as impoverished. The first kind of speaker is designated as trapped in a bubble, with the fissure of doubt at the heart of its self-enclosed reflexivity. The second is described as excluded, rather than excluding itself, from communication, only able to appeal or interrogate: "The subject who is apparently producing the message occurs only as the possible *object* of the person addressed" (1993a, 135). Again, this reiterates the concern about whether a subject we confront is, or is not, in the position of subject. If not, Irigaray asks, is an adequate dialogue between the sexes possible?

As Irigaray's research in the area evolved, she would claim in subsequent work that the pronouns "he" and "she" are used differently by the sexes. Men and women largely favor "he" in the subject position when asked to construct simple phrases. However, asked to construct a sentence with "you," male subjects tend to put a "woman, an anonymous other, or the Other" in the position of you-as-object. Women tend to construct more direct sentences of the form "I am cuddling you" (Irigaray 1996a, 82). Women tend not to place "he" or "she" in the plural. This is one of the indicators, Irigaray (1996a) suggests, of "the paucity of real or symbolic relations between women and men" (88). While both men and women are suffering from a lack of sexual difference, Irigaray claims that there is considerable variation in its expression. For example, linguistic analyses of syntactic formations suggest to her that "women seek communication with the other, the other-man in particular, and in this they are different from men" (80, translation modified).

Having negotiated in her approach to the history of ideas a concept of sexual difference as absent, Irigaray draws on the same approach in her linguistic analysis. She analyzes language in terms of its lack of an appropriate relationship to the feminine and to the other more generally. She uses language as evidence not just of how the feminine is seen but also of how it is not seen. For example, both male and female respondents usually refer to woman not as subject but as object and almost never refer to women in the plural. Rather than just telling what forms of communication occur, Irigaray attempts an analysis that demonstrates that communication is not occurring. This is seen in the different tendencies in male and female linguistic relations to the world, each other, and others.

What is missing from language is as important as what is present in it. Language does not just serve as the medium of expression or manifest a subject's relationship to identity or sexuality. It also expresses the absence of alternative relationships to identity and sexuality and can be analyzed in terms of its paucity in this regard.

Finally, just as in her more philosophical work Irigaray tries to invent an impossible concept of femininity and sexual difference, so in her linguistic work she proposes the introduction of reforms that might contribute to a culture of sexual difference. *I Love to You* discusses the possible substitution of verb formations such as "I speak to you," "I ask of you," "I love to you," and "I give to you" for "I ask you," "I give you," and "I love you."[11] Such formations could mark a constructive engagement with the possibility of restructured relations between selves and others. According to a utopian linguistic modification, "the 'to' is the sign of non-immediacy, of mediation between us. . . . The 'to' is the site of non-reduction of the person to the object. . . . The 'to' is also a barrier against alienating the other's freedom in my subjectivity, my world, my language" (1996a, 109–10).

Trying to change words or verb structure by fiat is more than difficult. Such proposed reforms are among the most ambiguous aspects of her work. So are proposals that those who engage in religious worship should do so in relation to a broad range of feminine figures including Anne, Ruth, Naomi, and Elspeth, and proposals for legal reforms that include the introduction of a new legal status of virginity. None of the proposed reforms need be taken at face value. For example, they can be interpreted as a negative reminder of just how much cultural change would be necessary for a society to evolve into a culture of sexual difference in the Irigarayan sense: reform at the level of religion, language, media, the economy, law, and so on. Thus the point of the reforms would be not that they sound plausible but that they do not. The implausibility of the changes can be interpreted as a reminder to us of the sexual indifference of our culture, an indifference to which we are usually oblivious. The proposed reforms can act as the rhetorical reminder that we live in a culture in which they are impossible. Alternatively, Irigaray's repeated demands for linguistic, social, legal, religious, and economic reform may be intended to change the reader's attitude toward a culture of sexual difference. Irigaray cannot expect that any one of the proposed reforms could have the intended effect. But through repetition of the proposals, she may heighten the degree to which the reader accepts her view that culture is impoverished to the extent that it does not better allow the possibility of sexual difference.

3

Rethinking the Politics of Recognition

The Declaration of Irigarayan Sexuate Rights

> But sexuate rights are impossible, isn't this the point she is making?
> Elizabeth Grosz, "The Future of Sexual Difference"

Surveying the extensive field of Irigaray commentary, Pheng Cheah and Elizabeth Grosz (1998) have noted that while she is "probably the only living feminist philosopher today who has articulated an elaborate program for concrete sociocultural, legal and political transformation," "Irigaray's contributions to political theory have largely been overlooked" (5). Few commentators have considered Irigaray's place in the context of historical and contemporary political philosophy, although some indications of how Irigaray might be so situated have been offered in the work of Iris Young (1990), Nicola Lacey (1996, 1998), Drucilla Cornell (1992a, 1992b, 1998), and Nicole Fermon (1998), amongst others.[1]

But Irigaray has been a frequent point of reference in debates about the recognition of sexual difference.[2] She has been grouped among those who argue for the recognition of feminine specificity.[3] In such contexts, the reality of actual differences between men and women is usually asserted so that it can be argued that difference should be recognizable by our political and legal institutions. The problem is located as one of blindness versus recognition: Can we restructure our formal and legal institutions so that they recognize the fact of sexual difference? In the words of Christine Littleton (1991, 44), "[C]urrent equality analysis is . . . inapplicable once it encounters 'real' differences." In "Polity and Group Difference," Iris Marion Young criticizes politics of equality that define citizens in terms of what they have in common as opposed to how they differ. In a legal context, she writes, universality means "laws and rules that say the same for all and apply to all in the same way; laws and rules that are blind to individual and group differences" (Young 1990, 114). However, legal treatment of sexual difference is not only a matter of its being recognized at law. As Vicki Schultz (1992) writes, "[F]eminists can remind judges that they too are the architects of women's work aspirations and identities. Courts can acknowledge their own constitutive power and use it to create a workworld. . . . [T]o create that world, they must abandon the fiction of the female subject already-fixed 'before' the law" (324). Schultz recalls that the role of the law is not simply to reflect social norms and conventional identities. The law's role is also to reshape civic and sexual identity.

But what sorts of identities might it be possible to legally invent? Can the law legitimately play such a role? Could Luce Irigaray's work be assessed insofar as it contributes to an understanding of legal creativity of this kind? These questions place under scrutiny the language of legal and institutional "blindness" versus "recognition" used by these scholars and their positioning of sexual difference as the potential object of legal, civil, and constitutional fields of vision. These writers assume that Irigaray is part of a feminist tradition that laments the sex blindness of contemporary and historical political culture, public policy, and legal and government institutions. It is true that she sometimes refers to recognition in discussing sexual difference. But to focus only on such formulations overlooks the crucial aspect of her work on sexuate rights and legal reform. This aspect is her concurrent argument that the recognition of sexual difference is impossible. If sexual difference ever emerged in our culture, we would cognize it, not re-cognize it.[4]

Many commentators (for example, Cornell 1991, Huffer 1995, Lacey 1996) have discussed Irigaray's philosophy in terms of a concept of performativity. They claim that Irigaray thinks we need a founding of sexual difference. But having claimed that sexual difference is (today, for us) impossible, she therefore claims that its legal recognition is impossible. Nonetheless, she does imagine the possible constitution of sexual difference. She imagines how it might involve a paradoxical legal recognition of its own possibility. Sexual difference would not precede the time of its legal recognition. It would be instituted by it.

To assimilate Irigaray's support for a legal recognition of difference to the position of those who posit women's differences as already fixed before the law and awaiting legal recognition is to overlook an important aspect of her argument. Irigaray finds value in arguing, not for a legal recognition of sexual difference that would be possible, but for a legal recognition of sexual difference that would not be possible. I want in this chapter to consider what kind of contribution she can make to debates about the politics of recognition.

In posing this question, I will first turn to a context in which the problematics of recognition have been thoroughly debated in recent years. This is a context in which figures such as Carol Gilligan are more likely to be cited than is Luce Irigaray.[5] Susan Wolf (1994, 76) has noted that the politics of recognition can be applied only awkwardly to gender politics. Think of the discussion of educational reform in the work of James Tully. Women do not share a distinct culture that could be affirmed by educational and institutional reforms. As Beauvoir (1988) wrote, women "have no past, no history, no religion of their own. . . . [T]hey live dispersed among the males" (19). Yet, Tully writes that in addition to claims by nationalist movements, a "politics of cultural recognition" includes multicultural or intercultural movements. He comments that this landscape is further complicated by

> the demands of feminist movements for recognition. . . . Because the constitutional institutions and traditions of interpretation were established long ago by men, it follows that they should be amended . . . in order to recognise and accommodate women's culturally distinctive ways of speaking and acting, so that substantive gender equality will be assured in the daily political struggles in the institutions the constitution founds. Making this task even more difficult, women's culture itself is not homogeneous, but multicultural and contested. (Tully 1995, 2–3)

Here, Tully refers to the idea that women might share distinctive ways of speaking and acting that should be recognized at law although women do not share a homogeneous culture. Tully's discussion falters as he associates women with "multicultural groups" and "linguistic minorities" as a set of those who "seek to participate in the existing institutions of the dominant society, but in ways which recognise and affirm . . . their culturally diverse ways of thinking, speaking and acting. What they share is a longing for self-rule" (4).

In "The Politics of Recognition" (1994), Charles Taylor's emphasis is placed more strongly on the law's potential to allow new possible identities through its recognition of them. He refers to "the thesis that our identity is partly shaped by recognition or its absence, often by the *mis*recognition of others, and so a person or a group of people can suffer real damage, real distortion, if the people or society around them mirror back to them a confining or demeaning or contemptible picture of themselves. Non-recognition or misrecognition can inflict harm, can be a form of oppression, imprisoning someone in a false, distorted, and reduced mode of being" (25). Taylor goes on to see the issue partly as one of esteem. Are public and institutionalized depictions of women and others demeaning, for example?[6] Taylor emphasizes the role of recognition by public institutions and the potential contribution of that recognition to the subjective possibilities of citizens.

But for a more sustained consideration of the role of feminism in the politics of recognition, I turn to his contemporary James Tully. In *Strange Multiplicities* (1995), Tully supports the institutional affirmation of cultural diversity. He refers to "protecting and enhancing the cultural differences and similarities of intercultural citizens. . . . The recognition and accommodation of these suppressed and persecuted citizens on equal footing with other members of a society marks the transition to post-imperial constitutionalism. It requires more than . . . mutual toleration and respect. . . . It requires that the citizens affirm diversity itself as a constitutive good of the association" (177). But the logic according to which one might undertake to protect cultural difference may be very different from the logic according to which one might undertake to enhance it. One model takes as its reference point difference posited before the protecting intervention. The other takes as its reference point difference as it might result from the enhancing intervention. Once diversity is affirmed as a cultural good, then a law that promotes diversity should be as justified as a law that recognizes it. But the language of the above passage refers to cultural diversity as preceding and calling for recognition, accommodation, tolerance, and respect.

Tully acknowledges that recognition can never be definitive because cultural identities are constantly contested, questioned, and renegotiated (25). He argues that "the politics of cultural recognition takes place on this intercultural 'common' ground, as I shall call the labyrinth composed of the overlap, interaction and negotiation of cultures over time. Of course, mutual recognition is not rendered unproblematic by the reconceptualisation and clarification of the ground on which we stand" (14). But he largely converts this acknowledgment into a point that "contract is an ongoing renegotiation." His argument is primarily that we should not see a nation's constitution as a static, original entity. His simultaneous point that identities are not static entities receives less emphasis.

This choice of emphasis is particularly seen in his comments on women. Tully refers to women's "feminine ways of speaking, thinking and acting" (47), citing Gilligan's work on the ethics of care and the distortion of women's voices by a tradition that privileges a principled approach to justice (49). He subsequently argues that because founding constitutions were established without women's contribution, it is insufficient for women to try to integrate their voice into them. Instead, women need to be able to have a say "in their own voice." Despite his recognition that women do not share a culture or language, as attributed to particular racial or cultural groups, Tully refers to women's voice. He asks how constitutional negotiations might come to recognize gender difference. Just constitutional negotiations would determine which gender differences are "relevant and worthy of being constitutionalised" (178). Such references assign women a possible preexisting specificity such as particular manners of speaking and acting. Consider this passage: "[W]ith this protection in place, women will be able to amend the political institutions they share with men so they can speak and act in their own ways on equal footing in everyday political struggles: that is, without assimilation to other ways of speaking and acting" (178). Tully acknowledges that "many male and female sceptics doubt that there are identity-related differences of gender which require constitutional protection" (179). At this point, he refers to the feminist view that there is a female specificity: "[H]owever, cultural feminists have brought forward sufficient evidence of their differences and their constitutional domination by men to establish that their claim warrants a fair hearing" (178–79).[7]

It seems the only kind of sexual difference the law might legitimately recognize must preexist that recognition. Any other kind of constitutionalization of sexual difference would, according to this supposition, be illegitimate. This is clear when Tully comments, "[I]f the participants [in periodic constitutional dialogues] reach agreement that no significant differences remain that cannot be recognised and accommodated in the prevailing constitutional order, then the sceptics will be proven correct. If not, then they must agree that the cultural differences that remain after the discussion ought to be constitutionalised" (179). The issue of sexual difference and its recognition at law is limited to existing differences between men and women.

It could be said that this limitation sits ill with references to the law's power to enhance difference and promote diversity. Such references imply that the law's role is not only to recognize difference but also to foster it. Tully plainly considers diversity to be a good. He rejects the view that the original nature and logic of constitutions must be respected. So it is not clear why a politics of difference must be limited to recognition. Why should we not value legal reforms that promote difference, playing an inventive, creative role in this respect? Not all theorists of recognition do limit its scope to real differences preceding legal recognition. Consider Nancy Fraser's formulation (1997) that "recognition claims often take the form of calling attention to, if not performatively creating, the putative specificity of some group and then of affirming its value. Thus, they tend to promote group differentiation" (16).[8]

As an alternative to Carol Gilligan's approach, how might Luce Irigaray's philosophy of sexual difference contribute to a rethinking of the politics of recognition? Tully's unsatisfactory references to women might suggest that the politics of recognition errs in extending the language of multiculturalism to women. But what of his suggestion that cultural difference should be constitutionalized (only?) if and where there is agreement from participants in constitutional dialogues that cultural differences exist among us "that cannot be recognized and accommodated in the prevailing constitutional order"? Is this formulation adequate to post-colonized cultural difference? Recall how Frantz Fanon (1970) depicted metropolitan France's erosion of Martinican culture in its promotion of "the mother country's cultural standards" (14).[9] Must our understanding of constitutionalizable cultural differences be restricted to those existing prior to their recognition? Fanon considered that much of what he valued in his culture had been undermined in the period of French colonialism. But he viewed a politics of restitution of lost culture as romantic, nostalgic, and frequently stereotyping.

Perhaps Tully's formulation cannot adequately take into account one's hopes for identities that might arise from institutional recognition of what does not yet exist. It is also inadequate to cultural identities that no longer exist. Discussing Fanon's reservations about privileging lost original identity, Homi Bhabha (1994) points out that Fanon "recognizes the crucial importance, for subordinated peoples, of asserting their indigenous cultural traditions and retrieving their repressed histories. But he is far too aware of the dangers of the fixity and fetishism of identities within the calcification of colonial cultures to recommend that 'roots' be struck in the celebratory romance of the past or by homogenizing the history of the present" (9). Bhabha is just one of Fanon's readers to emphasize Fanon's claim that "I am not merely here-and-now, sealed into thingness. I am for somewhere else and for something else. . . . I do battle for the creation of a human world. . . . [T]he real *leap* consists in introducing invention into existence. In the world in which I travel, I am endlessly creating myself" (Fanon, cited in Bhabha 1994, 8). If we return to Tully's concept of constitutional recognition, we see how Fanon's formulations exceed the question of whether legal institutions recognize existing differences. What of the ways in which legal reform can promote the invention of new cultural identities whose right to recognition need not depend on their being original or in their lying before the law? The language of the politics of recognition can be inadequate to the crucial work of invention, creation, and being forever "somewhere else and something else" in relation to identity.

In chapter 10, I am going to assess Irigaray's recent work on cultural difference in *Between East and West*. My interpretation will be critical of this work. I want in this chapter to contextualize my later criticisms. Irigaray is interested in the special rights and privileges that could be accorded to subjects engaged in a transformation of a culture of sexual difference. She should support a similar politics in relation to cultural difference, but, as I shall argue in chapter 10, her argument does not develop in this direction. Because I will argue that this is a problem in her work, I consider in this chapter some recent public debates about diversity and difference. I do not presuppose that Irigaray has an important contribution to make to these discussions. Because she addresses multiculturalism, I ask how her work might look when assessed from the perspective of public discussions about race and cultural difference as well as gender.

In Australia, debates about indigenous land rights have been forced by legal circumstances to ask what kind of original and unbroken connection to land would legally justify a land rights or compensation claim.[10] Urban indigenous Australians may be deemed less in a position to make land or compensation claims, despite reminders that "connection may be maintained in cultural or spiritual ways other than physical association" (Reconciliation Sheet 10).[11] The findings of a Saulwick and Muller survey on attitudes among nonindigenous Australians to reconciliation were that "[t]hose living in cities are thought not to be representative of all Aborigines and, indeed, not to be 'real' Aborigines, particularly if they have some white forebears. Indeed many of these people are accused of claiming Aboriginality in order to gain the welfare benefits which flow from this status. They are seen as more demanding, and somehow less 'genuine' than Aborigines living in remote areas" (Newspoll 2000, 36). Public debate seems equipped to think cultural difference only in terms of originality, and in terms of the opposition between the authentic and the inauthentic.

Obviously, such oppositions are inadequate to postcolonial identities and differences,[12] indeed to all identities and differences. Public institutions need to be adequate to the recognition of both eroded and reinvented identities, rather than casting an opposition between the original and the unauthentic. It is interesting to reflect on how land rights claims based on the right to transform and newly create indigenous culture as well as claims based on the right to continue traditional relationships to the land could be accommodated. In addition to recognizing indigenous identities, public institutions contribute to the forces that foster their reinvention.[13] The identities apparently recognized do not always precede their recognition at law.

One distinction made by Irigaray could be valuable in assessing appeals to respect for difference in public debate. Irigaray remains unconvinced by enthusiasm for sexual difference expressed by those who reify woman as mother, wife, muse, natural caregiver, sensitive companion. The apparent love of sexual difference has been the means of excluding adequate developments of sexual difference, she argues. This suggests what her approach should be to evaluating appeals to cultural difference. Has the political endorsement of cultural difference served as a means of avoiding an adequate thinking of cultural difference? An Irigarayan politics could provoke one to ask whether alternative modes of conceptualizing cultural difference are excluded by appeals to respect for difference.

Such an exclusion has not been infrequent in high-profile global politics of recent times. Take one of the most prominent contexts in which East Asian rights have been debated in the literature. In Malaysia, appeals to cultural specificity are said to have justified state repression of political opposition and cultural and sexual diversity. One could respond that while Mohamed Mahathir has spoken in the name of respect for cultural difference, his politics has been highly resistant to the affirmation of difference.[14] Perhaps an Irigarayan approach might interrogate the practical and conceptual exclusions on which a politician's appeal to cultural specificity is founded.[15] Does the long-term defense of "Asian values" by Dr. Mahathir interconnects with the suppression of plural perspectives on authoritarianism, the role of women, sexuality, religious expression, capitalist values, and worker's conditions?[16] Irigaray's question is whether qualitative discussions of difference are promoted. Speaking in the name of difference may be a means of avoiding a culture of difference. To return to the point made earlier, what is not said about difference is as determining as what is. It is useful to ask what concepts of cultural difference are disallowed, even by the very discourses that affirm cultural difference. Irigaray argues that of any context, historical or contemporary, "What differences are disallowed here?" is a good question. She also thinks one need not refer only to existing differences that are disallowed. It is also useful to ask what alternative possibilities for differences are disallowed in advance. An Irigarayan politics of the impossible asks what kinds of differences have not been possible in specific cultural and historical contexts. It analyzes the overall network of forces contributing to that impossibility. I will now look at one example of a concept that Irigaray considers has not been possible. I will then look at some criticisms of this concept.

In chapter 2, I mentioned one of the most controversial aspects of Irigaray's work. We saw that one of her strategies is to leave the contents of the term "sexual difference" open, a pair of empty brackets. Sexual difference is an anticipated, abstract possibility. But a second strategy is to mimic and amplify some of the most traditional representations of women so as to render them exorbitant. These include woman as sexual (amplified as the two-lips sexuality), as maternal (amplified as the ethical mother-child mediated by the placenta), and as virgin. Via this strategy of amplification, Irigaray proposes respect for women's virginity as a conceptual basis for legal reform instituting sexuate rights.

I want now to look further at Irigaray's interest in virginity as an impossible basis for legal rights. The use of the term virginity marks Irigaray's break with a politics of recognition. This use is not restitutive or nostalgic. It emphasizes that sexual difference need not precede its legal recognition. Because Irigaray anticipates the advent of sexual difference, she often leaves its content open. Sometimes it is an abstract notion. But sometimes readers will feel it is not abstract enough. Her poetic evocations of femininity do not evoke an entirely unrecognizable, nonsensical, or fantastic state because of her intermittent occupation, mimesis, expansion, and metamorphosis of conventions about women and sexual difference.[17] Her refigured understanding of female virginity as the philosophical basis for sexuate rights is a good example. She proposes alternative, new significations for virginity. She reworks these as an emblem of an ethics of nonappropriation of the other. But according to Drucilla Cornell, the content Irigaray gives to sexual difference as the foundation for legal reform causes the project to collapse and impedes the very creative effect it is meant to stimulate.

Irigaray's ideal for a legal remetaphorization of sexual difference as a basis for legal reform calls for many prosaic legal amendments including fair treatment of women in the areas of family allowances, media, advertising, taxation laws, and so on. But under the heading of the "right to human identity," we also find a startling affirmation of women's virginity as a legal right and as a crucial component of feminine identity (Irigaray 1994, 60; 1993b, 86–87).

When Irigaray argues for social respect for women's virginity, she has revalued it as a concept in terms of metaphors of integrity. Virginity would signify both a physical and a moral inviolability of women. The virginity to which woman had a right would not only be bodily but also mental or "spiritual" (*"droit à la virginité de corps et d'esprit pour la femme"*) (1989b, 16; 1994, xv). Indeed, in *je, tu, nous* and in other texts, she conceives of women as cultivating a kind of "becoming-virgin" (1993b, 117). As she writes, "There's no doubt we are born virgins. But we also have to become virgins, to relieve our bodies and souls from cultural and familial fetters. For me, becoming a virgin [*devenir vierges*] is synonymous with women's conquest of the spiritual" (1993b, 117). In *Between East and West*, Irigaray clarifies again that the virginity of which she is speaking is not an anatomical virginity ("once again, it is not a matter here of the presence or absence of a physiological hymen" [1999, 93]), and this makes greater sense of her claim that "if a woman does not keep her virginity, she loses her identity" (2002, 68).

Irigaray (2002) clarifies the conventional connotations of virginity from which she distances herself: "It would be worthwhile to make clear," she agrees, "that virginity does not then signify a woman's privation or abstention from her self-realization, her submission to a man's goodwill or becoming" (68, translation modified). Instead, she speaks of "psychic virginity [*virginité psychique*]," defined as a woman's aptitude to "conserve and cultivate her own identity" (68). Or in place of virginity, we could substitute Drucilla Cornell's concept of bodily integrity or inviolability (Cornell 1995). Irigaray reconceptualizes the term virginity to make it signify psychological and moral ideas of inviolability. Her argument is not exactly that women are radically different from men in body and mind. Rather, she analyzes contexts not able to accommodate such a conception and premised rather on sexual "indifference." Respect for women's equality (which carries the silent "with men," according to Irigaray) is more culturally plausible than a poetic, creatively refigured politics of virginity. What does the implausibility of the latter tell us about our cultural parameters? Many readers will find Irigaray's attempt to laud women's virginity regressive. But she asks what new meanings virginity could acquire. Shouldn't the project of transforming, rather than reiterating, its meaning be our task? Is it impossible for virginity to be refigured so that it no longer connotes the commodification of women for exchange between men? Is our culture premised on the exclusion of alternative connotations for women and femininity?

A revalued concept of virginity would interconnect with the other, more predictable financial and material rights supported by Irigaray. It would offer an alternative conceptual foundation for the rights with which we are more familiar. Otherwise, financial and other legal rights could too easily be appropriated in terms of a language of sameness and equality. In this sense, the interweaving of the mundane, the radical, and the poetic is pivotal to Irigaray's current project. It is for this reason that Cornell, and also Nicola Lacey, have distinguished a politics that attempts to remetaphorize the feminine from those that attempt to describe women (whether in terms of sameness or difference) (Lacey 1996, 139–40; Cornell 1991, 199–205). While extreme, the reappropriation of the term virginity and its reconceptualization serve an important rhetorical function, highlighting Irigaray's attempt to formulate rights that break with a politics of recognition in favor of remetaphorization.

Legal reform projects must ask whether there is sufficient room for poetic reinvention and the construction of new imaginaries, Irigaray is claiming. Have groups traditionally excluded from the shaping of social and political institutions had the opportunity to introduce new identities into law, in addition to appropriating traditionally recognized identities to whose shaping they did not contribute? What means might be used to generate new meanings in such contexts? Irigaray proposes those of reappropriation, mimicry, the implosion from within of traditional stereotypes, and the creation of unfamiliar notions of identity. Could we understand this as an important part of legal reform, interconnected with other, more obvious or practical questions? For issues of recognition are not, as Nancy Fraser has argued, opposed to issues of redistribution but intrinsic to them.[18]

But I want now to turn to the question of whether Irigaray is able to sustain an affirmation of an unfixed, undetermined concept of feminine identity, a concern eventually expressed by Drucilla Cornell after initial enthusiasm for Irigaray's work. Irigaray's concept of sexual difference as impossible does not imply that a culture that affirmed sexual difference could never come to pass. But it does mean that we cannot identify and pre-fix the identity whose recognition one might wish to see at law. Instead, the sorts of identities whose possibility is enhanced by legal affirmation of difference could arise from that legal affirmation rather than preceding it. Cornell, in her early writings on Irigaray, is among the commentators who have underlined in positive terms the impossibility of Irigarayan sexual difference in this sense.

Cornell has been one of those commentators most interested in Irigaray's concept of founding sexuate rights. In *Beyond Accommodation* (1991), Cornell writes positively about Irigaray's aim to remetaphorize the feminine. She emphasizes Irigaray's breaks with a politics of recognition. Performativity is the term that serves as the reminder of this break. For example, Cornell cautions that "[t]o reduce Irigaray's positioning *vis à vis* the 'sex' of feminine specificity to description of gender identity or of biological femaleness is to fail . . . to heed the specificity of Irigaray's literary language and its performative powers to crack open what 'is.' . . . [T]he affirmation of feminine difference . . . refigures the feminine" (17).

In "Gender, Sex and Equivalent Rights" (1992a), Cornell agrees with Irigaray that "we continually have to analogize our experience to men's if we want it legally 'recognized' as unequal treatment" (292). By contrast, a new formulation of equivalent rights that might apply to reproductive rights would "allow difference to be recognized and equally valued without women having to show that they are like men for legal purposes" (293). On the one hand, Cornell retains the concept of remetaphorization of the feminine, noting that the concept of equivalent rights "address[es] the value of feminine sexual difference" *as* "continually reimagined" (281). As she states in a later interview, "I did not see Irigaray at all as an essentialist. If anything, the feminine was a kind of radical otherness to any conception of the real or reality. More than anything else, here I found someone who was deploying the feminine unashamedly in a utopian manner, saying that there is a beyond to whatever kind of concept of sense we have" (Cornell 1998, 20).

On the other hand, the language of recognition repeats throughout Cornell's essay. "Equivalent rights recognize that the human species as currently constituted is composed of two genres" (Cornell 1992a, 282). "Sexual difference is recognized and valued" (282). But in her overall discussion Cornell emphasizes the retrospective status of this recognition. Recognizing a reimagined feminine sexual difference is not the same as recognizing a difference preexisting that recognition. Instead, such recognition contributes to the institution of the very sexual difference it apparently recognizes.

By contrast, Cornell's more recent *The Imaginary Domain* (1995) makes little reference to Irigaray, although it builds on her concept of the role sexuate rights might play in restructuring models of civic personhood. For example, Cornell argues for reformulated rights that ensure the legal "protection of the imaginary domain" (4, 105). They should ensure the right to have one's sexed being represented and to represent one's own sexed being. Emphasizing the retrospective nature of such rights, she qualifies, "[T]he recognition of the right of self-representation of our sexuate beings works backward. As beings entitled as a matter of right to represent their own sexuate being, women, for example, can no longer be identified in law as a naturalized class whose entitlement and duties flow from this status position" (43). In Cornell's description of the imaginary domain, she pulls back again from the notion of recognition, at least insofar as it implies the recognition of a static, pre-fixed identity. The right to representation of one's sexuate being means that we can no longer represent persons as neutered or as "pregiven" selves (61). And again, "a person is not something 'there'" (5). Instead, the person must be respected as a possibility that "can never be fulfilled once and for all" (5). Though it makes little overt reference to Irigaray, *The Imaginary Domain* bears some affinities with the Irigarayan concepts of sexual rights. Cornell understands the social process of legal reform and the legal reconstruction of sexuate identity as part of the ongoing process whereby my lived sexuate identity is transformed.

More recently, however, Cornell has come to express considerable reservations about Irigaray's project. In the subsequent work *At the Heart of Freedom* (1998), Cornell's references to Irigaray are more extensive, but Irigaray is now figured definitely, and critically, as a theorist who "naturaliz[es] sexual difference in sexuate rights" (30). Irigaray privileges sexual difference over difference of race, nationality, and sexuality. Cornell adds, "Irigaray's writings on sexuate rights seemingly contradict her philosophical work, in which the question of sexual difference is left as a question" (200 n. 67).

This position is most clearly articulated in Cornell's interview with Cheah, Grosz, and Judith Butler. Cornell explains her original interest in Irigaray: "I found someone who was deploying the feminine unashamedly in a utopian manner, saying that there is a beyond to whatever kind of concept of sense we have. And without that beyond being articulated, endlessly breaking up the real, we can't even get to a different kind of ethics" (Butler and Cornell 1998, 20). Cornell says that Irigaray never seemed to her to be an essentialist thinker but rather one who articulated a beyond without fixed content. Contrast with the Cornell of *At the Heart of Freedom* (1998), for whom it is precisely the way in which Irigaray refigures the imaginary—precisely the way in which she attempts to give content to sexual difference—that is the problem: "The attempt to give rights, thought through gender difference as a universal, denies women the freedom to reimagine their sexual difference. For Irigaray, there are naturally two sexes. Her ontologization of the two denies that women live their biology in infinitely different and original ways. In the imaginary domain, sexes cannot be counted because what we will become under freedom cannot be known in advance" (122).

Irigaray does attempt to think beyond sense. However, to criticize her very attempt to give content to that beyond of sense is a mistake at least insofar as Irigaray retains the notion of the impossibility of these attempts. How does one transgress sense? As with the earlier two-lips morphology of women, Irigaray piggybacks onto traditional concepts of femininity and maternity, in this case virginity, and elsewhere, as we shall see later, maternity.[19] Such concepts are blown out so as to become incredible. We are very far from giving cultural credibility to a legal privileging of virginity. Cornell takes Irigaray to be attempting to fix the meaning of sexual difference. But how does one occupy the position of "beyond sense"? Sometimes Irigaray does speak of sexual difference while leaving its content open. Sometimes she transforms traditional notions until they lose their sense.

It is indicative that when Grosz prompts Cornell, "But sexuate rights are impossible, isn't this the point she is making?" Cornell responds, "I have always read her as programmatically serious about sexuate rights, and seeing them as realizable" (Butler and Cornell 1998, 25, 26). Certainly, Irigaray speaks in the rhetorical mode of programmatic seriousness about sexuate rights. But the question is whether they function rhetorically for us as possible or impossible. What Cornell takes to be a mistaken attempt to give content can also be interpreted as a program of sexuate rights insisting on their own impossibility. This is notwithstanding—indeed, it is because of—the spirit of seriousness in which they are articulated. The more serious the spirit, the more they perform as impossible. While questions remain about the utility of an Irigarayan politics of impossible recognition, the assumption that the specific content of sexuate rights works to undermine their function as impossible is surely mistaken.

Irigaray's concept of sexual difference fails, on its own terms, not by providing specific content to sexual difference, or through omitting to give content to sexual difference, but only if these two aspects decouple. Her aim is to retain the double notion of sexual difference as impossible (lacking sense) and yet that which she would see legally recognized (yet how can we think a recognition of the senseless?). Sexual difference stands or falls on its ability to retain this contradictory status. The concept of virginity is a dovetailed hovering between the recognizable and the unrecognizable, as is the two-lips morphology.

Elsewhere, Cornell resists not the fact that Irigaray gives content to sexual difference but the precise content she gives. According to her argument in the passage previously cited, this content attempts "to give rights, thought through gender difference as a universal," and thereby "denies women the freedom to reimagine their sexual difference." This comment returns us to the term by which Cornell first assessed Irigaray's concept of sexual difference: performativity. In her earlier work, Cornell supported Irigaray's project by explaining its performative aspect. Irigaray's language, she argued, had the power to "crack open what 'is'" and refigure the feminine. Now Cornell questions not only the substance of Irigaray's work (that she gives content to the feminine) but also its performance. Irigaray's language acts to deny women the freedom of their imagination. These comments require some reflection on the status of performativity in Irigaray's work, to which the next chapter turns.

4

Irigarayan Performativity

Is This a Question of Can Saying It Make It So?

> Myth or fiction is not simply, for Irigaray, a *reflection* of social orga-
> nization, it also gives a shaping force to the conceptualization of
> rights and citizenship. . . . Plato's fiction is not just an expression of
> Ancient Greek class or sexual warfare; it actively contributes to
> women's exclusion from full citizenship.
>   The problem with the creation of myths, however, is that it is an
> aleatory process. Who can tell in advance which reworking, which
> creation, is going to crystallize a potential shift in the collective vi-
> sion and make a new configuration possible?
>   Margaret Whitford, *Luce Irigaray: Philosophy in the Feminine*

This chapter considers one set of problems that critics have raised about
Irigaray's program for sexuate rights. First, although intended to offer
a possible alternative imaginary for female embodiment, these rights may
restrict women's freedom to imagine another imaginary. Second, there is
no guarantee that they would act as Irigaray anticipates. Third, the rights
are illegitimate, unfounded, or unjustified.

In chapter 3, we saw Drucilla Cornell reconsider her initially positive
interpretation. Cornell's early view was that Irigaray is engaged in a poetic regeneration of the feminine. Irigaray's evocations of sexual difference perform a new metaphorization of femininity. Irigaray is not depicting the feminine sex with poetic language but attempting to "crack
open what 'is.'" Cornell's early view was that new possibilities for the
feminine are opened up by Irigaray's work. As we saw, Cornell's subsequent view is that Irigaray closes down new possibilities for the feminine.
I want now to consider this issue more closely.

We have seen that Irigaray proposes only very minimal content for the
concept of sexual difference. She defines it negatively. Its relation to the

masculine would not be one of sameness, complementarity, or privation. She also refers to sexual difference through a project of amplified mimicry. Here, she calls the bluff of the tradition that associates women with embodiment, virginity, motherhood, and the male citizen's helpmate. Her own depictions imagine alternative possibilities for women's embodiment (the two-lips sexuality), virginity (the conceptual basis for legal reform), and motherhood (a strong, mutually acknowledging and mediated relationship between mother and daughter). Such depictions refigure through exaggeration the traditional terms in which women have been represented.

Although their function is to open and unfix, Cornell has asked whether these exaggerating depictions do not narrow and fix. In her view, sexual difference is no longer posed by Irigaray as "a question" (Cornell 1998, 200, 67n). It has become an answer. To define sexuate rights in terms of the right to virginity (as reconceptualized by Irigaray) seems an answer that fixes. But Irigaray would claim that such imaginings still leave sexual difference an open question. They function as the question "Why not?" or "Why is this culturally impossible?" Where Irigaray posits a specific content (a different understanding of virginity or of the heterosexual couple), she asks us why that content is culturally impossible. She thinks it is worthwhile that we reflect on that cultural impossibility, and on the deep discomfort we have with the idea that virginity might take on new meanings, for example. Doing so may be a means of provoking readers to reimagine sexual difference, and not necessarily in the terms proposed rhetorically by Irigaray. But in Cornell's more recent view, "the attempt to give rights, thought through gender difference as a universal, denies women the freedom to reimagine their sexual difference."

At this point, Cornell makes claims about how we should understand the sexuate rights as performing. She claims that they work poorly, even infelicitously, if they are supposed to open up sexual difference to new possibilities. This returns us to the debates about performativity that have been pivotal to many feminist readings of Irigaray, and also to many criticisms of her.

Much literature about Irigaray's sexuate rights has evinced concern over the likely outcome of a declaration of sexuate rights. Some feel Irigaray places excessive confidence in rights talk. In the words of Nicola Lacey, "Irigaray borrows (unusually within her work) the language of . . . institutional reform. In doing so, she espouses a curiously naive and apparently instrumental optimism about legal reform" (1996, 149; 1998, 245). Lacey also consider Irigaray to be naively instrumental about the power of her rhetoric. Whitford (1991b) has argued that the utopian moments of Irigaray's philosophy should be understood "in terms of the imaginary, rather than as literal accounts of a possible future" (186). Debate about excessive confidence in legal reform shifts to concerns about excessive confidence in a program of utopian visions, in the politics of creating myths. There are really two questions here. Does Irigaray really think she has the power to create new myths? And does she place excessive confidence in the capacity of new myths and images to be socially transformative?

Irigaray might concede that the legal declaration of a bill of sexual rights would not lead reliably to the culture of sexual difference she hopes for. Perhaps she believes (more realistically) that to perform the declaration—for example, in her own published work—plays a useful role in contributing to the rhetorical conditions necessary for an eventual culture of sexual difference. In this case, some feel she is still being naively instrumentalist, not about legal reform but about her poetic rhetoric. In Nicola Lacey's words (1998), "[T]he question of whether particular rhetorics *can* move us forward is a relevant question. . . . [Can] rhetorical strategies . . . dislodge the dominant conception once they move from argument to legal institutionalisation[?]" (247). In all of these responses, instrumentalism troubles Irigaray's critics. Does Irigaray believe that as a result of legal reform, a refiguring of the imaginary, or her own writing, something willed or desired might happen: new potent and desirable images for women, if not extensive social reform? In the words of the epigraph to this chapter, "The problem with the creation of myths, however, is that it is an aleatory process. Who can tell in advance which reworking, which creation, is going to crystallize a potential shift in the collective vision and make a new configuration possible (or alternatively immobilize a tentative fluidity?)" (Whitford 1991b, 188–89).

In each case, these commentators raise concerns about the action of Irigaray's work. What events does Irigaray think might occur, either (hypothetically) from the legal declaration of sexual rights, or (hypothetically) from a declaration of sexual rights understood to be a poetic-rhetorical gesture, or (actually) from her own declaration of sexual rights in her published work? Whichever claim is attributed to Irigaray, critics ask what she thinks might result from her project. How does this critical reaction tally with the view that Irigaray's work is a politics of performativity? What is performativity?

John Austin's *How to Do Things with Words* (1962) famously discusses the infelicitous or unsuccessful speech act. Say that I pronounce the words "I hereby take you for my legally married husband." If I am not before a legally authorized marriage celebrant, the speech act is unsuccessful. Or I might say the words as an actor on a stage—again, no marriage takes place. But imagine that the celebrant is authorized to perform legal marriages and we are in the right conditions (the law might dictate that we must be of different sexes and that we must not currently be married to other partners). Imagine that we are also in the right context. We are not speaking the words of a marriage ceremony in the context of a play or a joke. Then, when I pronounce the words, the speech act may be described as performative.

In the performative mode of language, the words are said to do the marriage, to constitute it. The felicitous speech act brings into effect with its own enunciation the "thing" it apparently refers to. "In these examples," writes Austin, "it seems clear that to utter the sentence (in, of course, the appropriate circumstances) is not to *describe* my doing of what I should be said in so uttering to be doing or to state that I am doing it: it is to do it." He adds that this kind of utterance is neither true nor false. For "[w]hen I say, before the registrar or altar, etc., 'I do,' I am not reporting on a marriage: I am indulging in it" (Austin 1962, 6).

For Austin, the legitimacy of the words uttered does not inhere in their referring accurately to a situation to which the words correctly point. The words can be neither true nor false. Instead, through pronouncing the words ("in, of course, the appropriate circumstances") one effects what one says. So there are at least two issues here. There is an issue of referentiality and an issue of whether one can make things happen with words. This last might be described as "can saying make it so?" (Austin 1962, 7). These two issues—referentiality and making things so—have been key in the many discussions of performativity, feminism, and Irigaray.

Irigaray has little access to the institutional domains of legal reform and public policy in France. So her words of legal reform are pronounced, but apparently not pronounced in felicitous circumstances. They are not pronounced by a speaker authorized to effect legal reform. Saying the words of sexuate rights does not make the thing happen to which they refer: the social constitution of sexuate rights. From this perspective, Irigaray would be like the celebrant who performs marriages without being legally authorized to do so, or like the actor who says the words on the stage. There may be a performance of the words. But because the words fail to perform the act, they could be described as infelicitous. Nonetheless, commentators have thought that performativity is a useful concept for thinking about sexuate rights. In considering this issue, I offer suggestions for how Irigarayan sexuate rights might be assessed as performative by John Austin and Judith Butler.

A good example of the concern expressed by some critics about Irigarayan sexuate rights is seen in Lacey's otherwise fairly sympathetic response to them. She asks whether rhetorical strategies are capable of dislodging "the dominant conception once they gesture at a move from argument to legal institutionalization" (Lacey 1998, 247). For Lacey, the concern about Irigaray's work is exactly its striking naiveté with regard to the conditions necessary for legal reform. Does Irigaray think that performativity is, in the words of Judith Butler (1997), "the power . . . of an originating will" (51)? Does she think the declaration creates the sexual difference it declares? For Lacey, Irigaray's position is not that her simple declaration of the rights in her published works will make them happen. But Lacey does suppose it is Irigaray's view that the legal institutionalization of the rights, if it could be effected, would provide the conditions for a culture of sexual difference. This is what Lacey takes to be naive instrumental optimism, reflecting excessive confidence in the adequacy of legal reform for provoking change. But if one does read Irigaray's writings in terms of Austin's material on performativity, it is not clear that they are best interpreted as reflecting optimism in a cause-effect relationship between the institution of rights and a culture of sexual difference.

A return to Austin's distinctions may be useful in this regard. Consider his startling example, in which we imagine that someone says to me, "Shoot her," and I do (Austin 1962, 101). This is an example of how words can make things happen. Indeed, he qualifies, there are hardly any words that could not be said to make things happen. But, from the outset of *How to Do Things with Words*, this is not what Austin is most concerned with. Instead, he reflects on linguistic formulations that *are* simultaneously the deed they seem to refer to, such as "I declare," "I hereby name," "I promise," "I denounce." In such cases Austin proposes that "the issuing of the utterance is the performing of an action" (6). Questions about naive optimism would be inappropriate to such cases. Would one say, of the classic Austin performative, "Why should we think that because I enounce a promise, the promise will take place?" Certainly, someone might wonder whether I can be relied on to keep my promise. But the speech act that has happened is the promise itself. Performativity is not a concept about whether things will happen because of my words. It refers to the event my words have already constituted, such as a promise or a declaration.

Various effects may also result from my namings, declarations, and denunciations, but this is a different issue. To mark the difference, Austin distinguishes between illocutionary and perlocutionary speech acts. Speech acts may be thought of as perlocutionary insofar as they may subsequently lead to things happening. The speech act "Shoot her" is perlocutionary insofar as it may cause a gun to be fired. It is a different matter to assess a speech act insofar as it is illocutionary. Illocutionary speech has already accomplished an act regardless of its consequences. A promise has been made, for example, or a boat christened, or an order given, in the moment of these speech acts.[1]

Given that Irigaray's material has often been interpreted in terms of its performativity, how might this concept be brought most usefully to bear on her work? Perhaps Irigarayan sexuate rights should be interpreted not in terms of perlocutionary performativity (in terms of consequences that might or might not result from their enunciation or formal institutionalization) but in terms of their illocutionary performativity. What is their status as an act of declaration? Rather than asking whether the consequences would be all that Irigaray seems to anticipate, we would ask what kind of act this is already. This might be the better question, even if we cannot definitively determine the answer.

If we regard Irigaray's program as utopian, the discussion turns around consequences. Would the legal institutionalization of sexuate rights install a culture of sexual difference? The question arises because the performativity is interpreted in terms of the likely effects.[2] There is disagreement about whether the performativity in question pertains to a utopia in which sexuate rights would be installed (here the idea would be that the founding words are supposed, hypothetically, to have a possible effect, that of instituting a culture of sexual difference, and the question becomes, would they really have that effect?); or whether the performativity pertains, not to a utopian legal declaration of sexuate rights, but to Irigaray's own declaration of these rights in works such as *Thinking the Difference* and *je, tu, nous*. Either way, commentators have focused on likely consequences. Does rhetoric—new metaphors for identity to be written into legal reform—have the power to achieve cultural change?

Irigaray does not think that the institution of laws recognizing sexual difference would alone produce a culture of sexual difference. Instead, we are asked only to imagine this possibility. Asking readers to imagine that the effect could arise from the legal provocation is not the same as claiming that it really would. One strategy is to see Irigaray's rights as performing an imaginary performativity. The rights amount to a declared challenge: imagine that these rights could institute what was seemingly recognized, through that very legal "recognition" of sexual difference.

In other words, what if we think of Irigaray's declaration of sexuate rights as a declaration of a radical political perspective? Could it not be thought of as succeeding in this act of declaration? Lacking the authority, Irigaray declares that she too can declare new sexuate rights. Perhaps what is being performed is not the founding of sexuate rights but the founding of a critical perspective. The sexuate rights are a drag performance, Irigaray saying: "I can do law, I can do founding authority." We cut to the founding authority of law, and suddenly, to paraphrase Peggy Phelan (1993, 103), this law appears to be *more* unreal than the sexuate rights because it remains unaware of the artifice that the sexuate rights have made hypervisible.

An extensive debate has circulated about the degree to which imitation and parody should be seen as subversive.[3] Many commentators have argued that the drag ball performers in Jennie Livingston's widely debated film *Paris Is Burning* subvert but also reinforce and reconsolidate the norms they emulate.[4] One could ask whether Irigaray reconsolidates the importance of legal recognition by imitating its norms. The answer is similar to that given in these broader debates: it is not possible to determine a stable action. A parody or mimicry of legal foundation can both consolidate and reveal the fragility of what is copied.

If Irigaray appeals to the authority of law, she also tries to expose the illusion of founding authority. She does wish us to reflect on the original foundations of legal equality discourse. She does perform the "why not" function in relation to the legitimacy of the legal rights reform she imagines. Irigaray's sexuate rights can be interpreted as performative not because of what they might make happen. Rather the question is the act they constitute: an act of declaration. "I Irigaray declare sexuate rights. I declare they are not less legitimate than established rights."

This is why Cornell's interpretation has been exceptional in its interrogation of how Irigaray's discourse acts. According to Cornell's early reading, Irigaray's discourse refigures the feminine (rather than possibly leading to a cultural refiguring of the feminine). On Cornell's later reading, Irigaray's work acts as a denial that women should diversely imagine sexual difference. As performative, it is this act of denial.

In many ways, Cornell's interpretation is a useful break with much of the literature that interprets Irigaray's work in terms of performativity. She considers its action, rather than its possible effects. In other words, Cornell assesses Irigaray's discourse in terms of its illocutionary rather than its hypothetical perlocutionary effects. Most commentators have asked what effects a legal or rhetorical declaration might lead to (the perlocutive). Cornell asks what kind of an act the declaration already is (the illocutive). Once Irigaray's declaration is so assessed, it can be seen as performing the declaration "Why not?" for sexuate rights. What in our culture prohibits their viability? Is an equality discourse more legitimate than a difference discourse as the basis of rights? Why? Should we continue to accept the apparent self-evidence of equality as the best discursive basis of rights?

But this leaves us with the question of how stably we can determine the way in which a declaration acts. Cornell's position is that sexuate rights should be assessed in illocutionary terms. For her, however, the act is as follows. Irigaray declares that women shall not reimagine their sexual difference other than she imagines it for them. It may be, of course, that Cornell believes that Irigaray's discourse has the causal (perlocutionary) effect of inhibiting women's freedom to reimagine their sexual difference. I think a more plausible interpretation is that Cornell believes Irigaray does *declare* a limitation of those possibilities. Let us assume at least one important reason for this belief on Cornell's part. Irigaray's discourse is too little informed by diverse ways in which women wish to imagine that difference. Because Irigaray's voice is monodiscursive in this regard,[5] her discourse fails to act as a declaration that affirms diversity in how we reimagine sexual difference.

Much of the literature assessing the performance of Irigaray's work seems committed to fixing the question of how Irigaray's work acts in illocutionary terms. Let us assume that causal relationships are very hard to establish. It is, then, very hard to determine questions asked by Whitford and Lacey, such as whether modes of rhetoric, or indeed legal reform, could be sufficient to move us forward. But is it any easier to establish with certainty what the actual act of a speech act is? For example, does Irigaray's writing declare "I declare women do not have the right to reshape their sexual imaginary" or "I declare that they do"?

As many commentators have written, the apparently self-present and instantaneous nature of the speech act—such as the promise or the marriage vow—is mediated by social factors, context, the audience for or participants in the speech act. This mediation becomes apparent once we imagine the promise or marriage infelicitously performed on a stage or cited. Context dependent as it is, we cannot pin down exactly the action of Irigaray's discourse. It may well run the risk of declaring that women do not have the right to determine their own sexual imaginary. But it may also work as the declaration that women do have this right. The rights have the potential to work in both ways, in contradictory fashion, in a variety of different contexts, and indeed for a single reader. For example, by attempting to give content to sexual difference, isn't Irigaray simultaneously declaring both that women have the right to give that concept content (because she is in the act of hypothesizing such content) *and* that they do not—for example, because her own act of definition simultaneously forecloses an affirmation of alternative sexual imaginaries, or indeed because the very failure and infelicity of Irigaray's imagining amount to a different kind of declaration (perhaps a lament) that women do not have the right?

It is not clear that Irigaray makes her declaration of sexuate rights with the kind of optimism critics such as Lacey attribute to her. In a cause-effect assessment, one questions—as Lacey does—whether the recognition of sexual difference would ensue from legal reform alone. In an assessment of their imagined felicity, one asks whether the declaration of sexuate rights alone would suffice for the institution of sexual difference. Lacey's response is, surely not. Similarly, in an assessment of their actual felicity, the same approach would ask whether Irigaray's attempt to institute sexuate rights succeeds. The response would be no, because Irigaray is not authorized to perform it, because the declaration of sexuate rights is not socially or legally recognized, because it has no force. Both responses suppose that the appropriate issue, as we have seen, is the perlocutionary performativity of the rights. Both suggest that Irigaray's declaration of sexuate rights patently lacks the necessary force. In the here and now, Irigaray does not have the force to make her declaration of sexuate rights legally valid. And even in an imagined legal institution of the rights, such rights would still not (such is Lacey's suggestion) have the force to institute a culture of sexual difference. To think otherwise would be to exaggerate the cultural power of legal reform with respect to the transformation of identity.

In discussing felicitous performatives, Judith Butler (1997) interrogates the same issue of when one can be said to have the force to make one's sayings "so." It seems, she writes, that "performativity requires a power to effect or enact what one names" (49). But when one takes this position, one presupposes that "the subject who utters the performative is positioned on a map of social power in a fairly fixed way, and this performative will or will not work depending on whether the subject who performs the utterance is already authorized to make it work by the position of social power she or he occupies" (Butler 1997, 156). For John Austin, we saw that questions of optimism (will my saying make it so?) would be inappropriate in relation to illocutionary speech acts, because their logic is not that of the cause-effect. The speech act simply is the very deed it refers to; the promise is effected as it is said, as is the declaration, the confession, the order, and so on. This seems to suggest, in the case of the felicitous speech act, the oneness of the word and the deed. But Derrida and Judith Butler, in reflecting on performatives, have discussed the illusory nature of this apparent oneness between the speaker's performance of a felicitous performative and its success. This apparent instantaneity covers over the fact that performatives are felicitous only through context, citation and repetition of norms, the appeal to and recognition of conventions. The best example of this is Austin's own example of the way in which performativity is context dependent: if I have no authority to marry you, no marriage legally takes place. The context must therefore be folded within the event of the words for the self-presence or instantaneity of the word-act to manifest itself. Notice, also, how the judge who installs a situation seems to install it immediately with his or her very words, but in so doing the judge implicitly *cites* the law that he or she applies and speaks in the name of a certain authority.

In fact, Butler does not emphasize this need for authority in order to demonstrate the powerlessness of unauthorized speakers to effect felicitous performatives. Reminding us that the performative always invokes and relies on conventions, Butler reverses the issue. The point is not how I can be assured that the authority of my speech act is recognized. The point is to realize that this very lack of assurance also opens up the possibility that failure is not inevitable. When Irigaray is charged with naiveté, the supposition is that she has no authority to effect sexuate rights or any reason to assume that rhetoric, or legal reform alone, could move us forward. But by the same logic, Judith Butler has suggested,[6] conventional law has no ability to ensure that it will stay still. Because of its dependency on citation, context, and recognition, speech and speech acts are always somewhat out of the speaker's control, and it is this very fact that can be seen as politically enabling, not disempowering. It is precisely, argues Butler (1997), "the *expropriability* of the dominant, 'authorized' discourse that constitutes one potential site of its subversive resignification. What happens, for instance, when those who have been denied the social power to claim 'freedom' or 'democracy' appropriate those terms from the dominant discourse and rework or resignify those highly cathected terms to rally a political movement? If the performative must compel collective recognition in order to work, must it compel only those kinds of recognition that are *already* institutionalized?" (157–58).

As Butler reminds us, the same performative can "also compel a critical perspective on existing institutions." Butler's response suggests, first, that we need to reconsider the supposition that, even thought of in perlocutionary terms, Irigaray's declaration of sexuate rights is (from both an actual and an imaginary perspective) doomed to infelicity. As she argues, if a performative must compel collective recognition in order to work, there can be no guarantee that it will compel only those kinds of recognition that are already institutionalized. Because equal rights discourse is context, recognition, and convention dependent, there can be no assurance of exactly how it is recognized, or any assurance of how the language of rights can resignify once "re-territorializ[ed]" (Butler 1997, 158). Certainly, Irigaray has no means of controlling the consequences that may arise from declarations of sexuate rights, whether legal, authorized, recognized, or not, or how the declaration acts instantaneously in different contexts. But their very declaration may be thought of as the kind of unexpected result that can arise from conventional equal rights discourse. Irigaray's declaration of sexuate rights shows how conventional equal rights discourse will be reappropriated in unpredictable ways.

Finally, I want to return to the fact that the Irigarayan project for sexuate rights attributes a particular status to law and the French civil code. The Irigarayan rights could be seen as illegitimate insofar as they would recognize a sexual difference that is (according to Irigaray's own argument) excluded from the social given. This illegitimacy gives another connotation to to their impossibility. But Irigaray imagines that the law would recognize sexual identities whose cultural possibility it would thereby institute. A retroactive action would ground this legal recognition of sexual difference, she is arguing. The rights would recognize a state of sexual difference that cannot be recognized. Their justification is that the possibility of such a recognition has been excluded. Their operative logic would be the institutional recognition retroactively constituting their own conditions of possibility.

Is it appropriate to imagine legal reform operating outside the politics of recognition? And what does legitimate Irigarayan sexuate rights if not the politics of recognition? What could justify the founding of sexuate identity? It seems that we have no grounds on which to criticize a politics of sexual difference because Irigaray imagines its self-authorizing operation. Alternatively, we have no grounds on which to justify it, as opposed to any other politics we could imagine. Why would we support the ideal of an institution of a culture of sexual difference, rather than the institution of some other nonexistent politics? To answer this question, we need to think about the original legitimacy of the laws we have.

This leads us to a discussion of that legitimacy to which Cornell refers in her assessment of Irigaray's sexuate rights: Jacques Derrida's analysis of the legitimacy of the American Declaration of Independence in his article "Declarations of Independence." In looking at this material, I will ask how it relates to the Irigarayan demand that sexual difference be given legal institutionalization. I want to compare the original authority of a historical and a hypothetical bill of rights.

Asks Derrida (1986a), *"Who signs, and with what so-called proper name, the declarative act which founds an institution"* (8)? I have suggested that recognition of the founding of the Irigarayan rights would have a peculiar status. But, as Derrida points out, the recognition of institutionalized bills of rights also has a peculiar status. At first Derrida's discussion provisionally attributes the curiosity to the act's performative operation. It seems the act effectively accomplishes or enacts that which it describes, recognizes, or refers to. This, of course, is what Irigaray imagines a sexuate bill of rights could accomplish. In its intention, the American bill of rights institutes the rights of the American people that it invokes. The problem lies in what legitimates the constitution—the people signing it, whose authority to do so is effected only by the speech act in question:

Here then is the "good people" who engage themselves and engage only themselves in signing, in having their own declaration signed. The "we" of the declaration speaks "in the name of the people." But this people does not exist. They do *not* exist as an entity, it does *not* exist *before* this declaration, not *as such*. If it gives birth to itself, as free and independent subject, as possible signer, this can hold only in the act of the signature. The signature invents the signer. This signer can only authorize him- or herself to sign once he or she has come to the end *[parvenu au bout]*, if one can say this, of his or her signature, and in a sort of fabulous retroactivity. That first signature authorizes him or her to sign. . . .

In signing the people say . . . henceforth, I have the right to sign, in truth I will already have had it since I was able to give it to myself. (10)

The question remains. How is a State made or founded, how does a State make or found itself? And an independence? And the autonomy of one which both gives itself, and signs, its own law? Who signs all these authorizations to sign? (13)

Derrida's questions suggest one means of reconsidering the imaginary retroactivity grounding an Irigarayan bill of sexuate rights. Her formulation of these rights results from her argument concerning the impossible degree of structural, symbolic, and institutionalized mediation necessary to the generation of new sexuate identities. The rights also seem to be incoherent because they recognize what does not exist. But one can ask whether a conventional bill of rights, recognizing the equality of subjects, is grounded with any greater original legitimacy. Like the conventional bill, an Irigarayan bill of rights recognizing sexual difference would be authorized by its recognition of a referent that does not precede that moment of recognition. As in the Declaration of Independence, in Irigaray's imaginary bill of rights the subjects who authorize the bill acquire status only by the institution of the bill itself. Neither in the Declaration of Independence, nor in the bill of sexuate rights, do the subjects formally entitled to the declared rights precede their legal recognition.

Sexuate rights need not be considered less legitimate in their original formulation than equal rights. It is the case, though, that legitimization would come after the fact, only with the eventual cultural possibility of sexual difference. Cornell (1992b) proposes that Derrida's analysis of justice offers an account of the "justificatory language of *revolutionary* violence." This justice depends on "what has yet to be established, and of course, as a result, might yet come into being. If it did not depend on what was yet to come, it would not be *revolutionary* violence" (167–68). She continues by citing Derrida's comments in "Force of Law" that "a 'successful' revolution . . . will produce *après coup* what it was destined in advance to produce" and that it may be a matter of generations before it is known "if the performative of the violent founding of the state is 'felicitous' or not" (168; see also Derrida 1992, 36). Perhaps the validity of the sexuate rights is not yet something we can assess; perhaps it would be conferred by the future, not the present.

Cornell's implicit suggestion here is that the same deconstructive analysis that destabilizes conservative law by demonstrating how it generates the effect of its self-authorization can be used to formulate the conditions of possibility of revolutionary change. If it is possible to make this parallel, the first point to be noted is that the impossibility *relied* upon in Irigaray's utopian project, and that *exposed* by Derrida in "Declarations of Independence," are related in status. If Cornell thinks one can gain a critical lever on the law in its function as a conservative force by emphasizing its mystical foundations, then how could the same notion of the mystical foundations of any institutionalization of sexual difference be used to affirm the Irigarayan project?

With this question open, I turn to the rejoinder directed by David Farrell Krell to Cornell in the debate that was provoked by Derrida's "Force of Law" essay (Derrida 1992). Krell (1990) objects, "Is it not the case that ethics, metaphysics and ontology alike are structured with a view to the Good—to the ultimate, infinite, and universal form of the capital G Good, the capital G that summons and that punishes capitally? Does not an ethics of the Good, precisely in its infinitely good intentions, reproduce the worst violence of the tradition of which it is not only a piece but the keystone? . . . Is it impossible that the guardian of the machine should be a woman? Or perhaps more neutrally put: What is the possibility of *justice* we call *woman*?" (1723–24).

Krell is asking if sexual difference has been elevated to an intrinsic Good. How is this elevation legitimate? Cornell and Irigaray are operating outside of the politics of recognition. Have they left themselves trapped in the abyss Balkin (1990) describes: "What can deconstruction possibly tell us about our choice of values if all texts are deconstructible? . . . What is the source of moral authority to deconstruct in one way rather than another? . . . Deconstruction . . . has nothing in particular to tell us about justice, or ethics, or any questions of value" (1626)?[7] One might argue that sexuate rights are not illegitimate for having been established without recognition. One might argue that sexuate rights would be authorized only after the fact. But what gives sexual difference and sexuate rights some special entitlement to be justified in this fashion, rather than any other rights?

Despite the utopian nature of the Irigarayan bill of rights, is it less legitimate in its founding status than the American Declaration of Independence? Both are grounded in a paradox of recognition. But Irigaray emphasizes the impossible status of her sexuate rights. Conventional law disavows its own mystical foundations. The American Bill of Rights invokes God to claim its divine authority. In the context of that claim to authority, it is a destabilizing and critical gesture to indicate its mystical foundations. Conventional law is grounded in unavowed retroactivity. By contrast, Irigaray emphasizes the retroactivity of her utopian bill of rights. The difference is not that one would be grounded less in the logic of retroaction that the other. Rather the difference occurs at the level of avowal.

Conventional law obscures its grounding in a paradoxical impossibility of recognition. Irigaray highlights the formal impossibility of the recognition of the sexuate rights of the sexually different subject.[8] The underlining of impossibility clarifies their ethical status. It can be argued that the strength and not the weakness of Irigaray's work on legal reform is precisely her avowal of its impossible status. The Declaration of Independence contains a reference to its legitimization by divine authority. To the extent that Irigaray does not justify her sexuate rights by reference to a transcendent, authorizing sexual difference, she rightly avoids a similar structure.

Does deconstruction tell us nothing about our choice of values? If so, the best one could say is that the paradox of recognition that forms the basis of the imagined institution of sexuate rights is no less legitimate than the constitutive action of any institutionalized bill of rights. But there is at least one set of criteria for legitimacy for the rights, and one form of deconstructive ethics. Is one prepared to avow, negotiate, and work with the founding aporia of the politics one favors? A position that does not rely on mythical foundations may be more ethical because less duplicitous than one that does. It is more prepared to recognize the difficulty of its own politics and the impossibility of an ultimate legitimacy. One suggestion arising from the debate around deconstruction and law is that Irigaray's sexuate rights are not less legitimate than other rights in their imagined original founding. A second is that they would be legitimate only after the fact. A third is that they could never be reliably legitimate. A fourth is that their strength is their greater preparedness to acknowledge this.

Their hypothetically future anterior or retrospective status does not undermine but sustains the legitimacy of the sexuate rights *insofar as it is avowed*. That sexuate rights are grounded in a logic Irigaray might understand as performative has recently provoked further discussion. What kind of political responsibility attaches to concepts of performativity? The issue has already been seen in the preceding discussion. The point of Irigaray's concept of legal reform may well be to exchange the politics of recognition for a politics of performative rights. But if so, what makes the rights she would see instituted politically responsible? In much discussion of this issue, the issue of referentiality (what is the referent for the sexual difference recognized by sexuate rights) slides into one of "making things so." Is it appropriate, is it justified, and is it possible that Irigarayan sexuate rights would make sexual difference "so"? In addressing this issue, I have first returned to the most well-known philosophical articulation of the concept of performativity, asking what kind of act the sexuate rights already are, rather than what effects they might lead to.

I have interpreted Irigaray's bill of sexuate rights in terms of performativity in several ways. I asked how Irigaray's bill of sexuate rights is justified,[9] given that hers is an impossible politics. The concept of performativity helps in the first instance to emphasize that sexuate rights have a circular logic. They would be justified only by the sexual difference they would institute. This is not to say that the legal institution of sexuate rights would necessarily institute a culture of sexuate difference, or that their current, literary declaration leads to the increased material possibility of the Irigarayan rights. The Irigarayan rights are no more or less illegitimate insofar as they would recognize that which does not precede the act of recognition. But this legitimacy does not make them legal or effective in other reliable ways. Their imagined performativity highlights that Irigaray's sexuate rights are not justified by a prior state of sexual difference. Further, Irigaray does not argue that as a cause-effect relation, the rights would produce sexual difference. But if a culture of sexual difference ever materialized, it might justify the rights.

Is Irigaray able to justify the position that sexual difference is a good? Yes, at least insofar as the overdetermined and highly invested exclusion of sexual difference does lead to an argument in "its" favor that she would not make on behalf of all kinds of identities that might be deemed absent from culture. In this sense, the politics of sexual difference is not arbitrary. But no, to the extent that a substantive culture of sexual difference would be justified after the fact, not before it. Irigaray is at her best when she does not "make justice a woman." Sexual difference is sometimes depicted by Irigaray as a fact to be recognized. But her work is at its most rigorous when it is prepared to bear its own paradox: in a politics of the impossible one recognizes what cannot be recognized.

For some commentators, an unjustified politics is irresponsible. A feminist politics of performativity would constitute an example of such a politics.[10] For others, a politics is irresponsible because of the uncertainty of what it would produce.[11] But Judith Butler has noted that we need the uncertainty of how speech acts operate and signify, both from a perlocutionary and from an illocutionary perspective, for it to be possible for existing discourse to signify differently. Irigaray's politics is subject to that uncertainty. Only because of that uncertainty in relation to both existing rights discourse and her own work does the possibility of her politics open up.

Lacey's response focuses on the lack of power of language to move us forward. However, Butler would ask us to focus on the way in which sites of apparent power such as institutionalized equal rights discourse are open to unexpected forms of response that can open them to recontextualization, reinterpretation, and transformation. This is the risk to which all speech acts are open. A good instance can be seen in Irigaray's declaration of sexuate rights. There is some degree of unpredictability in the way in which these rights may travel, and be read, in different contexts. Rather than seeing them as weakened by this unpredictability, one should affirm the way in which they are as dependent on their own fragility as they are on the fragility of institutionalized law. Both institutionalized right and reappropriations of legal formulae are open to this degree of unpredictability.

Butler offers the means to reconsider the illocutionary infelicity of the bill of sexuate rights. Butler's concept of the "'*expropriability*' of the dominant, 'authorized' discourse" is not just that in a perlocutionary sense it has the power to provoke unexpected consequences (as when others, for example, rework or resignify terms such as rights to rally a political movement). Butler's concept questions the apparent instantaneity of speech acts thought of as illocutionary. The marriage and the order work only because they cite conventions of ceremonies and orders that we recognize. If we do not recognize these conventions and ceremonies, or not in the same way, they act differently for us. Context dependent as they are, there is no guarantee of how Irigaray's sexuate rights can work even in their instantaneity as a declaration of radical political perspective. For some, her work may act as such; for others, it may act as naiveté or poetry, or the declaration of a limitation of women's possibilities for reconceiving a sexual imaginary. But again, Butler would argue that we need this level of unpredictability. It is this unpredictability that allows for the possibility that the equal rights ethos acts for Irigaray not only as that which we recognize as authorized but as that tradition which we want to displace. As Butler (1997) writes in response to Catharine MacKinnon and Rae Langton, "That the utterance can be turned, untethered from its origin, is one way to shift the locus of authority in relation to the utterance. And though we might lament that others have this power with our language, consider the perils of not having that power of interruption and redirection with respect to others" (93).

What impact might this point have on the interpretation of Irigaray's work? One cannot control how the discourse of law and rights will be used, or exclude the possibility of their being reappropriated by individual feminist theorists such as Irigaray. Irigaray's gesture usefully highlights this point. This said, Irigaray herself also can not entirely determine the ways in which her own discourse is read, interpreted, and strikes us, the force it has, and for whom. For some, her discourse acts as subversion. For others, it acts as reconsolidation of the language of law or indeed of conventional notions of virginity and sexual difference. For some, Irigaray's discourse acts to exclude difference.

I suggested that Irigaray's discourse is too little informed by diverse ways in which women wish to imagine sexual difference. Monodiscursive in this regard, it could be said that Irigaray's discourse does fail to act as a declaration that affirms diversity in how we reimagine sexual difference. Can we resolve the question of whether Irigaray's text acts as the statement "I Irigaray declare that women have the right to diversely reimagine sexual difference (because I am doing it)" or "I Irigaray declare that they do not (because I am doing it for them)"? I think not. But I think there is a way to reroute this question. We can ask how a writer avows within her writing the multiple and diverse contexts in which she will be read.

Writers give themselves up to the unpredictability of multiple contexts. Irigaray's call to difference may strike some readers as an effective closure to difference, and Irigaray has to admit the importance of this possibility. This said, we also cannot pin down or predetermine which of these possibilities constitutes the force of her work. (Neither can she.)

Nonetheless, perhaps the ethical call for a philosopher is to engage more directly with the possibility of those multiple contexts. Irigaray retains a responsibility to open up her writing through an avowal of and sensitivity to its possible multiple interpretations, actions, events, forces, and contextualizations. And the question would be, what might that responsibility look like, once one relinquishes the hope of maximal control over the interpretations, actions, and events one's work constitutes? The author inevitably fails if he or she tries to control, predetermine, or have authority over those contexts. But the author also cannot, on the grounds of their indeterminacy, disavow responsibility for the diversity of possible contexts and ways in which the work will strike the reader. Without fixing the issue of whether Irigaray's texts act as "I declare that women do" or "I declare that women do not," we can still criticize their monodiscursivity, for example, her textual supposition that author and reader are western, and thus her rhetorical failure to avow maximally diverse contexts for the action of her writing (see chapter 10).

Indeterminacy of speech acts opens up the discourse of law and rights to Irigaray's reappropriation of them. But it also opens up the possibility that Irigaray's writing will act very differently in a multiplicity of contexts. This possibility limits our ability to say with definite resolution that the texts certainly work to limit or close the possibilities of sexual difference. I suggested that Cornell seems overly eager to settle this question. But setting aside the question's resolvability, I agree that the ethical call to avow plurality of possible contexts does apply to Irigaray's own work. We can criticize her prose for its assumption of a racially and culturally neutral reading subject, who is, of course, anything but. At one point in her work she offers a discourse about India—and this will be discussed further in chapter 10—that patently does not suppose an Indian reader but speaks with the reader about India as (favored) other. To make this point is not to suppose that we can determine how her writing strikes different readers. But it is to point out that this writing seems insufficiently aware of the differences of those readers.

5

Sexuate *Genre*

Ethics and Politics for Improper Selves

> Is the same notion of sexual difference still operative after *An Ethics of Sexual Difference*? It seems to me that there, Irigaray's idea of sexual difference changes dramatically, and it is formulated as a generative interval that exists between the two sexes.
> Pheng Cheah, "The Future of Sexual Difference"

Despite her own claim that there is no break between her earlier work and the later texts (Irigaray with Hirsch and Olson 1995, 106), Irigaray recently suggested that her work could be divided into three phases. There was, she explains, a first, critical phase, of decentering the dominance of a masculine perspective on the world. There was a second phase, of defining "those mediations that could permit the existence of a feminine subjectivity." A new, third phase corresponds to the construction of an intersubjectivity respecting sexual difference. Here, the governing question would be "how to define a philosophy, . . . an ethic, a relationship between two different subjects"? (97).

In her early work, Irigaray distanced herself from those who might try to define the identity of women. A greater interest in problems of identity is manifest in her later work. She argues that women's identity, including a civic identity, needs to be cultivated. The prologue to *I Love to You* (1996a) comments that what is required is "more than the attainment of the immediate needs and desires of a woman. . . . It is, rather, a question of awakening her to an identity and to rights and responsibilities corresponding to her gender [*genre*]" (4).[1] Irigaray, by adopting the term *genre*, wants to give a new sense to belonging to "men" and "women" as sexuate identities. This intention is lost where the term is rendered by the English "gender."[2]

74

Speaking of sexuate genre in *Thinking the Difference* (1994), Irigaray comments that "woman must be able to express herself in words, images and symbols in this intersubjective relationship with her mother, then with other women, if she is to enter into a non-destructive relationship with men. This very special economy of woman's identity must be permitted, known and defined" (20). The reshaping of sexuate identity into belonging to one of two sexuate genres would inflect the quality of inter-subjective relations with others of the same sex, including those with whom one shares a genealogy. Such a reshaping of identity is, in Irigaray's view, also crucial to the quality of one's relations with those of another sex.

As we have seen, Irigaray considers that women as a symbol and as a group have been exploited in the representation of masculinity. Woman has been object and other. Women have been the object of men's exchange, use, procreation, investigation, and objectification. Other of the norm, nature to man's culture, emotion to his reason: woman has been man's inverted specular mirror. Irigaray critically analyzes the modalities of narcissism. She is particularly sensitive to the price paid by others, and particularly by those in the position of cultural other, in the attempted self-loving, idealizing self-capture by the subject. A subject who identifies with too phantasmic or impossible an ideal—of masculinity, of unified subjectivity, or of autonomous identity—displaces the specter of lack all the more thoroughly onto the figure of the other. To this end, certain subjects come particularly to be represented as those who have not, or are not.

In an alternative identity structure, privileged subjects might be better reconciled with the ways in which they have not, and are not, and less dependent on depicting others in terms of atrophy, lack, and negation. Instead, subjects tend to identify with idealized images of themselves as complete and whole. Irigaray has investigated the way subjects try to identify with desirable reflections of ideal identity. She counsels against the confusion of *identity* with *identification*, describing the latter as "idealistic delusion that produces a great deal of social entropy" (1994, 19). Identificatory structures are illusory, and also appropriative of the other.[3]

To appropriate is to render something one's own. To relate to a woman appropriatively is to fail to consider her insofar as she may differ from one's field of expectation. It is to subordinate her to one's field: of knowledge, for example, or exchange, or speculation, or self-relation. It is to consider her as a mirror, sending back a reflection as opposite, complement, or same. A male subject who relates to femininity in such terms does so only insofar as it seems to tell him something about himself: what he hopes he is not like, or perhaps what he might possess, know, control, or trade.

Appropriation is in this sense a "making mine." Irigaray understands identification as one of the appropriative modes. One identifies among the possibilities of others only what relates to one's self. The other becomes that in which I find myself, that which I take to be like me, or my opposite. Considered as same, women are appropriated as flat mirrors. Considered as opposite, atrophy, or lack, women are appropriated as inverted mirrors. They serve as a kind of negative identification, representing that which is not-like a man. As such, they are still subordinate to the logic of identification. Irigaray considers identification to be an unethical mode that fails to affirm the greater possibilities of the other. Irigaray locates unethical relations in the exploitation of women by men to serve the latter's self-identificatory purposes. Women also identify with other women, and men with other men. All these modes may be considered failures to consider the other outside the identificatory field in which one locates oneself.

In her earliest work, Irigaray assesses the price paid by marginalized others acting as contrasting inverted images to consolidate the ideal identities of privileged subjects. A masculine "phallic currency" circulating in this way, she writes in *Speculum* (1985b), needs *"its* other, a sort of inverted or negative alter ego" (22). This poses the question: Out of what matter is the reflecting surface fashioned? What must have happened to that matter in its subordination to the self-capture of the privileged subject? Irigaray describes the feminine as a remainder exceeding its appropriation as the other. She formulates questions such as: What has been appropriated? What has been atrophied? Were it not for the atrophy, she argues, feminine others might be otherwise, not subordinate to the self-capture of the masculine subject. With such questions, she carves out the hypothetical conceptual space for alternative representations of femininity. Irigaray makes this move without having to essentialize the notion of a feminine that has been atrophied. She does not posit the latter as a specific identity subsisting in its atrophy.

In *This Sex Which Is Not One* (1985c), Irigaray refers to the expropriation of women. "How," she asks, "can [women] free themselves from their expropriation *[leur emprise]* within patriarchal culture?" (119). To expropriate is to take something out of the owner's rightful hands, to deprive someone of his or her property wholly or in part. To appropriate is to make something one's own. Certainly Irigaray thinks that women have been made men's own. They have served as object of exchange between men, and representations of women have been as man's complement, opposite, or like. In that sense, women have been appropriated. But have they been expropriated? Has that which is proper to them—for example, their identity—been stolen from them, converted into a phallocentric representation?

A similar question will arise in relation to the suggestion that all forms of identification are appropriative. Certainly, we make the other our own. We subordinate them to our field of self-location. But is the other expropriated? Is something which is properly theirs wrongfully appropriated by me? To theorize appropriation, need Irigaray be committed to positing expropriation of subjective property? My argument is no, because she replaces the concept of an expropriated identity with the concept of appropriating the possibility of unnamed and unformed alternatives.

We have seen that in Irigaray's work, appropriation is not seen merely as a matter of constructing a phallocentric false representational overlay that could be stripped away again to expose an expropriated proper or true feminine underneath, waiting to be uncovered. Irigaray has attempted, from her earliest work, to take up this question of how we can speak of a missing X that "has been" appropriated. X stands not for the misrepresented truth of woman but for the *absence* of such a truth—for the truth that there is no truth. X, in other words, stands not for an identity but for a foreclosed possibility. But what is that possibility? Is it that ideally, according to Irigaray, women should have a "proper" identity—in other words, an identity that properly belongs to them, that never had the chance to develop? While some commentators do interpret Irigaray along these lines, I shall in this chapter offer an alternative proposal.

I have argued that Irigaray defines sexual difference as impossible. So far, I have defined the impossibility of sexual difference as the excluded possibility of a femininity that exceeds its subordination to the masculine. But in Irigaray's more recent work sexual difference is also the name for relations between women and men that are not possible so long as femininity represents atrophy. As Pheng Cheah writes, in Irigaray's later work, sexual difference is "formulated as a generative interval that exists between the two sexes" (Butler and Cornell 1998, 27). Sexual difference is still an excluded possibility. It is still considered culturally impossible today. Connoting an impossibility for female identity, it also connotes the impossibility of an ideal relation between men and women. But in Irigaray's work, the problem of an adequate relation between men and women would assume increased emphasis, to the dismay of many readers. Irigaray's priorities seem to have become heterosexist. The impossible relation between men and women is given emphasis in her work.

Sexual difference in this sense is not an ideal for monolithic, radically distinct sexual identities occupied by women and men. It is an ideal for a culture in which sexed subjects would be primarily oriented toward the other, as opposed to drawing on the other only to provide succor for their own identity. They would be turned outward toward the other, rather than being primarily fixed on whether the other is turned toward them. A new relation to sexed identity might facilitate this outward orientation, in Irigaray's view. She imagines a reconstruction of society. In belonging to the community as a citizen, one is situated in the context of one's sexuate identity. In addition, in encounters between "a sexuate two," each would understand the other as irreducible to him or herself. Rather than appropriating the other, each would be more likely to see the other as "You who'll never be me or mine" (Irigaray with Hirsch and Olson 1995, 110). Irigaray's ideal for the reconstruction of relations between the sexes should not be decontextualized. Because the feminine has been accorded the position of lack and atrophy in relation to the masculine, she considers that male-female relations must be reconceived as a cultural imperative. The imperative for this reshaping derives from this historical context, rather than from a global privileging of heterosexual and heterosocial interrelations in an Irigarayan politics. In this chapter, I shall consider the cultural imperative of reshaping male/female relations as a destabilizing intervention into a social-historical context in which women have been associated with the atrophy of qualities attributed to masculinity. I shall consider in chapter 8 the privileging of heterosexism in Irigaray's work.

Irigaray emphasizes that appropriation is not limited to the masculine appropriation of the feminine. It is seen in any subordination of any other to one's field of knowledge, expectation, possession, imagination, identification, and so on. Irigaray's recent work often analyzes women as appropriating subjects. Both men and women are prone to the day-to-day appropriative relations in which I am less interested in the other than in the recognition, love, or identity the other seems to give me. In *I Love to You* (1996a) Irigaray describes such relations as cultural cannibalism, ethical failure between subjects. She offers as instances a series of self-other relations that risk "annihilating the alterity of the other," transforming him or her into the object, or the "mine," that which comprises "my field of existential or material properties." This series of relations includes: "I love you, I desire you, I take you, I seduce you, I order you, I instruct you, and so on" (110).

In fact, women are prone to this appropriative tendency according to Irigaray precisely because they are caught up in the specular self-capture of masculinity. Already appropriated in male self-capture, abandoned in that sense to atrophy, they are likely to turn to the other with the question "Am I loved?" Irigaray's description of women apparently concurs with Freud's view that there are "fundamental differences between [the male and female sexes] in respect of their type of object choice" in love. Women's love, Freud (1914, 88) claimed, lies most in the desire to be loved. We have seen Irigaray's proposal (1993a) that "[t]he typical sentence produced by a woman is: *Do you love me?*" (134). Her analysis of woman as appropriative leads her to depict women as narcissists or hysterics turning to others to sustain their egos.

The emphasis on woman as appropriated in Irigaray's early work seems to shift in her later work to an acknowledgment that women appropriate. However, elements in the early work sometimes suggested an interest in figuring women as appropriating, not only as expropriated. For example, in "And the One Doesn't Stir without the Other" (1981), Irigaray's retelling of the oedipal narrative, she describes an archetypal mother who appropriates her daughter in her desire to "vanquish [her] own infirmity" (64). In Irigaray's narrative, the young girl turns away from her mother toward her father not because of her discovery of her mother's lack but because her mother suffocates her. Irigaray describes a woman unable to relate to her daughter in any but a paralyzing and engulfing mode that subordinates her daughter to the needs of her own atrophied identity. As the daughter laments to the mother:

> [D]idn't you quench my thirst with your paralysis? And never having known your own face, didn't you nourish me with lifelessness. . . . Of necessity I became the uninhabitable region of your reflections. You wanted me to grow up, to walk, to run in order to vanquish your infirmity. So that your body would move to the rhythm of your desire to see yourself alive, you imprisoned me in your blindness to yourself. . . . Imprisoned by your desire for a reflection, I became a statue. (1981, 64)[4]

Irigaray reminds us that when they are left in a cultural position of atrophy, women also do turn to appropriate the other—feminine or masculine—for sustenance. To say that sexual difference is impossible is also another way of saying that women are in a position of atrophy, or cultural other. To sustain an impoverished relation to identity, men turn to women for succor as a negative mirror. But this pushes women to turn to their children, or to other women in identificatory need. Irigaray criticizes identification in general. Our attachment to the identificatory mode is connected to the impossibility of sexual difference, which leaves both men and women in atrophied and unsatisfactory positions.

However, Irigaray's designation of knowledge, merging, possession, and all other modes in which others are subordinated to one's own field of expectation or self-capture as unethical identification will be problematic from the perspective of any psychological, psychoanalytic, or philosophical theory according to which such modes are constitutive of the subject. Take the mode on which Irigaray focuses, identification. Theorists from Freud though Merleau-Ponty and Lacan consider that the subject is founded in its identification with the other. Through identification we locate ourselves in the other. It is describable in this sense as a subordination of the other to my self-location. But to designate this mode as ethically problematic is to say that human subjects are constitutively unethical. How will Irigaray respond?

This raises the question of what an appropriate relation to the other might be. In *I Love to You* (1996a), Irigaray depreciates as cultural cannibalism taking the other as object, as prey, or as possession, or as the "you" becoming "mine" or "same" in a mode of "I ask myself if I am loved." This is "an introverted intentionality, going toward the other so as to return ruminating, sadly and endlessly, over solipsistic questions in a sort of cultural cannibalism" (110). But can we relate to the other without subordinating him or her to our knowledge of, expectations about, or identification with him or her?

With these questions raised, I turn to the politics Irigaray has offered in this regard. She imagines a culture of mediation between subjects. This ideal prompts her call for the reorganization of codes of laws, civic duties, and ethics to mediate relations between women and between women and men (Irigaray 1996a, 2–5). In chapter 2 we saw Irigaray's turn from the analysis of language to hypothetical proposals for linguistic modification. In *I Love to You* Irigaray marks the relations I would have with the other in ideal circumstances with the emblematic linguistic modification eponymous with the book title. It will be recalled that my relations with the other would exchange an "I love you" for an "I love *to* you," an "I give you" for an "I give to you," "I tell you" for "I speak to you," and so on. The linguistically mediating "to" is the symbolic emblem of the necessary mediation between self and other, of the nonreduction of the other to my self-capture. Such intersubjective relations might avoid cultural cannibalism. Irigaray (1996a) designates the role of the emblematic "to" as follows:

> *I love to you* thus means: I do not take you for a direct object, nor for an indirect object by revolving around you. It is, rather, around myself that I have to revolve in order to maintain the *to you* thanks to the return to me. Not with my prey—you become mine—but with the intention of respecting my nature, my history, my intentionality, while also respecting yours. . . .
>
> The "to" is the guarantor of two intentionalities: mine and yours. (110)

Irigaray's ethics of mediation was not always so overt. Some of the chapters in *This Sex Which Is Not One* privilege a model of interconnectedness between feminine subjects. "I love you," says Irigaray in "When Our Lips Speak Together" (1985c), "body shared, undivided. Neither you nor I severed," "One is never separable from the other" (206, 209). In this essay, the speaker's voice mocks the logic it considers masculine, whose concern is with the exact number of subjects: the fact that there are two. "In their calculations, we make two. Really, two? Doesn't that make you laugh?" asks the speaker (207); "I'm touching you, that's quite enough to let me know that you are my body" (208). Because of these early, well-known evocations, the reader might be surprised at the ideals Irigaray defends in her latest work: the politics of mediation between selves and others, between women and men, and between women. The ideal of mediation seems to imply an ideal of being in a position to keep one's distance from the other, instead of becoming confused with the other. The earlier work seems to evoke an ideal of being submerged in the other in a loss of boundaries between us.

In fact a politics of mediation is also locatable in the early work. For example, "And the One Does Not Stir without the Other" (1981) imagines a relation between women in which "the one doesn't disappear in the other, or the other in the one." As the daughter says to the mother: "I would like both of us to be present. So that the one doesn't disappear in the other, or the other in the one. So that we can taste each other, feel each other, listen to each other, see each other—together" (61). The consumption/cannibalism metaphor can also be seen in this essay. Irigaray writes, "We've again disappeared into this act of eating each other. . . . Will there never be love between us other than this filling up of holes? To close up and seal off everything that could happen between us indefinitely, is that your only desire? To reduce us to consuming and being consumed, is that your only need?" (62).

Some kinds of loss of boundaries occur on the basis of identity positions that might be deemed impoverished, as when one turns to the other to supplant insufficiency. But other kinds of unstable boundaries between subjects occur in more positive encounters with the world and others. Irigaray imagines the possibility of positive sexuate identities in an interconnected relationship to others of the same sex and genealogy. Perhaps such identities could afford the encounter that involves the sharing of bodies and subjective positions, and afford such an encounter better than atrophied identities of different sexes. There is, for Irigaray, a qualitative difference between these different kinds of unstable boundaries. Some are grounded in a positive relationship to one's sexuate identity. Others are grounded in an atrophied relationship to one's own and the other sex.

Because "When Our Lips Speak Together" was the best-known, most discussed paper in the initial period of reception of Irigaray's work in the 1980s, commentary initially focused on the Irigarayan ideal for merging between feminine subjects. Yet Irigaray also valued distance and separa-

tion between those subjects. The politics of mediation consolidated by institutional reform that she introduces in her later work is consistent with
those early directions. With an institutional, public discourse of sexual
difference mediating relations between subjects, one might turn less to
the other in a fragile need for love and recognition. In the context of social institutions constituting a field of law, language, and representation
mediating between subjects with a language of sexual difference, subjective relations between subjects might be quite different. The instability of
boundaries that occurs out of need and anxiety is distinguished from the
playful, pleasurable, or stimulating instability of boundaries that might
occur between subjects with adequate social mechanisms of consolida-
tion and mediation. In other words, when Irigaray in "When Our Lips
Speak Together" characterizes an ideal relationship with the other as one
of "I love you, body shared, undivided," we have to imagine that the
lover whose relationship to her partner is that of the mediated "I love to
you," not "I love you," is also the lover in a stronger position to experience indistinct boundaries because her position is less that of lack and
alienation. Love grounded in atrophy and "Do you love me?" or "I ask
myself if I am loved" is to be distinguished from love grounded in "I love
to you."

However, I have suggested that some elements of Irigaray's concept of
the constitution of the subject bring into question how the ideal of mediation and nonappropriation of the other is to be grounded theoretically in
her work. Irigaray was trained in Lacanian psychoanalysis, although she
is also its critic.[5] A first principle of Lacanian psychoanalysis is that the
neonate begins life as a fragmented body in bits and pieces, a conglomer-
ation of flows of incorporation and expulsion, with no discrete bodily or
subjective boundaries. What begins to give us a sense of unity is our identificatory encounter with an image of a whole, unified body—an encounter with a mirror image or with an image of another. Any sense of
recognition or primordial identification is illusory since the unified,
whole, discrete image is not an accurate reflection of the uncontrolled, dis-
unified body. The sense of recognition is misleading in that we do not recognize ourselves as such. Rather, through the process of recognition in the
image of another, or of one's own body as other, we develop an internal
image of a unified body with which we identify.[6] Our unified body-sub-
ject does not precede our own recognition of ourselves in these terms but
is the eventual product of that recognition. In identifying with an exterior
image, we are produced as subjects who never quite meet up with, or coincide with, our images and social identities—our self-images, our body
images, or our symbolic, social positions. Identity—both imaginary and
symbolic—will always be that with which we are never at one.[7]

At the most primordial level there is no unified subject prior to or separate from the other, on this account. The subject is originally the syncretically sociable infant who "lives as easily in others as it does in itself" (Merleau-Ponty 1964, 119). Merleau-Ponty points out that the adult never entirely resolves the initial lack of boundaries between self and other. Evidence of this is to be found in many adult emotions and responses: in jealousy and empathy, for example, in pride in the other's achievements and in love. "To love," says Merleau-Ponty (1964), "is inevitably to enter into an undivided situation with another" (154). Love "impinges" on the other, by which he means that one's beloved becomes intermingled with one's subjective boundaries: "From the moment when one is joined with [*lié avec*] someone else, one suffers from her suffering. . . . One is not what one would be without that love. . . . One can no longer say 'This is mine, this is yours'; the roles cannot be absolutely separated" (154).

Does this depiction not seem echoed in Irigaray's descriptions of everyday infringements of self-other boundaries as appropriations, cultural cannibalisms, "I love you" as opposed to "I love to you"? If so, the following question arises. If love, empathy, pity, jealousy, pride, and other adult forms of transitivism are manifestations of breakdowns of boundaries between self and other, what justifies the moral loading on expressions like infringement, appropriation, and cannibalism? How can Irigaray's transformation of this material into an ethics of nonappropriation be legitimate? Isn't the impingement on the other, in this sense, inevitable? Is there any kind of subject that is not an impingement on the other? Does Irigaray have a utopian vision in which we would not be jealous, envious, empathizing, identificatory, appropriative, impinging, loving, hating subjects?[8]

Is it realistic to imagine a subject who does not, in Irigaray's sense, appropriate the other? If we are inevitably identificatory selves, should we consider identification inappropriate? And a second question: Does an ethics of nonappropriation and nonexpropriation suppose an understanding of subjects as having discrete, proper boundaries from each other, discrete identities? What are the proper boundaries of the subject? Irigaray must offer an alternative to inevitable appropriation of the other. She must also offer an alternative to the constitutively identificatory subject. If the ethics of nonappropriation implies some concept of proper boundaries between subjects, this pulls Irigaray back into depicting subjects as having proper identities. Yet from her earliest work she is at pains to distance herself from such depictions.

There is no subject who has not incorporated the other. Given this, ethical ideals of recognizing the proper boundaries of the subject are in question. When I turn to the other with the plaintive "I ask myself if I am loved," how shall we say I have appropriated him or her? Irigaray deems certain formulations of love inappropriate. But how to question the subject's confusion of those boundaries when we are always improper selves? How to distinguish between inevitable incorporations and unethical appropriations of the other?[9] Here we see Irigaray's politics of the excluded X go to work.

In proposing an ethics of nonappropriation, she avoids the assertion that what is proper to a subject has been appropriated. She does not refer to a pre- or nonappropriated other or self. What has been appropriated is not one's identity but a possible alternative identity structure. The substantive account given is not of the real or discrete subject but of the form that a utopian mode of mediation between subjects would take.

Let's think about Irigaray's claim more practically. I have appropriated the other when I turn to her or him with the question "Am I loved?" I engage with the other only insofar as she or he may have something to offer my self-understanding. This does not amount to attributing a fixed identity to the other. It is not the other's proper identity that is expropriated. Instead, possibilities for alternative relations to the other are excluded. Such alternatives are exchanged for my appropriative concern about the other's relation to myself. Narcissistic love is by definition an exclusion of alternative modalities of love and exchange with the other. Irigaray theorizes appropriation without theorizing proper identity. For example, jealousy and envy take place as the appropriative exclusion of a more mediated relation with the other that would allow the other's existence in alternative ways.

I cannot be jealous, in other words, except *as* the failure of such alternatives. I cannot be jealous except as the failure of improved structures of mediation, for example. Alternatives would require differently structured subjects. So when Irigaray argues that I cannot be jealous except *as* the failure of the possibility of mediation, she also argues that my jealousy appropriates the possibility of radical institutional reform promoting the development of more mediated relations between subjects. In this way, Irigaray adds a politics of institutional reform to a politics emphasizing the remainder and excess of the other. Possible institutional reforms take on the status of the excluded X.

Those who have been cast in the position of other—such as Irigaray's emblematic, atrophied woman—cannibalize another other to sustain their own attempt at self-capture. We would need, so the theory goes, mechanisms to interrupt reactive cannibalizations of the other in compensating attempts at plenitude.

In her later work, Irigaray develops a program for these social mechanisms. She imagines men and women cultivating a field of sexuate be-

coming as a horizon of significance for their individual sexed subjectivity. As sexed, male or female, I would participate in a collectivity: sexuate genre. As a woman, I would be participating in the genre of women; as a man, in the genre of men. Sexuate genre would have to be recognized at a social and institutional level through modifications to legal, religious, economic, linguistic, political, and civil institutions—hence the bill of sexuate rights declared in *je, tu, nous* and *Thinking the Difference.* Participation in one's genre would operate as a mediating factor in all kinds of relations between selves and others.

One of the most controversial aspects of Irigaray's recent work is her view that women must be roused to an identity. She also considers male identity to be in need of renovation. In the words of Mary Anne Doane, "[I]n an era . . . in which the ego is seen above all as illusory in its mastery, what is the status of a search for feminine *identity?*" (Doane 1987, 9, discussed Fuss 1989, 104). On Irigaray's view, participation in one's sexuate genre would enable the formation of a new, sexuate identity (constitutively interconnected with that of others). Critics are startled to see Irigaray take this position when the metaphysics of identity has been the target of deconstructive analyses over the past two decades, and when ego psychology's ideal of a strong ego has also been the critical target of Lacanian psychoanalysis.[10] By her own argument, the ideals of a strong ego or a self-present subject involve, first, the disavowal of the necessary fragility and failure of such a subject, and second, the disavowal of the dependence of a subject with pretensions to strong identity on the cannibalized other to sustain these pretensions. These appropriative modes of reinforcing identity could be described as the product of the subject's inability to reconcile itself with lack.

Although participation in sexuate genre would reinforce identity, Irigaray imagines such a participation very differently. It would aid reconciliation with being not-whole. Being sexuate is a hypothetical identity mechanism that would not collapse into ideals of wholeness and totality, imaginary specular capture of the other, and disavowed identificatory props. Remember, she states, not to confuse identity with identification. In this ideal identity structure, the self would not cannibalize either a negative or an ideal other to the ends of self- reinforcement.

This position can be summed up in five points. First, Irigaray understands the reimagining of identity structures to be a political ideal. Second, the subject would be situated in the context of his or her sexuate genre, as a nonidentificatory identity structure in which he or she participates and to which he or she contributes. This would provide alternatives to distancing oneself from opposites and identifying with ideals. Such structures consolidate alienation, and we make others pay the price for that alienation. Rather than identifying with their genre (for example, as an ideal), subjects would be co-extensive with their sexuate genre, thought of as an infinite and unfinished series. Third, two sexuate genres would be recognized at the level of all social institutions, thus Irigaray's interest in institutional and policy reform. Fourth, the significance of two should be understood as a critical intervention into a history dominated by one kind of subject. Irigaray emphasizes that there are two sexes because she considers that western culture has been particularly resistant to the "two." Political thought has favored the mode of "one" subject (often a subject who is assumed to have a politically invisible domestic help-mate). Fifth, a subject situating him or herself in the context of his or her genre would be less impelled to appropriate the other to sustain the self. Rather than identifying with an ideal or idealized genre, one would participate in the sexed series that constitutes one's genre.

If we return to the theme of love, we see how Irigaray connects a different amorous structure with the problematics of institutional reform. In her view, only the rights of men (and women occupying the position of like-men) are inscribed in the legal code. She argues that love "requires that the rights of both male and female be written into the legal code" (1993c, 4). Irigaray's ideal for legal reform connects with her ideal for individual subjects' restructured relationship to love, friendship, and family genealogy. Situating oneself in the context of the sexuate genre with which one is co-extensive might enable one to better respect the other as different. Accordingly, she claims that "[b]ecause I'm able to situate there [i.e., as sexual difference] the difference and the negative that I will never surmount . . . I'm able to respect the differences everywhere: differences between the other races, differences between the generations and so on. Because I've placed a limit on my horizon, on my power" (Irigaray with Hirsch and Olson 1995, 110).

Given that Irigaray argues against appropriative and identificatory identity structures, is she to be aligned with those who espouse identity politics?[11] She defends the need for an identity structure. But her insistence that "we need identity" is compatible, at least in its spirit, with an important critique of identity politics. According to this critique, identity politics appropriate the other woman as she who is the same as myself or she for whom I speak, or she whose truth I presume to know as woman. Irigaray asks readers to imagine a hypothetical identity as sexed through an alternative identity structure. They need not assume that all women are the same. Rather, they are to imagine women as differently contributing to the fluid spectrum of sexuate genre in which they participate. Grounding feminist politics in an ideal of women's identity has often been seen as problematic because, in the words of Diana Fuss (1989), "to the de-

gree that identity is a radically *destabilizing* force and not at all a stable guarantee of a coherent politics, the current tendency to base one's politics on a rather vague and imprecise notion of identity needs to be rethought" (105). Irigaray does not consider identity to be static or a common, stable thread of commonality running through all women. Rather, one's relationality to women—an infinite play of the differences among women—is what she envisages at the heart of the apparent identity of women.

It is one's differences from other women, not one's fixed sameness as woman, that lie at the heart of what Irigaray names one's "identity." She supports a transformed model of identity as an open-ended, deferring spectrum of difference to which we contribute and in which we participate,[12] not a static model with which we identify.[13]

Does Irigaray ignore the differences among women in favor of what they may share as women? Critics wonder, for example, if Irigaray "fails to recognize that female sexuality is experienced differently, at different times, in different cultures" (Suzanne Moore, cited Chanter 1995, 175). Others have come to her defense. Tina Chanter (1995) emphasizes that "Irigaray's refusal to identify with any group that 'purports to determine the "truth" of the feminine, to legislate as to what it means "to be a woman," and to condemn women who might have immediate objectives that differ from theirs' [Irigaray 1985c, 166] is a testimony to the seriousness with which she takes differences at all levels. She is just as concerned to acknowledge the differences among women as she is to assert sexual difference" (175). Chanter (1995, 175) defends Irigaray by locating her earliest refusals to define women from *This Sex Which Is Not One*.

Irigaray's project for cultivating women's identity in terms of their sexuate genre reopens the same questions. For some commentators, such as Ellen Armour, the later work bears witness to Irigaray's turn away from the best aspects of her early concept of identity. Where, Armour (1999, 132) asks, is the "differing/deferring" woman in the later work? The differing, deferring woman is diffused through phallocentric reproductions of masculinity. According to Irigaray's early analysis, male identity projects its negation onto femininity. Representations of women are the locus of that from which the male differs, and his ideal identity is deferred through them. Woman is not defined in terms of presence or self-identity. Having analyzed women as aiding the differing and deferring of male identity, Irigaray refused in her early work to counter with fixed concepts of female identity. Rather, she criticized as an illusion bolstered by ideal and atrophied others any concept of identity as self-present and fixed. When Armour asks where the "differing/deferring" woman is in Irigaray's later work, she suggests that Irigaray has now attributed to women the presence and self-identity that should be no more than an illu-

sory ideal for any sex, according to her own earlier argument. Furthermore, Armour argues, the differences among women are suppressed in
the account of their identity as women. For Armour, projecting an ideal of
women's identity is precisely to project an image of women's self-sameness (132). For all Irigaray's promise, Armour argues, "Woman is returned
to a logic of sameness in the name of . . . thinking *genuine* sexual difference" (130).

Yet some of Irigaray's depictions of mediation by genre suggest that the
differing, deferring sexuate subject has not been abandoned. She describes belonging to genre as "differentiation within ourselves" (Irigaray
1996a, 145). And what of the intended function of the concept of genre: to
promote a culture of nonappropriation—of men by women, of women by
men, of women by women and men by men? Appropriation takes many
forms, which include the supposition that the other is like me. Irigarayan
politics seeks a model according to which I would be less likely to assume
that other women are like me or are my opposite (both modes being variations on the economy of sameness). She writes that "the pact with a
person of my own gender [*genre*] is paradoxically less straightforward
due to the risk of objectivity dissipating into sameness" (1996a, 145). Her
hypothesis is that if I were situated in the context of genre, I might love
the economy of sameness less. I would have less requirement for the identificatory props of same, negative, and complement, if I were situated in a
horizon of significance of infinite sexuate genre. According to some commentators, genre assumes the sameness of women. But through her notion of genre, Irigaray imagines that my situation in the field of the differences among women might enable my willing and searching less for
sameness. Genre is the very structure Irigaray believes might interrupt assumptions about the sameness of women and about the likeness of the
other to the self. Sexuate genre would be the conceptual structure allowing a woman to value another woman's possible difference.

It is useful in this regard to compare the accounts of this point proposed
by Armour and Margaret Whitford. For Whitford (1991b), Irigaray's ideal
is for a female identity to come. It has not come yet, it is of the future: "Irigaray is positing an identity that still has to be created" (136). For Whitford, then, Irigaray is saying that woman's identity is not yet but it could
"be." Armour (1999) emphasizes that in an Irigarayan politics, woman "is
not/will not be subject to the order of the 'is'" (110). Her position is not far
from that of Whitford, since Whitford emphasizes that giving women an
identity would change what identity is. But for Whitford, what would
change is that there would be two identities: "[T]o give women an identity
(however problematic the concept) will change our notion of what identity means. The existence of two 'kinds' would have an effect on *man*kind"

(136). Whitford emphasizes Irigaray's resistance to what Irigaray deems a deconstructive politics. Irigaray claims that "[p]hilosophy is very interested in the deconstruction of ontology, in the anti-, in the post-, but not much in the constitution of a new, rationally founded identity" (Irigaray 1993c, 205, as cited in Whitford 1991b, 123). Whitford points out Irigaray's own concern about the phallocentric fragmentation and dispersal of feminine identity and for this reason thinks the invention of two identities in Irigaray's work may potentially disrupt existing ideas about identity. It seems that for Whitford, Irigaray would redouble identity but not fragment it. By contrast Armour includes among the positive aspects of Irigaray's work her understanding of identity as dispersed and fragmented. All subjects should recognize identity as necessarily dispersed and fragmented; women should not aspire to a fixed, stable field of identity. So, for Armour, the best aspects of Irigaray's work are lost in what she sees as the later turn away from the notion of identity as "endlessly deferred and differing." But this judgment may underestimate the extent to which Irigaray proposes genre as such a notion.

6

Anticipating Sexual Difference

Mediation, Love, and Divinity

> This need not turn the figure of Woman into a religion, unless of
> course religion is reinterpreted as a desire for intimacy, and that, I
> think, corresponds nicely to what Irigaray means by the divine and
> to what Derrida has recently called a "religion without religion."
> John Caputo, *More Radical Hermeneutics*

In chapter 5, we saw that Irigaray does not reject all ideals of identity. She favors the cultivation of an alternative identity structure, genre, in which we would participate. Although "my *genre* remains partially exterior to me in that I belong to a historical community, of women particularly," it is also a collectivity to which I contribute. It is the source not of my personal identity but of my differentiation from myself: "I thus differentiate myself within myself through the facts of my being a particular individual and of my belonging to a gender [*genre*]" (1996a, 145). This genre would constitute an alternative to identificatory suspension between ideal and negative egos.

In this chapter, I will consider why Irigaray considers such suspension problematic and pins her hopes for a new sexuate culture on the renegotiation of identity structures. This question is not disconnected from a politics of economic redistributive justice. No isolated modification of law or language would be sufficient to produce a culture of sexual difference. No account of any individual change, such as the legal reforms discussed earlier, should be understood in abstraction. Individual measures do not guarantee structural change.

We have seen the account of how ideal legal and linguistic reforms mediate relations between subjects. This chapter considers the third major domain on which Irigaray focuses: religion. In the anticipation of a culture of sexual difference, women need a feminine divine. This argument arises from her analyses of the interconnection between negative and ideal egos as unsatisfactory identity structures. Irigaray considers that in the western tradition, depictions of divinity play a key role in these unsatisfactory structures. Masculine-paternal Gods have served as male ideal ego figures, implicated in male identificatory mechanisms. Irigaray argues that the appropriation of women as man's negative alter ego interconnects with his identification with the impossible ego ideal represented by the Judeo-Christian God. According to Irigaray, unsatisfactory historical structures of law, language, philosophy, and identity cannot simply be abandoned, or simply be reappropriated by women. Neither abandonment nor reappropriation is an effective means for women to change their symbolic role as other to the subject, the citizen, or the philosopher. Irigaray argues instead for the invention of new imaginary bases of law, language, and identity. In this chapter, we will see a similar argument in relation to the history of western religion.

From her earliest to her most recent publications, Irigaray has, as Morny Joy (1990, 9) and others have emphasized, shown an ongoing interest in religious themes. This interest has taken diverse forms. Irigaray has asked why traditional readings of the gospels and ancient mythology tend to ignore their more women-centered elements, for example, "the good relations between Mary and Anne, Mary and Elizabeth, etc., Mary and the other women. Even though this corner of society does form a part, of the 'Good News,' few texts or sermons transmit or teach its message" (Irigaray 1993a, 68). She asserts as an often forgotten fact of ancient mythology that "most of the gods of the *universe* start out as goddesses. The solar goddesses are effaced or papered over when the universe is taken over by the men-gods, especially by Zeus and his son Apollo. This domination of the cosmic world by the gods by means of the couple of a unique God-Father and an all-powerful son, erases the fact that mothers and daughters once presided as goddesses over the solar seasons and, together, protected the fertility of the earth in its flowers and fruits" (1993c, 80). In such ways, Irigaray supports feminist reinterpretation of traditional religious myths and texts, so as to highlight the role they attribute to women. In texts such as *Sexes and Genealogies* (1993c) and *An Ethics of Sexual Difference* (1993a), we also find the hypothesis that a feminist reconceptualization of divinity could have a broader cultural significance. As Margaret Whitford points out, "whatever one's personal beliefs about the reference of transcendental statements," one might redress male-centered religious myths simply because those myths remain "an extremely powerful discourse," and she quotes Irigaray: "It seems we are unable to eliminate or suppress the phenomenon of religion" (Irigaray 1993c, 75, cited in

Whitford 1991b, 140). This might be sufficient reason for a feminist theorist to engage critically with religion. However, Irigaray goes beyond arguments that religious philosophies should be reshaped by feminist reflection. A substantial reshaping of sexuate identity structures would
require a reshaping of social conceptions of divinity.

Ellen Armour and Elizabeth Grosz have noted the reluctance with
which many feminist theorists have greeted Irigaray's material on divinity (Elizabeth Grosz, cited Armour 1999, 131). But Irigaray (1996b) insists that the imperative of this material is not negotiable: "I don't think
anyone among you could say, 'I'm not going to consider the problem of
God.' For we are, notably, in a monotheist cultural economy, subjected to
a culture of the male God, the masculine Trinity. Philosophy, art, most of
the western representations of the body since classical Greece, are connected either directly or indirectly to this idea" (212). In the context of Irigaray's argument that all male-centered traditions would have to be
reimagined as the prerequisite to a new sexuate culture, resistance to her
work on religion in particular makes little sense.

In the piece "Divine Women," included in *Sexes and Genealogies* (1993c),
Irigaray makes strong claims for the role of divinity in the cultivation of
human subjectivity and culture. She declares, "Divinity is what we need
to become free, autonomous, sovereign. No human subjectivity, no
human society has ever been worked out [*élaborée*] without the help of the
divine" (62, translation modified). She asserts that there is a connection
between the absence of an autonomous subjectivity for women and the
fact that "woman lacks a divine made in her image" (63). "If women have
no God," she argues, "they are unable either to communicate or commune
with one another" (62). As long as a woman lacks a divine appropriate for
her, "she cannot establish [*accomplir*] her subjectivity according to the
goals that suit her. She lacks an ideal that would be her goal, and she lacks
a route for her becoming" (63–64).

Three claims are made here. First, figures of divinity have played a crucial role in relation to formations of human identity. Man is "able to exist"
because of his identification with a masculine-paternal God (Irigaray
1993c, 61).[1] Second, nothing has played an equivalent role for women.
Third, the absence of a feminine divinity contributes to the atrophied state
of women's identity, subjectivity, and community. Consequently, if a culture of adequate sexual difference is desired, one in which women would
not be "cut . . . off from themselves and from one another" (64), one necessary factor would be the generation of a feminine divine or some kind of
equivalent.

Irigaray is most known for her argument that man / woman oppositions
rely on the (auto-destabilizing) exclusion of any feminine in excess of that

opposition.[2] But she has also emphasized the crucial relationship between man/woman oppositions and cultural representations of mythic ideals such as the masculine-paternal God. Mythically transcendent figures offer a paradoxical identificatory structure. The relationship to an idealized masculine-paternal God produces a fragile structure for masculine identity: "[A]s man seeks to rise higher and higher—in his knowledge too—so the ground fractures more and more beneath his feet" (1985b, 134).

Male identification with God as an impossible, transcendent masculine-paternal ideal provokes a compensatory displacement of devalued qualities onto the feminine. For this reason, Irigaray deems the representational schism between man and God a "source of evil." We see this interpretation in texts such as *Marine Lover* (1991a) and *An Ethics of Sexual Difference* (1993a), for example. The *real* "original sin," Irigaray claims, consists in dissociating the human and the divine, and "[i]n setting up God as a distinct and transcendent entity. With the expulsion from the 'earthly paradise' corresponding to the will to know God as such. To the desire to produce him as a 'suprasensory' reality? God—Different? And this would be the source of evil, in the beginning" (1991a, 173, translation modified).

The tragedy of man's "banishment" is not, for Irigaray, that he is expelled from a state of innocence, as many biblical traditions would have it. Rather, it is his discontinuity from the God/father with whom he identifies. The fate of the feminine (as man's other) is interconnected with man's identification with an ideal from which he is severed. This is how we must interpret Irigaray's account of the divine "'suprasensory' reality," "God—Different" as the real "source of evil." The conceptualization of a schism between man and God is the "source of evil" from a feminist perspective because the division between man and a projected transcendent entity has been fatal for the role of the feminine as man's other.

In Christian and biblical tradition the projection of a divine transcendent realm serves to legitimate the hierarchy ranking man, woman, the material/sensory realms, and the animal.[3] The depiction of man as "made in God's image" is well known, and, as Elaine Pagels notes, this depiction has sometimes been interpreted to include women and slaves also, insofar as they too have souls or minds.[4] But just as strong in the tradition of biblical commentary has been the argument that woman represents the flesh that tempts man away from righteousness, as in Tertullian's account of every woman as Eve, the "devil's gateway."[5] The representation of man as both divided from and yet aspiring to draw nearer to God is supported by the representation of femininity in terms of the temptations of the flesh. It is in avoiding excessive indulgence in this temptation that man draws nearer to the God from which he is divided.

Women are banished to the role of man's other, that which thwarts his ascetic ideals, for example. This subordination occurs in conjunction with man's mode of "being like unto God." "Sin" and "suffering" do not occur because men and woman are cast out of paradise, Irigaray declares in *Marine Lover (1991a)*, but because man takes on God as his ideal, an extraterrestrial (impossible) ideal: "How does banishment occur? In the mode of the 'being like unto God.' The position of God as model to be repeated, mimicked. Thus, set outside the self. Surely evil, sin, suffering, redemption, arise when God is set up as an extraterrestrial ideal, as an otherworldly monopoly? When the divine is manufactured as God-Father?" (173). Irigaray proposes that new cultural models of sexual difference would require a reconceptualization of both woman/divine and man/divine relations. If men did not identify with a transcendent divine from which they were severed, they might draw less on women as the negative mirror. From this point, it becomes for Irigaray a feminist task to represent the divine as continuous with the human, rather than severed from it.

We have seen Irigaray's proposals for more adequate forms of law and language. In similar vein, she makes suggestions for an alternative, hypothetical structure of relation to divinity. What if women had their own divine, a feminine-divine? It should not occupy the same structural role as the masculine-paternal God. It should not be an ideal that is radically exterior to the individual, from which one is severed but with which one identifies. Irigaray (1991a) probes the possibility of a relationship between the feminine and the divine where women and men might have a "perception of a divine that was not opposed to them, perhaps? That was not even distinct from them" (173). Men would need an alternative relationship to divinity also. Irigaray has diagnosed as problematic the representation of schism between man and God. For this reason men, like women, would need a new relationship to divinity as that with which they are interconnected, rather than that from which they are severed.

Irigaray's project is based on her view that traditional models of divinity reflect not just an unsatisfactory role for women but also an unsatisfactory identificatory structure more generally. We have seen her argue that there is a difference between identity and identification. She criticizes identification with ideals from which we are also alienated. She considers the relationship between men and the masculine-paternal God of western Christianity to be an example. We have seen her argument that others pay the price to sustain such identificatory ideals. We are liable to depreciate and objectify negative others to sustain our identification with alienating ideals. When Irigaray suggests alternative models of divinity, she suggests alternative models of sexed identity. An alternative concept of divinity would substitute for the masculine-paternal God. It would not adhere to the man/God schism. In Irigaray's work the concept of divinity is stripped of its supernatural connotations. It is given a diverse breadth of definition.

Divinity is reformulated in Irigaray's work in at least the following ways. Sometimes it simply refers to an "opening onto a beyond" or a "limit" (1993a, 17). Sometimes it is the material texture of beauty (1993a, 32). Sometimes "God" is that which women would become for themselves (1993c, 71). Sometimes it is used by Irigaray to refer to the "wonder" there might be between the sexes in a culture of sexual difference. In *To Be Two*, Irigaray imagines how transcendence would exist between men and women rather than between human and divine, proposing my "becoming the woman I am" as an alternative to the "completely masculine" ideal of becoming: becoming God (2001, 92). And sometimes it refers to a certain ideal form of love: "[W]here the borders of the body are wed in an embrace that transcends all limits . . . each one discovers the self [*se découvre*] in that which is inexpressible yet forms the supple grounding of life and language. For this, 'God' is necessary, or a love so attentive that it is divine. Which has never taken place?" (1993a, 18–19, translation modified). Irigaray so redefines the notion of divinity that it is sometimes interchangeable with the concept of sexual difference.

Certainly, Irigaray argues that "women need their own divine." But this statement is best interpreted in the context of her plural redefinitions of the term. She speaks of the need for women to cultivate their own identity. The difficulty, as Margaret Whitford (1991b) points out, is that Irigaray attempts to "change our notion of what identity means" (136). The same problem also arises with the related Irigarayan material on the divine. Irigaray attempts to change our notion of what divine means. Some readers assume Irigaray argues for a female relation to divinity parallel to the traditional relation between man and the paternal God. To the contrary, she is arguing that women need an alternative, as do men. Anne-Claire Mulder (in Irigaray 1996b) asks, "Does a 'fixed' divinity exist for women? Wouldn't the projection of our ideals, the creation of female Gods carry with it the perils of reimprisoning ourselves rather than liberating ourselves?" (234). But Irigaray does not envisage a fixed divinity for women or the projection of imprisoning ideals. Camille Mortagne has asked Irigaray, "God's name is, in my Catholic tradition, inevitably associated with God-the-Father, which excludes me from being a divine woman. Don't we need to look for another name?" (Irigaray 1996b, 214). But Irigaray's ambition is to find a substitute for the cultural role of God in relation to sexed identity. Her use of the same term is an argument for such a substitution.

However, the occasional interchangeability of the terms "divinity" and "femininity" provokes questions. Why deploy the concept of divinity so redefined? Why provoke confused interpretation of statements such as "It is essential that we be God *for ourselves*" (Irigaray 1993c, 71)? Irigaray's view is that the concepts of God and divinity need to be used otherwise, disrupted, reimagined, and resignified. Avoiding the terminology would not achieve the same substitutive effect.

It is imperative, Irigaray concludes, to refigure divinity so as to question its connotations of schism from the human. Irigaray retains the term "divine" while redefining it as connection between humans. When women's becoming or relations between the sexes are deemed divine, divinity has evolved into another term for Irigarayan sexual difference. Transcendence is located not between humans and immortal beings but between humans.

What then of the potential role played by divinity in relation to male identity? Consider the following formulations from "Divine Women" (in 1993c):

> No human subjectivity, no human society has ever developed without the help of the divine. (62, translation modified)
> Man is able to exist because God helps him to define his gender [*genre*], helps him orient his finiteness by reference to infinity. (61)
> In order to become, it is essential to have a gender [*genre*] or an essence (consequently a sexuate essence) as *horizon*. (61)
> Man is supposedly woman's more perfect other, her model, her essence. The most human and the most divine prospect [*perspective*] for woman lies in becoming *man*. If she is to become woman, if she is to accomplish her female subjectivity, woman needs a god that would represent the perfection of *her* subjectivity. (64, translation modified)

Traditionally, man relates to a transcendent, masculine-paternal God as a horizon of perfection. Both men and women need an alternative horizon of becoming (or a field of infinite, open-ended sexed identity or identities) in the context of which to situate themselves. Irigaray insists in "Divine Women" that she does not envisage a feminine analogue of that God which has acted as ideal ego to the masculine. By contrast to the traditional relationship to the masculine God, women would not be severed from the Irigarayan divine. As Irigaray asks in *An Ethics of Sexual Difference* (1993a): "Why do we assume that God must always remain an inaccessible transcendence rather than a realization—here and now—in and through the body?" (148). She speaks for a divine that would be "an inscription in the flesh" (1993a, 147). If sexual difference were cultivated, and genre allowed to develop and become individual, collective, and historical, then, she says, genre "could mark *the place where spirit entered human nature*, the point in time when the infinite passed into the finite, given that each individual of a gender *[genre]* is finite and potentially infinite in his or her relation to gender *[genre]*" (1993c, 139). The term employed by Irigaray to express her conception of a divinity from which we are not severed is the "sensible transcendental." She describes this concept as "[a] birth into a transcendence, that of the other, still in the world of the senses ('sensible'), still physical and carnal, and already spiritual" (1993a, 82).

The feminine divine is not figured as an ideal ego that the feminine is both aligned with and yet simultaneously opposed to. The feminine divine does serve the function of an infinite horizon in terms of which women can identify themselves. But, for Irigaray, it is crucial that one participates in the divine so conceived. The divine is not an ideal from which a woman is severed. Irigaray defines the feminine divine interchangeably with the concept of the feminine genre. Women are said to situate themselves in the context of a horizon of "becoming women," which is constituted by the notion of women as the collectivity named as genre. Finally, Irigaray introduces the terminology of sexed subjects participating in horizontal and vertical axes of relations.

Belonging to their sexuate genre would be a means for women to situate themselves as finite in the context of the infinite. Here infinite does not mean the supernatural, or that which I am not, but that which exceeds my own limits but in which I participate and to whose infinite range of senses I contribute. As we saw in chapter 5, the connotations of feminine genre are those of the collective of feminine identities in an open-ended process of becoming. Irigaray promotes the ideal of our situating ourselves in the horizon constituted by our genre, without arguing that women would definitively become themselves, or accomplish themselves. Because Irigaray affirms the notion of the infinite as always in a state of becoming, women participate in this notion of infinity. It is another figure for a divinity from which women are not severed. Irigaray exchanges the vertical relationship between man and the masculine-paternal God for women's relationship to their sexuate genre. This is a different kind of vertical relation, in which there is no radical schism between women and the feminine genre, as there is between man and the figure of the masculine-paternal God:

> This world of female ethics would continue to have two vertical and horizontal dimensions:
>   —daughter-to-mother, mother-to-daughter;
>   —among women, or among "sisters."
> . . . Female genealogy has to be suppressed, on behalf of the son-Father relationship, and the idealization of the father and husband as patriarchs. But without a vertical dimension . . . a loving ethical order cannot take

place among women. Within themselves, among themselves, women need both of these dimensions. (1993a, 108)[6]

Any woman would always be involved concurrently in self-other and in self-divine relations. She would always be situated on both axes, horizontal and vertical. Any (horizontal) relation between self and other would always be mediated by divinity, or one's relation to the vertical axis, insofar as the vertical axis of self-divine relations intersects with, and mediates, the horizontal self-other axis of relations. Any relationship a woman has, either with another woman or with a man, would be mediated by the field of her relations with other women, in the context of which a woman would situate herself. In this way, a woman's relationships both with men and with other women would not take place from the starting point of women's position as atrophy. And in his relations with other men and women, a man would similarly situate himself in the context of the vertical axis of a male sexuate genre that is to come.

Irigaray relocates transcendence as occurring between men and women in a culture of sexual difference. Although relations between men and women occur in the horizontal dimension, transcendence between men and women is due to the fact that the man and woman are situated along a different vertical axis of male or female sexuate genre. Relations among those of the same sex are also mediated by the vertical axis of their belonging to sexuate genre. There would be a degree of mystery between men and women because they participate in different genres. But our relationship to transcendence would not arise from an impoverished structure of identificatory identity with mystic ideals.

To summarize, Irigaray reformulates the divine so that there are no connotations of identification with an inaccessible supernatural entity. Instead, Irigaray's divinity may simply consist in the experience of wonder at alterity in this hypothetical sexual difference. We see the substitution of transcendence between the sexes for transcendence between man and God in the following passage:

> To arrive at the constitution of an ethics of sexual difference, we must at least return to what is for Descartes the first passion: *wonder.* This passion has no opposite or contradiction and exists always as though for the first time. Thus man and woman, woman and man are always meeting as though for the first time because they cannot be substituted one for the other. . . . [T]hey are irreducible one to the other. . . . Who or what the other is, I never know. But the other who is forever unknowable is the one who differs from me sexually. This feeling of surprise, astonishment, and wonder in the face of the unknowable ought to be returned to its locus: that

of sexual difference. The passions have either been repressed, stifled, or reduced, or reserved for God. (1993a, 12–13)

The sexually different other is transcendent for me.[7] This returns us to
Irigaray's objective: imagining an alternative to appropriative relationships between self and other. In recent essays in *Sexes and Genealogies* and
An Ethics of Sexual Difference Irigaray uses the terminology of horizontal
and vertical relations in the context of her ethics of mediation in human
relations. Intersecting axes of horizontal and vertical relations would enable mediation between self and other such that one would not appropriate the other in the generation of one's own self-identity. As we have
seen, in Irigaray's view, relations both between women, between men,
and between men and women tend toward the appropriation of the other.
I suggested in chapter 5 that appropriative relations occur wherever I relate to the other in a narcissistic mode, using her or him to tell me who I
am and whether I am loved. Irigaray proposes her utopian formulations
for mediated self/other relations as an alternative to relations where the
other is both appropriated in the production of my self-identity and also
overridden such that I am unable to go out toward the other qua other. I
am left in a mode of self and (the other appropriated as) version of the self.
What might provide this field of mediation between subjects? Ethico-
legal-linguistic transformations would enable the recognition and institutionalization of sexual difference and sexuate genre. A subject's participation in sexuate genre would constitute the mediating vertical plane in
which we could participate at the same time as interacting with the other.
The mediation of my relation with the other by this vertical plane would
render my encounter with the other less inclined to appropriation.

Many feminist theorists have criticized the Christian biblical tradition
for the sex bias of its representations of women. The contrast with Irigaray's approach is instructive. Irigaray assesses this tradition in terms of
the quality of the identity structures it offers to men and women. It has
posited men as made in God's image and women as spiritually equal to
men insofar as they are sex-neutral souls. The tradition renders the account of man as made in God's image in tandem with the positioning of
God as radically not-man. Making God man's ideal is a means of severing
man from his ideal. The projection of the masculine-paternal God results
in an alienating identificatory structure for man. Irigaray concludes that a
subject might respect the possible specificity of the other, rather than appropriating the other, if an alternative horizon of sexuate genre inter-
sected with the subject's identity. We see sexuate genre serving as the tem-
plate for mediating vertical dimensions between nonappropriative
individuals in her comment "I am often asked if man and woman will be

able to communicate if two different genders [*genres*] are affirmed. Perhaps they will be communicating for the first time!" (1993c, 120).

The comment allows us to better understand the Irigarayan definition of love between men and women as divine. The divine refers not just to the dimension defined by Irigaray as vertical (women in the context of their genre) but also to horizontal relations insofar as they are mediated by the vertical dimension. Love between men and women in a culture of sexual difference would be divine if mediated by vertical axes constituting a positive symbolic context for women and men. Thus in the essay "Questions to Emmanuel Lévinas," Irigaray speaks favorably of a model in which love could become "spiritual and divine." She laments, however:

> But what chance has it to exist in the genealogical economy of patriarchy? Without relationships between both natural and spiritual mothers and daughters, that are relationships between subjects, without cultural recognition of the divinity of this genealogy, how can a woman remain the lover [*l'amante*] of a man who belongs to the line of a Father God? And does not the latter need a Mother God? The two genealogies must be divinized in each of the two sexes and for the two sexes: mother and father, woman and man, for it to be possible for female and male lovers [*amante et amant*] to love each other. (1991b, 186)

In chapters 3 and 4, we considered the seeming instrumentalism of Irigaray's work. Does she think that desired social change could be brought into being through (legal or other) revolution promoted by agents? Is there a connection between the social changes that might arise from such reforms and the volitional agent who intends them? As I have argued, when Irigaray's sexuate rights strike us as implausible, they may not be striking us infelicitously. Perhaps we should understand them as working. They highlight the impossible extent of cultural reform that would be required to bring about an Irigarayan society of sexual difference.

For clearly this society could never arise as a result of the social reform indicated. One can implement some specific legal and religious reforms. Even linguistic reforms are sometimes implemented. But Irigaray's point is that any such reforms would be insufficient to bring about an Irigarayan culture of sexual difference. Such a change would require overall structural reform in relation to every conceivable domain: the media, religion, language, law, government, fiscal policy and economics, interpersonal relations. Some individual reforms are possible by decree, but not all reforms at all levels. Irigaray's sexuate rights are in this literal sense impossible. In this sense also hers is a politics of the impossible. It declares the plausibility of the rights it describes, but it describes their implausibility. The rights declare the impossibility—in the practical sense—of structural reform. They say, forget it! What you need is too much! Imagine what you're talking about! You'd need to invent a feminine divine, reinvent the whole of language, sexual identity, psychic structures, the economy, history, tax reform, and the legal system! While they do not declare, they perform a critique of instrumentalist feminist reform politics insofar as the latter could not implement an Irigarayan culture of sexual difference.

In chapter 4, I questioned the founding status of Irigarayan sexuate rights. They assume the retroactive time that any new bill of rights instituted by citizens whose authority to do so arises only as a result of that bill relies on. This is the founding aporia of any institutional regime. This aporia is often concealed by such regimes—for example, if one appeals to divine authority to justify the founding of rights, as occurs, Derrida points out, with the American Declaration of Independence.

In the light of the material presented in the present chapter, it is all the more pertinent that we ask whether Irigaray justifies the founding of sexuate rights through an appeal to divine authority. Of course, that divine authority would not be a supernatural God. It would be sexual difference, if presupposed as a transcendent, authorizing force irrespective of whether sexuate rights are instituted.

In chapter 4, I argued that Irigaray's emphasis on the impossible status of sexuate rights is not a disavowal of their founding aporia. Drucilla Cornell seemed to take a similar position, referencing Irigaray's sexuate rights in the context of Derrida's discussion of revolutionary violence. We can interpret Irigaray as arguing that we cannot know in advance that sexuate rights are justified. Only *après coup* would they be, and there may never be the *après coup*. In this sense, they are a leap of faith. To anticipate a proposal to which I will turn in a moment, perhaps they may be described as a form of religion without religion.

But one is not called upon to make an arbitrary leap of faith. To ask us to believe in the desirability of sexuate rights is not the same as asking us to believe in any kind of imaginable rights no matter how implausible or impractical. When women are said to be man's helpmate, that statement is considered by Irigaray an active exclusion of alternative possibilities for women. By contrast Irigaray does not believe that the statement "I am now going to empty out the contents of my bag" is similarly an active exclusion of alternative possibilities for a relationship to my bag. My emptying is not importantly traced, ethically or politically, by the absence of those alternative possibilities. Irigaray does believe that our culture is meaningfully marked by the absence of sexual difference, as it is not meaningfully marked by the absence of bag rights. She does believe we can read many texts in the history of philosophy and culture for their active exclusion of sexual difference, their active reduction of women to same, complement, or opposite. She does not believe we could meaningfully read contemporary culture as actively excluding the possibility of bag rights. In this sense, our culture is traced by the one exclusion, as it is not traced by the other. She thinks we do have an experience of the exclusion of sexual difference to which we can respond ethically and politically. This is the case even though sexual difference has no identity. I draw the distinction to point out that Irigaray's notion of active exclusion is more than a logical possibility. She would consider that what is said about women and femininity does constitute a legible opening to the future. What is said about bags has little ethical status and is not legible (is certainly less legible) as an opening to the future.

I suggested that Irigaray's diagnostic readings are the most convincing on this point. Figures such as Freud are diagnosed as repeatedly insisting that women are opposite, same, or complement, and these oppositions are so widely repeated as to be meaningfully interpretable as "active exclusion." The advent of a culture of sexual difference takes on an ethical status. This is not the case for any arbitrary and nonexistent rights one cares to mention. Sexuate rights are a leap of faith, because sexual difference has no content. But the absence of sexual difference is culturally significant, and Irigaray does think this significance is empirically demonstrable. Because of this, the leap of faith is not—as some may consider— ridiculous or arbitrary. However, it must be made without attributing content to sexual difference. In that sense, sexual difference is to come.

I have mentioned the discussion of Irigaray's work in terms of a notion of revolutionary violence and democracy to come attributed to Derrida. Drucilla Cornell interprets Irigaray's female imaginary in terms of Derrida's call to the future, to new forms of democracy, or to revolution, "the turn of the ethical toward radical alterity, toward the *tout autre,* which is also toward the justice to come . . . innumerable genders to come." "The unknowable of the essence of Woman is the figure not of a lack but an excess and an opening to the future" (Caputo 2000, 140, 141, discussing Derrida, Irigaray, and Cornell). Both Cornell and John Caputo have acknowledged Derrida's own reluctance, despite a politics affirmative of the possibility of new sexual idioms, to name new metaphors for women, which might lock the reference to such idioms into a politics of presence. Cornell's earlier suggestion (1991, 110, 118, discussed in Caputo 2000, 142) was that Irigaray's remetaphorization of the feminine was not the same thing as fixing a new concept of woman and could instead be affirmed as an opening toward the new. John Caputo joins the discussion at this point.[8]

As a commentator on Derrida's politics of the *"à-venir,"* Caputo cites Cornell's interpretation and Irigaray's politics of the imaginary. Things cannot happen without risk and anxiety, he reminds us. True, attempts at a new feminine imaginary might essentialize it, promoting the fixing of female identity, the metaphysics of presence. But "the risk of reinstating, not displacing, oppositional schemata . . . is a risk worth running, part of the aporetic or risky axiomatics of the question of sexual difference. Who ever said that things could happen without risk or anxiety?" (Caputo 2000, 142–43).

This argument would question any attempt to lock down Irigaray's politics in terms of its political and rhetorical operation. I mentioned this problem in chapter 4, and it returns here. We cannot assume the failure (even the successful, rhetorical failure) of Irigaray's politics any more than we can its success. We cannot lock down the context in which it works. Both Caputo, and Drucilla Cornell in her earlier interpretation have seen Irigaray's work as open rather than closed to the unpredictability of an opening. Neither would have said that Irigaray's work performs the rhetorical function of "Forget it!" For one thing, even if the gesture "Forget it!" does takes place, it necessarily undermines itself, simultaneously saying "Think about it!"

But, having made this point, I would like to think further about some comments made by Caputo about Irigaray in this regard. Discussing Irigaray's concept of divinity, Caputo (2000) suggests that we need not think it turns "the figure of Woman into a religion" (143–44). We have seen Irigaray use the concept of divinity in two interconnected senses. On the one hand, my existence as divine is, for Irigaray, my situation of myself in the context of my sexuate genre. It is the intimacy of difference at the heart of my self-identity: it is my deferring and ceaseless relations with those of my sex around which I could never draw a boundary. Genre is that which is most infinite to me, and most intimate. It is my intimate relation to the infinite: the sensible transcendental. Divinity is also sometimes associated with (redefined) love, and sometimes it is particularly associated with love between the sexes. Again I am in intimacy with infinity. In my relations with the sexed other, I have relations of the greatest proximity with that which is transcendent to me. Divinity among those of the same sex occurs in their deferring and differing relation to the genre they share, that belonging then mediating their relations with each other. But divinity among those of different sexes is seen in one's proximity to an entity who bears a differing and deferring relation to a different sexuate genre.

In brief, Irigaray rethinks divinity as intimacy, offering this as a conceptual alternative to being severed from an unknowable and alienating God. Irigaray's divinity is, continues Caputo (2000, 144), religion without religion. In this regard he recounts Derrida's discussion of a tale from Blanchot,[9] this time reworked by Caputo to suit a discussion of Irigarayan sexual difference:

> That is why I suggest we could, in the spirit of Derrida's citation of the story of the coming of the Messiah in Maurice Blanchot's *The Writing of the Disaster,* reimagine this tale as *her*story, as the story of a 'messianic Woman.' Once, when the messianic woman was to be found disguised, dressed in rags, among the wretched of the earth, someone approached her and, identifying her as the Messiah, said, "when will you come?" The point of this story, Blanchot comments, is that we not confuse the *coming (venue)* of the Messiah with his—we rewrite—*her* presence. For the Messianic Woman is always to come, structurally to come, so that she cannot be identified or reduced to her presence, and indeed is meant to confound the present, to disturb and disrupt the present. Thus in a way that Lacan never dreamed, it is true to say that the Messianic Woman does not exist. She can never exist, and this is because she is always to come. (Caputo 2000, 144)

This tale gives us another sense of the intimacy of divinity in an Irigarayan "religion without religion." We have seen Irigaray's strong commitment to a divinity from which we are not severed. But what does this mean? A radically transcendent divinity—that which is radically "not man" to man or "not woman" to woman, radically God-like to the human—would be a divinity about which, by definition, we could know nothing at all. This is the insight of any negative theology, and of Irigaray's philosophy of sexual difference is not the God of negative theology.

Caputo uses the formulation "religion without religion" to consider Irigaray's desire—like, Caputo suggests, that of Derrida—to welcome the *"tout autre."* This is religion without religion for various reasons. It is no accident that the parable used repeatedly to depict this philosophy is that of a Messiah's impossible coming. Caputo's point is that Derrida and Irigaray are anticipating the *tout autre* only in some of the ways that the devout have waited for the Messiah. Derrida uses the concept of the messianic, as opposed to messianism, to delineate this kind of anticipation.[10] Those who wait for the Messiah usually are waiting for the completely other: that which is most radically "not-man" to their man, or "not-human" to their humanity. Those who wait for the Messiah think they can name it: God. But waiting for the Messiah is surely founded on a paradox. If the Messiah really were radically other, we would not know him if we met him. If we could recognize him, he must have complied with the way in which we could have anticipated his coming. Yet the Messiah, by definition, would have to exceed that anticipation. If we are waiting for the Messiah, we must not know what we are waiting for. To name what we are waiting for, to think "It is the Messiah," is to disavow this point. Messianism—like those who give content and identity to sexual difference—involves the disavowal of this paradox. It is the conviction that although we wait for radical alterity, we know what we are waiting for. Derrida distinguishes from this the messianic, to connote knowing better the necessary paradox of anticipation. We know we anticipate—we know this very profoundly, ethically, politically—yet it still may be true that we do not know what we anticipate. We cannot give it identity, content, fixity.

Yet messianicity is also a kind of intimacy. It is intimacy, not with any Messiah, but with anticipation. We have no intimacy with the exclusion of bag rights, but we do have intimacy with the exclusion of sexuate rights and sexual difference. This is a mood or mode or willing "Come!" that we direct to an impossible *tout autre* of sexual difference. This intimacy with the ethical domain of an exclusion of sexual difference can be described as alterity at the heart of our identity. Judith Butler (1998) has asked the question, is it by "appropriating a Lévinasian view of the ineffability of the Other as radically Other that multicultural understanding might be significantly advanced? . . . Does such a casting of alterity beyond the domain of the thinkable not reconstitute the radically alien character of 'the other' and continue to cover over the ways in which the 'other' may well be more properly a constitutive part of the self?" (43). But the structure of anticipation is a structure according to which the "other" is a constitutive part of the self. Anticipation is a mediation by alterity that interrupts self-sameness. I think it probably is the case that in Irigaray's work sexual difference is "radically Other, as beyond the reach of reason" (Butler 1998, 43). But that which is beyond the reach of reason need not for all that be radically alien. It is the locus of anticipated change and transformation, of openness to alternative possibilities, though they cannot be named. For this reason, the notion of an intimacy with the otherness of impossible sexual difference is useful as a means of counteracting a depiction of that otherness as transcendent or alien.

Irigaray's divinity is, Caputo argues, religion without religion. Why? We have seen him raise the problem that a politics that names the *tout autre* as a specific configuration of sexual difference risks converting the philosophy of sexual difference to a philosophy of named (sexual) identity. In chapter 8, I am going to pursue this problem further. But it is worth noting Caputo's argument that this risk is worth running. A feminist philosophy is not to be belittled for its hopeful desire to name the *tout autre* with the language of sexual difference.[11] Religion without religion is a politics founded on the inevitability of anticipating in the name of such im-

possible namings. Any provisional name we give to a pair of empty anticipatory brackets will necessarily seem to shut down some of their possibilities. It may be that this is the necessary price for an attempt to keep
them open by naming them at all.

The difference between the messianic and messianism is the difference
between an impossible politics that cannot (but must) name what it
knows it anticipates, and a disavowing politics that will not admit its impossibility in these terms. This brings us to an interesting problem, for it is
Irigaray's politics that I have, throughout this work, named the politics of
the impossible. Impossibility has meant many things. Irigaray's political
program literally could not take place. Her program of political reform
can be read as impossible in this sense. Impossibility also refers to the
structure of recognition on which Irigaray relies. She calls for sexuate
rights that would recognize and be legitimated by that which does not
precede that recognition. But we turn now to a new sense of impossibility.

The *tout autre* is impossible for us. Any content-based anticipation of the
tout autre inevitably reduces the *tout autre* to anything but. The *tout autre* is
in this sense paradoxical, impossible, anticipating that which can not be
anticipated. But impossibility itself does take place: we are intimate with
it. It is the very fact of anticipating the *tout autre*—change, the new, another democracy—that places us in proximity with impossibility. So, argues Derrida, we are in a kind of intimate proximity with the anticipation
of that which cannot be anticipated. In the next chapter, I am going to
argue that Irigaray's concept of sexual difference is thinkable as impossible in this sense also. This argument will give a new inflection to the notion of an Irigarayan "politics of the impossible." But I am also going to interrogate the extent of Irigaray's acknowledgment of the impossibility of
her philosophy of sexual difference in this sense.

7

Interrogating an Unasked Question

Is There Sexual Difference?

> Sexual difference has not had its chance to develop, either empiri-
> cally or transcendentally.
>
> Luce Irigaray, The Ethics of Sexual Difference

In chapter 2, we saw the suggestion, based on Irigaray's linguistic analysis, that men and women are sick or suffering from an absence of sexual difference, and her suggestion that "[f]or some time now, sexual difference has not played a part in the *creation of culture*, except in a division of roles and functions that does not allow both sexes to be subjects. Thus we are confronted with a certain *subjective pathology* from both sides of sexual difference" (1993c, 172). Irigaray's diagnosis of contemporary culture is that it has excluded the possibility of adequate sexual difference.

The very thinking of its impossibility is a kind of thinking of sexual difference. We are asked to imagine a pair of empty brackets, "sexual difference," whose emptiness is necessary to phallocentric culture and the source of its ailment. Irigaray deems the empty brackets to be filled with meanings yet to come. She proposes that just thinking of sexual difference as a set of empty brackets is a therapeutic improvement on a culture that places a premium on discourses of equality, sameness, negation, and complementarity. Thinking about the emptiness of these brackets is already the beginnings of a thinking of sexual difference. Sexual difference is, at least, thought of as absent.

I think the inevitable instability of this project adds to its force and interest. Irigaray (1996b) also emphasizes its constructive outlook: "We do have to smash our chains and prisons, but we need to construct our identity, and our divine identity, and seek out traces and scraps of it, wherever they may be" (232–33). The project of thinking impossibility would, in principle, generate more cultural possibilities for a thinking of sexual difference. But wherever we lose sight of the impossibility of the project, its specific character has been exchanged for a simpler version of the politics of difference according to which there is difference, men and women are different, and this is a fact that should be recognized.

Introducing *An Ethics of Sexual Difference*, Irigaray presents us with sexual difference as a possibility, but not as a question of ontology of the sort "Is there sexual difference really?" Her philosophical framework is constructed by taking both these positions, each of which can be argued with equal vigor: that there is no sexual difference; that there might be sexual difference. Historical attempts to think sexual difference, such as a Rousseauist thinking of women as the natural opposite and complement of man, are anything but. There never has been a thinking of sexual difference that did not subordinate it to a masculine benchmark. Furthermore, there never has been sexual difference because its cultural conditions have never existed. As we know, Irigaray elsewhere lists these conditions as a revolution in law, language, media, philosophy, the economy, religion, and so on. Thus, "there is no sexual difference."

But Irigaray does claim that the thinking of sexual difference has been repeatedly avoided, or ignored, or foreclosed, or reduced into a thinking of the same. One constant of Irigaray's work is the view that western culture has been engaged in the constant process of actively not thinking sexual difference. On that basis, while there is not and has not been sexual difference, there is the trace of a possible sexual difference in that active and repeated cultural action of "not that." The need to think sexual difference in terms of the simultaneous "there is not" and "there might be" precludes Irigaray from posing a simple question, "Is there sexual difference?" Rather than introducing it in such terms, she presents sexual difference as a foreclosed conceptual possibility that has not yet been recognized as culturally significant.

For whom is this foreclosure a problem? According to the diagnostic aspect of Irigaray's work, we are all suffering from sexual difference, from its failure to come, from our failure to pose it. The steps of her argumentation are as follows:

1. "There is" must be relinquished in favor of a structure of reflection on a simultaneous and inseparable "There is not" and "There might be" to enable an adequate reflection on sexual difference.

2. Sexual difference must be reformulated not as a fact but as a cultural impossibility.

3. This impossibility is significant, whereas many impossibilities may not be. Sexual difference is a problem with the highest stakes. Indeed "the

stakes are so high that everything is subject to denial, incomprehension, blindness, rejection" (1993a, 134).

4. Sexual difference is everybody's problem in all of culture and all cultures.

5. Cultures and texts may be analyzed as expressing the symptoms of their malaise of an absence of sexual difference.

Irigaray considers the absence of sexual difference to be a crucial underlying issue of culture and thought to which we do not attend. The ramifications of this claim are first seen in Irigaray's methodological approach in *Speculum* (1985b). The claim that sexual difference might have this double status leads to a particular reading of Freud and Plato. Irigaray interprets their texts as biographies of an excluded sexual difference lurking in their conceptual schemas. Sexual difference lurks as the major issue of these authors, and yet the issue to which they will not attend. On Irigaray's reading, Freud's concerns of identification, desire, castration, libido, object substitution, and repression are symptoms of his failure to deal with the major issue, sexual difference. With some ingenuity, Irigaray also interprets Plato's concern with ideal immaterial forms, symmetry, the sun, light, the good, a knowledge transcending the domain of physical desire and procreation, the love of truth, the devaluation of mimesis, the image, the copy, matter, and procreation as symptoms of a neglect of issues of sexual difference.[1] Plato's texts are reinterpreted as the tracing of a conflict about the major issue to which he will not attend. Irigaray is not arguing that sexual difference is a philosophical issue for Plato. Instead we should consider his failure to think of sexual difference as a key philosophical issue. This failure is his problem, and his texts constantly manifest symptoms of this failure.

This kind of interpretation enables Irigaray's claims concerning the status of historical philosophical texts. These texts are conflictual. They are engaged in a constant, disavowed failure to think sexual difference. Does any text from the history of philosophy escape this conflict? Few, if any: Irigaray attributes its symptoms to Plato, to Aristotle and Plotinus, to Spinoza and Descartes, to Kant and Hegel, to Nietzsche, to Heidegger, Sartre, Lévinas, and Merleau-Ponty. Tina Chanter (1995) offers a good summary of this Irigarayan account of the overinvested absence of sexual difference from the history of philosophy:

> Irigaray reads the history of Western philosophy as a history in which the question of sexual difference has been obliterated. What this means is not only that philosophers—from Plato to the present day—have failed to pose the question of sexual difference, but that the question itself has been buried, suppressed or banished from the arena of legitimate philosophical

consideration. Irigaray's insistent emphasis on the question of sexual difference is not simply a matter of drawing attention to an area that happens as
a matter of empirical fact to have been neglected. The question of sexual
difference has been excluded from philosophical orbit as a matter of principle. Irigaray's concern is to investigate the dynamics of this systematic rel-
egation of sexual difference to the sidelines of philosophical discourse, and
to ask why and how sexual difference has been written out of the history of
philosophy. (140)

To be sure, sexual difference seems to be an overt philosophical issue
for some of these philosophers. But its unsatisfactory treatment by figures
such as Nietzsche leaves Irigaray concluding that such texts are still failures to think sexual difference, little better than the simple omission of the
question.[2] Whether omitted or mistreated, the very absence of sexual difference from the texts of the history of philosophy is deemed by Irigaray a
presence in the text, a present, interpretable absence. Where and when,
she asks, is sexual difference absent? In relation to what themes, in which
locations? With such questions Irigaray establishes a fragile foundation on
which to build up a philosophy of sexual difference, pulling it up by its
own bootstraps.

In *Speculum*, Irigaray reconstitutes the failure to attend to sexual difference in Plato's concept of ideal forms. In more recent work, Irigaray locates in the following contemporary cultural phenomena a similar failure:
the many forms of destruction in the world, nihilism, the proliferation of
status quo values, consumerism, cancer, the end of philosophy, religious
despair, regression to religiosity, scientistic or technical imperialism "that
fails to consider the living subject" (1993a, 5). These are not posited as failures in the face of a sexual difference considered as a cultural fact. They
are interpreted as expressions of the cultural failure to posit the possibility
of sexual difference, let alone to allow sexual difference to develop as a
cultural reality. Irigaray (1993a) diagnoses "everything" as "resist[ing] the
discovery and affirmation of such an advent or event" (6).

One of Irigaray's boldest philosophical contributions is her diagnosis of
every aspect of culture, from a scientific discovery, to a Platonic text, to a
day-to-day relationship between a man and a woman, a woman and a
woman, or a man and a man, as:

1. a constant failure to attend to sexual difference, and
2. a state of conflict, tension, or resistance in relation to that failure.

While sexual difference is the question of "our age" (1993a, 5),[3] the am-
plitude of the series of philosophers she considers makes clear that Irigaray

views it as the problem avoided by all ages.[4] But we have seen that she does not posit sexual difference as a fact that has been ignored throughout the ages or as a universal thing that has persisted throughout the ages, taking on different permutations, expressions, or interpretations.[5] Irigaray does not claim in this sense that there has been sexual difference going back to the Greeks. So the founding problem of her work might be as follows: Can one claim instead that there has been the refused issue or the foreclosed question of sexual difference throughout history? In other words, if sexual difference is not an entity, is the *absence* of the question of sexual difference a continuous phenomenon going back to the Greeks, whose symptoms we might plausibly find in the philosophical texts of history?

The issue is not whether sexual difference as a question or a problem could have been considered throughout the ages. Irigaray is not arguing that reflections on sexual difference have a long history, any more than she is arguing that sexual difference persists throughout the ages. She is not reconstructing a continuity of sexual difference *as problematized.* Sexual difference has continuity as a problematic no more than it has continuity as an entity. Instead, we have never come to pose the question. An absence is not an entity. But can it have a continuity nonetheless?

Asking whether Irigaray is uncharitable in her apparently ahistoricist treatment of Aristotle, Cynthia Freeland (1998) comments, "[R]ather than treating Aristotle as a philosopher with potential contributions to the history of physics and metaphysics, [Irigaray] sees him as a 'neurotic,' his text a symptom of a collective repression" (85).[6] While Irigaray does not quite describe Aristotle as a neurotic, Freeland's comment nicely incarnates the problem. Irigaray does not universalize a concept or essentialize a reality of sexual difference throughout the ages. By contrast, does she want to universalize a collective disavowal throughout the ages relating to sexual difference? The commentators who have accused Irigaray of essentializing sexual difference may have missed the point.[7] If she is essentializing anything, she is essentializing its absence throughout the ages, as when, on Freeland's formulation, she interprets all of the texts of the history of philosophy as evidencing a collective repression, a connected neurosis. Given that sexual difference does not run throughout the ages, could its collective avoidance, or the constant failure to think it? To ask whether one can narrate a continuous story, we would have to distinguish between a phenomenon problematized and a question that never came to be posed. If anything, it is the latter that has continuity throughout history, on Irigaray's model. This notion of active failure may be one of her most ingenious maneuvers. In her view, the absences, failures, and continuous disavowals are legible as the constant cultural admission that "there might be" sexual difference.

I want to offer one final example of the status of sexual difference in Irigaray's work. If there is one domain in which Irigaray seems to consider that sexual difference exists, it is that of language. In *An Ethics of Sexual Difference* and elsewhere, Irigaray reports on linguistic findings based on the analysis of spoken discourse by men and women. Without much ambiguity, Irigaray (1993a) argues that "discourse is sexed" (133, translation modified). She acknowledges that because the stakes are taken to be very high, the claim that discourse is sexed is always given a rough reception, although it incites curiosity (134). Irigaray attributes sexedness to linguistic structures and to the mode of address of the speaker's utterance. She claims that masculine discourse is typically self-reflexive. The speaker muses to himself or to a generalized other akin to himself. The speaker does not assume that a different other is going to speak back to, or with, him. Thus, typically masculine discourse positions both the "I" and the "you" as "two unequal parts of the world that are capable neither of exchange nor of alliance. . . . This leads to social crises, to individual illnesses, to schematic and fossilized identities for both sexes, as well to a general sclerosis of discourse, a hardening of language" (135). When she makes such reflections, Irigaray seems to consider that there is sexual difference indisputably. She states, "[A]nyone who denies that discourse is sexed is advised to carry out a statistical investigation of taped materials and analyze the results. If one still claims to discern no difference, then one's own interpretation would have to be analyzed to see how it reproduces one of the patterns of the taped material, even, or perhaps especially, in the denials" (136, translation modified).

Irigaray takes the sexedness of language to be empirically irrefutable for anyone with a tape recorder. But her point is not that the sexedness of discourse is evidence of the reality of sexual difference. To the contrary, it is evidence of the absence of sexual difference in the Irigarayan sense. It demonstrates that there is no adequate exchange or communication between sexed subjects. Irigaray (1993a) proposes a formulation according to which "man and women have not spoken to each other—not since the first garden"(140). In this sense, her linguistic samples may demonstrate the sexedness of discourse, but they do not demonstrate the presence of adequate sexual difference in our culture. They demonstrate the contrary. Perhaps this point clarifies the status of Irigarayan sexual difference. Sexual difference is usually taken to mean differences between men and women. But this is not what Irigaray means. She means an ideal, alternative, transformed sexual difference, not culturally impoverished relations between men and women or existing differences in their status, equality, or psychology. The latter indicate the absence of sexual difference in our culture.

Is there sexedness of philosophical discourse, according to Irigaray's interpretations of philosophers such as Plato, Descartes, Spinoza, Merleau-Ponty, and Lévinas in *An Ethics of Sexual Difference?* Yes, but according to Irigaray's analysis it is not an unambiguous sexedness. The works of the historical philosophers are not monolithic, unmitigated, masculine discourses. They contain thinkings of the other, of difference, of sexuality, of wonder, surprise, mediation, and the in-between, all of which could contribute to an eventual thinking of sexual difference.

As a result, Irigaray seems to claim that the philosophical texts discussed in *An Ethics of Sexual Difference* (1993a) are ambiguously sexed. Elements of an eventual thinking of sexual difference can be located in certain aspects of the work of such philosophers as Plato, Aristotle, Descartes, Spinoza, and Merleau-Ponty, in their thinking of touch, the interval, astonishment, eros, and the envelope.[8] She presents Plato as a philosopher who "gives the floor to a woman" (20), Diotima. This female character thematizes thinking the intermediary in the midst of Plato's dialogues. These may be masculine in many of the respects discussed by Irigaray, but they are not homogeneously so. We can value a philosophy of the intermediary briefly articulated in the *Symposium*, even though it subsequently "miscarries," collapsing into a binary separation between the mortal and the immortal, with love losing its temporary status as the divine intermediary between opposites. Descartes depicts wonder as the first of the passions. This too could be a valuable contribution to an eventual thinking of sexual difference. Descartes rarely distinguishes between men and women as reasoning beings. He formulates the passions in terms of a sexually neutral subject. His subject "reconstitutes the world in solitude on the basis of one fixed point: Descartes' certainty that he is a man" (116–17). Nevertheless, Irigaray can connect "the issues relating to passion and its ethics," as she understands these, to "Descartes' *wonder*." She can do the same in relation to "Spinoza's *joy*," despite the concurrent sex bias of Spinoza's account of why men and women should not mutually assume political authority (117).[9] Merleau-Ponty depicts prediscursive experience in terms of original mystery. Irigaray affirms this aspect of his work, even though he eventually retains a model of binarized divisions between viewer and viewed and fails to consider the possibility of an alterity ontologically different from one's own (157). Lévinas articulates a relation of original immersion in the world, a relation prior to eros and marked with wonder and astonishment, even though he formulates eros by subordinating the feminine to man as his beloved.

Irigaray considers that sexual difference has been avoided throughout the history of philosophy. Yet its possibility is half thought in ambivalent, self-contradictory, and fragmentary ways. These ways are not only seen in what philosophers have or have not said about women. They are also seen in brief formulations of certain concepts, despite their concurrent collapse, such as the intermediary, the envelope, mystery, and wonder. Along these lines also, *An Ethics of Sexual Difference* argues that the philosophers who exclude sexual difference also envelope the elements or potential for such a thinking, while also counteracting that potential. In reading these philosophers, Irigaray refigures them as already enveloping Irigarayan themes, or at least the possibility of those themes.

The reader will observe that some ingenuity is needed to locate the elements for a possible thinking of sexual difference in historical philosophical discussions of the intermediary, the envelope, and so on. The scope of the problem broadens beyond what might usually be associated with a feminist problematics: questions of what is said about men and women.

In addition, *An Ethics of Sexual Difference* asks how a philosophy of sexual difference can adequately theorize sameness. Somewhat surprisingly, Irigaray asks how we may have not only adequate structures of difference but also adequate structures of self-sameness.

Formulations offered at the beginning of the third section of *An Ethics of Sexual Difference* and in many other contexts convey her view that to engage with the other, even with the best of intentions, is to reduce the other to the same. Of course, this argument implies a negative connotation of love of sameness, as when Irigaray (1993a) argues that "love of sameness becomes that which permits . . . a customarily autarchic discourse which opens up only toward a dialogue-monologue with God" (100). This would suggest another sense in which we can say there is no sexual difference. There is merely love of the same, love of what seems to be like me, to have something to tell me about me, or to be in relation with me. Apparent love of the different or the other collapses into a love of the same. Love of the same is another indication of the impoverishment of our culture. We might well conclude that Irigaray devalues love of the same. It is so dominant that we are forced to answer "no" to the question, Is there sexual difference?

Complicating this picture is that Irigaray also asks whether there is sexual sameness, any more than sexual difference. With this question, she widens again the concerns of a philosophy of sexual difference. This widening will be apparent to the reader who opens her *An Ethics of Sexual Difference* (1993a) to the chapter "Love of Self," as opposed to the apparently key introductory chapter, "Sexual Difference." The latter chapter introduces us to reflections one would predict: the importance of sexual difference, its deemphasis by philosophers, the need for "a revolution in thought and ethics [that] is needed if the work of sexual difference is to take place" (6). But the chapter "Love of Self" is also critical to the work. It opens with a reflection on the problems and possibilities arising from the expression "love of self." Irigaray muses on the complexity of that expression:

> *Love of self.* The status of this *of* is complex. Who is loving whom? Or who is loving a part of whom? How in this case is the relationship between subject and object to be determined? The relation between two different subjects?
>
> *Love of self.* I am supposed to relate to my self, but how? The *I* is supposed to relate to the *self,* but how? (59, translation modified)

What is the role of self-love and of love of the same in an Irigarayan philosophy of sexual difference? Why does Irigaray also ask whether there is love of the same, really? While theorists have focused on the status of sexual difference in Irigaray's work, the concept and status of sameness are an equally problematic issue. If Irigaray asks whether there is difference really, she also asks whether there is sameness. An Irigarayan question is whether love of the different ever succeeds. Do we not fail at it with our inevitable love of the same? But she also asks if love of the same is ever a success. We have reason to think that according to her interpretation, love of the same also fails. It fails in the sense that it is an impoverished form of love, to be sure. But, like sexual difference, it is also an impossible form of love. Love of the same is a fragile, collapsing form of love. We have seen her argument that it is sustained by a self-undermining identification with the divine, or by opposition to a negative other. It is dependent on the other's confirmation, which is never definitive.

But in *An Ethics of Sexual Difference* (1993a), Irigaray also introduces a different and more positive sense of a possible love of the same. This kind of love of the same would make sexual difference possible. At one point she describes this sameness as "the maternal-feminine which has been assimilated before any perception of difference" (98).[10] The reader might expect Irigaray to be entirely critical of this kind of love. Certainly she criticizes nostalgia for a lost maternal, expressed either overtly or in the desire for other forms of unity. But she also attributes a potentially positive connotation to love of the same. She assigns it a crucial role in an ethics of alterity and a philosophy of sexual difference. In this regard, she allocates it "one of the most essential places for an ethics of the passions: *no love of other without love of same*" (104). Elizabeth Grosz has drawn attention to Irigaray's position "I believe that you can love the difference but only if you're also able to love those who are the same as yourself" (Irigaray 1983, 199–201, cited Grosz 1994a, 348). Forms of failed and impoverished self-love become the context for Irigaray to speculate on restructured, reconceived forms of self-love.

The sections "Love of Self" and "Love of Same, Love of Other" in *Ethics* demonstrate that positive concepts of "sameness" and "love of self" constitute a crucial component of Irigaray's formulations on sexual difference. In chapter 1, I referred to a comment from Joan Scott that "the apparent need to choose sameness *or* difference (which can never be satisfied by either alternative)" is symptomatic of the problems faced by feminism in relation to its conceptual heritage. Neither sameness nor difference can be satisfied by either alternative. In chapter 6, I considered Irigaray's concept of sexuate genre. We could see this concept, and the interest in an adequate sameness expressed in *An Ethics of Sexual Difference*, as an illustration of Scott's formula. The relationship between a qualitative sameness and a qualitative difference redoubles in Irigaray's work. Sexuate genre is a model for a qualitative sexual sameness, enabled by difference and also enabling difference. The relationship of positive difference between two subjects is mediated by their relationship to those of the same genre. But that qualitative relation of sameness is in turn mediated by difference, insofar as it is the differentiation between those of the same genre that constitutes genre. My relationship to genre allows a form of self-identity, but one posited only on the endless deferral of differences constituting a genre. A differently conceptualized sameness relies on difference, and difference fosters structures of self-sameness as Irigaray imagines these. In chapter 1, I raised the question of why Irigaray favors a politics of sexual difference. She suggests that concepts of equality may presuppose inequality, such as the inequality of women and nonwhites. I acknowledged a critic's possible view that discourses of sexual difference may also have built-in presuppositions about women's inequality. I pointed out that Irigaray's project is to transform concepts of sexual difference and noted a likely question: Why not transform concepts of equality and sameness? In this chapter I am suggesting Irigaray's position that these politics are not so very different. She considers the projects of reconceptualizing sameness and difference as intertwined and dissociable.

Unlike traditional oppositions between sameness and difference, a deconstructive interpretation typically locates a generalized concept of difference at the heart of concepts of sameness. This is a gesture undertaken by Irigaray also. But her work on sameness is interesting for its concurrent reverse move. Irigaray locates the necessities of (modified versions of) sameness and self-love at the heart of her formulations of difference. Sameness will always have enveloped difference: Love of same, she writes, is a relation which takes place in a "horizon of sexual difference" (1993a, 99). Perhaps the more surprising model is that sexual difference will always have enveloped a restructured relation to sameness. A self should and could be, Irigaray argues, "open in the present" and yet "closed and enveloped enough to make a self" (62, translation modified). The envelope structure is taken by Irigaray as an ideal for a generalized understanding of subjectivity as internally separated, inevitably, from itself. Her alternative model of self-sameness remains a model of internal separation from oneself, but affirmed as such.

Irigaray articulates this envelope structure in her analysis of the split between the "I" and the "self" and of the various ways in which we might think of a "doubling of the self" (1993a, 59), which gives rise to a structure of original division, or lack of self-identity. The "I" is originally a redoubled relationship to itself, and the possibility of love of self expresses the duplicity of that original non-self-identity. "Love of self," as Irigaray reflects on it, is not the pitfall of narcissism. It need not be the failure to attend to the other. This pitfall is elsewhere condemned in her work. But Irigaray also offers an important analysis of the self as an original enfolding or envelope of difference rather than an original, static identity: "Love of self . . . neither the subject nor the self is fixed in its position or its given, otherwise the two would be separated without any possibility of love" (59). In chapter 6, we considered Ellen Armour's suggestion that at her best Irigaray conceptualizes an infinitely deferred, displaced, fragmented sexuate identity. In this chapter, I have addressed aspects of Irigaray's work that try to present such an infinite displacement as mediating but still allowing the possibility of (an enveloped, non-self-coinciding) sexuate identity, rather than invalidating it. Although she considers that it would never finally become, and never be static, Irigaray privileges a notion of self-sameness mediated by infinitely deferring differences, rather than no notion of self-sameness at all.

Since refigured models of self-sameness are important to a qualitative relation of sexual difference, I want finally to reflect on the further breadth of definition allocated by Irigaray to sexual difference and its concerns.

Let's return to the extended list she provides of contemporary culture's failures to think sexual difference. We saw that she locates this failure in forms of world destruction, nihilism, status quo values, consumerism, cancer, the end of philosophy, religious despair, regression to religiosity, and scientistic or technical imperialism. Irigaray diagnoses "everything" as resisting "the discovery and affirmation of such an advent or event" (1993a, 6). What of this "everything"? Is it so open as to be a weakness in her work—too open to be meaningful? I'd like to suggest some reasons why it makes sense that the concept be this open.

I have already noted that in *An Ethics of Sexual Difference* (1993a), the scope of the conceptual field of sexual difference becomes very broad. The book's description of Irigarayan sexual difference is as follows:

[A] revolution in thought and ethics is needed if the work of sexual difference is to take place. We need to reinterpret everything concerning the relations between the subject and discourse, the subject and the world, and the
subject and the cosmic, the microcosmic and the macrocosmic. (6)

The transition to a new age requires a change in our perception and conception of *space-time,* the *inhabiting of places,* and of *containers,* or *envelopes of
identity.* It assumes and entails an evolution or a transformation of forms, of
the relations of *matter* and *form* and of the interval *between.* (7)

As I suggested earlier, this is a field that vastly exceeds the problematics of
men, women, the relations between them, the representation of them, and
the representation of the masculine and the feminine. Irigaray clarifies
that time, space, matter, and form share a history of gender connotations,
whereby the feminine has been associated with space and matter and the
masculine with time and form. But this is not her only reason for an interest in space and time. We saw that her drive to locate the possibility of
a thinking of sexual difference in its very nonthinking of sexual difference
leads her to conceptualizations of materiality, envelopes, intervals, inter-
mediaries, place, space, time, wonder, the touch, and identity in historical
philosophers. Sexual difference could now be thought of as a term substi-
tuting for the thinking of the cosmos, time and space, divinity and the universe. The conceptual point we think of as "sexual difference" becomes an
envelope into which Irigaray enfolds reflections on the universe, its dimensions and physics, and our capacity to think these things. This is a
kind of becoming-all of sexual difference. Ironically, at the most radical
point of a thinking of sexual difference, there is again no sexual difference.
There are alternative possibilities for thinking the cosmos, the universe,
everything, enfolded within the term "sexual difference."

Insofar as subjects have suffered from the absence of sexual difference,
they have suffered from their failed or impoverished relationships to the
envelope, self-love, sameness, the interval, the intermediary, space and
time, and so on. Think then of the breadth of scope finally attributed to
our neurosis and the neurosis of philosophy going back to ancient Greece.
It is seen in this philosophy's treatment of identity, self-identity, different
conceptualizations of the interval, the intermediary, and envelopment, in
relation to which we have all, always, been suffering. What have we been
sick from? The impoverishment of identity and difference, relationality,
space and time, the formation of the cosmos and our place in it.

What then is sexual difference, and is there sexual difference? We have
seen that it is not a thing, an entity, or a notion. This becomes graphically
clear at the point at which the field of sexual difference becomes the field

of a thinking of the envelope, matter, the intermediary, and the universe. There is no unitary or self-identical sexual difference for this reason also.

Dorothea Olkowski is one of Irigaray's commentators most alert to the exponential expansion of the meaning of sexual difference in Irigaray's work. Irigaray argues that the development of alternative possibilities for women is inhibited. Possible alternatives are prejudged nonsensical. Olkowski notes the implications for embodiment, which may be lived as inhibited. This point can be extended beyond discussions of gender oppression. The same phenomenon occurs in the embodiment of poverty and race. One does not only live a devalued embodiment. One lives an inhibited embodiment marked by one's sense that a more diverse range of possibilities is prohibited in advance. In class, race, gender, and age oppression, one does not know the ways in which one might be otherwise, but one knows that one anticipates them and one knows they have been rejected in advance by the social forces inhabiting one.

> Irigaray must recognize, even though she does not usually posit this as an aspect of sexual difference, that other relations than those between man and woman are at stake here, too, and that the interval is a crucial element in transforming situated spatiality in a manner that *exceeds* the body and even a morphology of the body. (Olkowski 1999, 81–82)

Olkowski reminds us that the exclusion of sexual difference is not just the exclusion of an idea. This is a lived corporeal, not just a conceptual, exclusion. The one is the other. Olkowski underscores the corporeal implications of a body physically lived as the exclusion of its broader possible permutations. She points out that this is part of what a marginalized embodiment is. This offers a response to Iris Young's now classic discussion of "throwing like a girl" (1990). On Young's reading, the marginalization of women manifests itself in women's lived embodiment as a body that "cannot" (throw with agility, for example). Living marginalization as an awkward, conspicuous body goes deeper still, points out Olkowski, as she articulates an Irigarayan response to Young. One is aware of not just a devalued body but a body prevented from developing in ways we cannot anticipate, so easily is it seen as nonsensical, abnormal, or wrong.

Once we try to imagine those alternative possibilities, we cannot assume that we are speaking of another variation of sexual difference or classed or raced embodiment. Imagined more expansively, those alternative possibilities might amount to a transformation in what we understand as "a body" or "power," "interval," "differentiation," or "difference." Olkowski (1999) traces the reach of Irigaray's work, whereby

"Irigaray calls for a transformation of the relation of matter to form and the *interval* between them, in which interval operates the concepts of power, act, force, energy, and desire" (81).

Irigaray reaches a watershed moment in her project when sexual difference is given this expanded scope of alternative possibility for embodiment and existence. Some readers may feel that the project is no longer identifiably feminist. Shouldn't a philosophy of sexual difference be primarily concerned with representations of women and men? It seems what we assume to be gender and sex have been lost from the focus of the project. Instead, sexual difference becomes highly abstract, folded inside out so that the parameters of possible alternate universes are enveloped at its heart. Some may be relieved to find that Irigaray did not continue this direction. The remaining chapters of this study of her later work will not consider such an abstract definition of sexual difference. From this point on, she would rein in its definitional scope. As we will see in the next two chapters, the philosophy of sexual difference would become increasingly concerned with everyday relations between men and women. Should we be relieved to see her return from the edges of space and time? Is this a prudent focusing of the terrain? For my part, I am not convinced by this return.

As Irigaray writes in *An Ethics of Sexual Difference* (1993a), "[S]exual difference has not had its chance to develop, either empirically or transcendentally" (15). We have seen that she can not call for a simple politics of recognition of difference, since sexual difference does not have the status of a preexisting, simple given subsisting in its integrity throughout culture and history irrespective of its failure to be recognized and represented. Though in her later work, published after *Ethics*, Irigaray does propose reforms mandating the recognition of sexual difference by the domains of law, language, religion, and the civil code, we have seen that the status of her reforms is paradoxical. She argues both that sexual difference is excluded from culture and that sexuate rights should recognize sexual difference.

And certainly Irigaray wants to say "Come! Come!"[11] to sexual difference. Yet, by definition, she can not know or name what she anticipates. Does she even know it is sexual difference? This is the paradox of an Irigarayan philosophy of sexual difference: the emptiness of its own brackets. A politics of the *à-venir* needs to affirm its impossibility in this sense. We do not know the definitional limits of sexual difference. This is the advantage of an open definition prepared to enfold the possible edges of an alternative thinking of the cosmos into its heart.

In chapter 6, I discussed John Caputo's interpretation of the messianic structure of sexual difference. Perhaps sexual difference takes on the status of the woman (or the man) "found disguised, dressed in rags, among the wretched of the earth," to whom the other, approaching, could only say "When will you come?" By definition, the two subjects could not know (within the limits of reason) with what, and with whom, they engage. Irigaray defines their relationship in terms of mystery. This suggests one would never be confronted with the presence of sexual difference. Sexual difference could only be that which is to come. Difference does not lie between two identities, the male and the female. That should not be sexual difference. In a necessary thought experiment, I start with the relations between men and women with which I am currently familiar. I place some brackets around them and imagine something else to come in their place. But there is no guarantee that this replacement would fit perfectly over the vacant space represented by men and women. If it is too much like—identifiably like—what I think of as men and women, then something is wrong in this thought experiment.

Instead, in a messianistic sexual difference subjects are confronted with infinite, unfixed continuums that can be affirmed only through that paradox, as to come. Transcendence would not lie between two self-present identities, male and female. Irigaray situates it between two infinitely deferred series of displacing relations. Since these relations are infinitely displacing, the trajectory of their movement cannot be narrowly circumscribed. And it is also plausible that these two series could not be clearly distinguished from each other. We must imagine each intimately implicated in the articulation of the other. In her later work, Irigaray would depict a man and a woman, understood as foreign to each other, knowing each other as two foreign entities, secure in their recognition of the other as different, the difference lying between them. Difference also lies at the heart of each. This is the very point of Irigaray's concept of belonging to a sexuate genre. This being the case, why are we sometimes presented with images of a peaceful, comfortable encounter between a man and a woman, each saying of the other, with confidence: here is difference? Where the encounter is formulated in such terms, some may be reassured that they are in the presence of an identifiable "philosophy of sexual difference." But many critics have noted the risk that difference becomes instead identity and loses its status as the *à-venir*. Perhaps the answer to the question "What is sexual difference?" must be left open.

In making this proposal, I have returned to Drucilla Cornell's suggestion that something goes wrong when Irigaray defines sexual difference. Insofar as she does, her work acts so as to declare a limitation of its possibilities, Cornell argues. In answer, I suggested that not all forms of definition work this way. For example, a declaration of sexuate rights declares its own impossibility, even as it seems to declare its own viability. The very broad definition of sexual difference discussed in this chapter acts so as to declare the impossibility of a definition of sexual difference. I think such gestures are appropriate to a philosophy of sexual difference. But in the following chapter, I will discuss a tendency that goes in the opposite direction: the focusing of sexual difference in the encounter between a man and a woman imagined as saying to each other: "Here is difference."

8

The Impossible Friend

Traversing the Heterosocial, the Homosocial, and the Successes of Failure

> Locating difference *outside* identity, in the spaces *between*
> identities . . . ignore[s] the radicality of the poststructuralist view
> which locates differences *within* identity.
> Diana Fuss, *Essentially Speaking*

In chapter 7, I considered an increasingly abstract interpretation of the open brackets represented by Irigarayan sexual difference. In this chapter, I am going to return to a more practical context in which she discusses sexual difference: relations between lovers and friends. I will ask how Irigaray tries to sustain the abstract openness of sexual difference at the heart of some of our most intimate relations. Toward the end of *I Love to You* (1996a), Irigaray evokes an ideal other, lover or friend, as one who resists my knowledge and appropriation of him or her. Now a pair of empty brackets is fitted around the friend or lover to anticipate alternative, impossible possibilities for love and friendship. Imagining friendship otherwise, she suggests that listening

> to you, as to another who transcends me, calls for a transition to a new di-
> mension. I am listening to you: I perceive what you are saying, I am atten-
> tive to it, I am attempting to understand and hear your intention. Which
> does not mean: I comprehend you, I know you, so I do not need to listen to
> you and I can even prescribe your becoming. No, I am listening to you as
> someone and something I do not know yet . . . *with* you but not *as* you.
> (116–17, translation modified)

The last comment reflects an important aspect of Irigaray's depictions of difference. The other whom I value is someone who transcends my knowledge of and my relation to him or her.

How does this point compare with Irigaray's early thinking of sexual difference? According to her early argument, male-centered appropriation of sexual difference necessarily fails. It never completely succeeds: the range of potential possibilities for the existence of femininity is not exhausted by its role as man's other. This is intended as a politically enabling interpretation. The feminine may be appropriated as the masculine mirror, but it is not reducible to that role. It remains open to alternative possibilities for its own reimagining. From the perspective of imagining sexual difference, the failures and fissures of an appropriative account are a success for a possible sexual difference.

Now consider Irigaray's musing on love, friendship, and day-to-day relations with the other, cited above, which includes the formula, "I am listening to you as someone and something I do not know yet." We can compare the idea of a possible sexual difference exceeding historical depictions of femininity with the idea of my friend or lover's exceeding the ways in which I understand him or her. Again, my failures of understanding are a kind of success. They represent the fissures opened up by the excess of my friend to my depiction of him or her. The successful excess of my friend to my depictions is also signified when we think of my depictions as a kind of "failure." One dissimilarity between the appropriation of sexual difference and appropriative love or friendship is that our intentions in the latter cases are usually better. This observation could be seen as an affirmation by Irigaray of the necessary failure of my attempts at successful listening, or an affirmation of the success of my failure. Assume that I have good intentions. Assume that I want to listen to you, as to another who transcends me. Assume that I am attentive to what you are saying, that I am attempting to understand you. With all these good intentions, I can't fully comprehend you. I must listen to you as someone and something I do not fully know. To say that this failure of full understanding is a kind of success is to mark the excess of my friend's possibilities to me. In the success of failure, I listen to you as someone and something I do not know. Irigaray's formula "someone I do not know yet" suggests that the other, like sexual difference, is always to come, never fully present. According to the structure of identity associated by Irigaray with the field of sexuate genre, the other would never be fully present before me. The other's identity would always be infinitely deferred in the relations of genre, and so would mine. Always to come means anticipated but never transparently here. In the transition from an abstract thinking of sexual difference to a thinking of love, friendship, and interpersonal relations, an emphasis on excess, remainder, and anticipation remains important. The possibilities of the other always exceed my own field of knowledge and consumption, just as the possibilities of sexual difference always exceed any male-centered depiction of them in the history of philosophy.

In this chapter, I am going to discuss an alternative inflection that is given by Irigaray to friendship and to sexual difference. This alternative inflection could be discussed in relation to a number of passages. I introduce it by its manifestation in one of Irigaray's discussions of friendship. It may appear to be a small moment in her corpus, but I will argue that it indicates another status for sexual difference in her work.

In one passage in *I Love to You* (1996a) ideal friendship is figured in the person of the Italian politician Renzo Imbeni. Imbeni is someone whom Irigaray claims to be able to recognize. He is described as a man who can save a city, a man who is unsubmissive, respectful, innovative, who shares without complacency, is prudent and daring: "He only makes promises he can keep. It is possible to have faith in him. One can take from him without renouncing one's self" (15). Irigaray realizes that her reader may believe that she has been projecting onto Imbeni: "You are probably thinking that I must be blinded by some sort of passion for him, some projection onto him?" (16). This is a perturbing question. Obviously the reader does assume that Irigaray is projecting onto Imbeni. And to project onto the other, one must implicitly position the other as she or he who can provide the succor and screen for my projections. I reduce the other to the domain of my self-same, but the other exceeds this reduction. When I project onto the other, this excess is lost, effaced, denied, or submerged. Perhaps it is also implicitly recognized by the very action of projection, just as it is simultaneously disavowed, in this sense, by the same action. This is the "success" of failure. Can we appropriate, without an implicit recognition that the other we appropriate as screen or projection is more than that? Is appropriative projection not a simultaneous recognition and disavowal of appropriation of alternative possibilities for the other?

Trivial as the question may appear, why might Irigaray assure her readers that she is not projecting onto her friend? Does she hope for the possibility of a friendship that does not involve some degree of being blinded, some degree of projection? This would return us to questions asked in chapter 5. What sorts of ethics for friends are possible from the point of our acknowledgment of the impossibility of formal boundaries between us? Can we hope for the absence of projection in friendship, and should we? This is a question opened up by Irigaray's own work. Perhaps the politics of friendship must be prepared to negotiate the inevitable play of projection in friendship. Perhaps we should not disavow that play.[1] At the same time, we can try to read in our very projection the recognition of an excess to projection. For this reason, one queries Irigaray's denial that projection onto Imbeni is involved in her friendship with him, if the denial implies that an ideal friendship contains no projection. When the brackets around my friendship anticipate a more ideal friendship, must that ideal be one of nonappropriation? We might ask how we shall be friends in the context of the inevitable failures of our friendship. Rather than ask this question, Irigaray affirms that ideally her friendship need not fail. Of course, Irigaray might be reminding us of the impossibility of a nonappropriative friendship. More generally, marking the impossibility of sexual difference, Irigaray demarcates the vast extent of structural change that would be required for something she argues we would want, sexual difference. Is the right ideal, even as an impossible ideal, nonprojection or transparency of the friends to each other, as when we are told that Imbeni is the perfect listener?

In one refrain about friendship, Irigaray proposes an account of the ways in which we can never be sure of the identity of the friend. The other always resists and exceeds my certainty about him or her. I might specifically value in the friend what he or she could least comprehend about me and I about him or her, a refusal or inability to be my perfect listener. When Irigaray comes to laud a friendship, we might expect her to laud a friendship in which the other is depicted as she or he who is not my perfect listener. Instead, Irigaray idealizes Imbeni as the patient, perfect listener. By her own definition, Irigaray's depiction of Imbeni is appropriative.

When the brackets anticipating an ideal friendship are fit around Imbeni, Irigaray seems to propose the possibility of a friendship in which we would not project onto each other, and I asked whether we could interpret this gesture as marking the impossibility of what it appears to declare. Does Irigaray declare the possibility so as to declare its own impossibility? Does she remind us of how much cultural change—unimaginable cultural change—would be necessary for a nonappropriative, nonprojective friendship to be possible? Imagine that this is the correct interpretation. The problem is that even within an ideal deemed impossible, the friend is depicted as my perfect listener. Even in an anticipated friendship to come, the depiction of my friend as someone I would know with confidence—someone whose role would be my perfect listener—seems wrong.

I am going to suggest that the depiction of the friendship with Imbeni be considered as symptomatic in Irigaray's more recent work of a transition from an other depicted as unknowable to an other valued as known and—particularly troubling—as receptive. Its analogue, which we are about to see, is a transition from a sexual difference that is impossible to a depiction of a possible and static sexual difference. The possibility of sexual difference affects her depiction of sexual difference in friendship.

When Irigaray comes to tell us of the possibility of friendship, critical to her account is the friends' sexual difference, now similarly designated as possible.[2]

Consider the way in which her homage to Imbeni occurs in the context of an evocation of an ideal for

the encounter between woman and man, women and men. An encounter characterized by belonging to a sexed nature to which it is proper to be faithful; by the need for rights to incarnate this nature with respect; by the need for the recognition of another who will never be mine; by the importance of an absolute silence in order to hear this other; by the quest for new words which will make this alliance possible without reducing the other to an item of property. (1996a, 11)

It is the sexual difference between Irigaray and Imbeni that is, in her work, emblematically crucial to the possibility of ideal friendship between them, where ideal friendship is characterized by "the recognition of another who will never be mine; by the importance of an absolute silence in order to hear this other."[3] Irigaray imagines an impossible possibility in which the significance of the encounter between herself and another as sexually different could be as she depicts. She asks us to reflect on what in our culture prohibits this encounter. She marks the excluded possibilities hovering at the limits of her relationship with Imbeni. Their very impossibility is the trace of their possibility.

Having offered this interpretation, let me try to locate where I believe a problem lies even within this politics of impossibility. Although Irigaray wants to write in alternative possibilities for sexual difference within the space of a relationship between a man and a woman, sexual difference is also overly reduced by the supposition that it represents alternative possibilities for the relationship between a man and a woman. This reduction must provoke reflection on the status of heterosociality and homosociality in Irigaray's philosophy of friendship, identity, and difference. There is a significant difference between wishing to write alternative possibilities into the brackets represented by heterosexuality and taking heterosexuality as the privileged emblem of what would be written into the open brackets represented by sexual difference. Why is heterosociality so particularly figured as critical to encountering the other? This privileging has been resisted by many wary commentators.

In chapter 5, I made the point that the priority Irigaray allocates to reformulating the male-female relation could be interpreted as an intervention into the history of women's traditional representation as lack and atrophy in this relation, rather than a privileging of the hetero over the

homosocial. In chapter 9, I argue that her attempt to resituate the philosophical subject as primarily dual (as the pair "man and woman") does
work effectively as a means of displacing the philosophical tradition of
which, we will see, Irigaray considers Jean-Paul Sartre as a particularly
good representative. Irigaray's focus on alternative possibilities for
friendship between the man-woman couple can also be interpreted as a
displacement of conventional philosophical depictions of ideal friendship
as occurring between two men.[4] These arguments notwithstanding, I will
in this chapter discuss the widespread concerns about the privileging of
the man-woman couple.

Difference and sameness have often been attributed to the specificity of
heterosocial and homosocial bonds, respectively. Consider that famous
depiction of ideal friendship between two men. After the death of his
beloved friend Etienne de la Boétie, sixteenth-century essayist Michel de
Montaigne described their friendship in terms of "resemblance and har-
mony," which, he claimed, "gives rise to true and perfect friendships"
(Montaigne 1958, 93). He deemphasized the fact that he and La Boétie had
been two different selves, using the language of "one soul in two bodies"
or the "complete fusion of the wills" (99). He suggested that no difference
or boundaries existed between the two friends: "[The friendship] left us
with nothing that was our own, nothing that was either his or mine" (98).
When I promise to reveal to "no other" a secret, he wrote, "I may without
perjury communicate [it] to him who is not another—but is myself" (101).
They were as one: "In the friendship I speak of [the friends] mix and blend
one into the other in so perfect a union that the seam which has joined
them is effaced and disappears" (97). Imagine that my friend helps me.
Then it is as incoherent to talk about loving the friend more because of
help he gives me as to talk about loving myself more for help I give myself. There is no difference between the friends, the other *is* myself (101).

From Montaigne's perspective, one of the crucial points about this ideal
friendship is its homosociality. His essay "On Friendship" depicts perfect
friendship as more possible between two likes—such as two adult men—
than between adults and children, or between men and women. Here,
Montaigne supposes that we know the like and that the like occurs in
male friendship. Montaigne has "not survived whole," mourning a half of
himself. So we surmise that La Boétie had already been reduced to Montaigne's (same as) self. Notice how, from Irigaray's perspective, the friendship might be deemed unethical in the context of her ideal for love and
friendship. She condemns as appropriative the transformation of my
loved other into "my property, my object," "what is mine, into mine,
meaning what is already a part of my field of existential or material properties" (Irigaray 1996a, 110).

But for both Montaigne and Irigaray, the subject's sex is the key indicator of sameness or difference in the relation with the other. For Montaigne, the sexual sameness of the two friends makes their perfect friendship more possible. Irigaray replaces this sexual sameness with sexual difference in her idealizing discussion of her friendship with Renzo Imbeni. As sex (sex sameness or sex difference) is apparently critical to an ideal rapport, both writers share an implicit conviction that they are capable of pinpointing sameness and difference. Montaigne has no doubt of the sameness or identity of his friend to himself. In her account of an alternative friendship, Irigaray would not be in doubt that her relation with Imbeni represents the presence of sexual difference. Irigaray is as little in doubt that she would be in the presence of difference as Montaigne doubts he has been in the presence of sameness. Both writers also suppose their friend to be the ideal listener. Both friends are reduced to their knowability. Irigaray criticizes the conviction "I know you, so I do not need to listen to you" (1996a, 116). But she identifies the friend so assuredly as the site of difference and perfect listening.

Neither Irigaray in her archetypal ideal friendship between a man and a woman, nor Montaigne in his archetypal ideal friendship between two men, doubts his or her friend. One early thematic that is slightly deemphasized in Irigaray's later work is the inevitable resistance of the (feminine) other to its cultural appropriation. For example, if we look back at the thematic of mourning introduced in *Speculum of the Other Woman* (1985b), Irigaray uses the term to destabilize a sense of what exactly has been lost by the emblematic girl/woman deemed by Sigmund Freud to be melancholic. In this case, Irigaray moves from Freud's discussion of mourning to melancholia because Freud uses the latter term to indicate a context of loss in which "'one cannot see clearly what it is that has been lost. . . .' The little girl, obviously, does not know *what* she is losing in discovering her 'castration.' . . . In more ways than one, it is really a question for her of a 'loss' that radically escapes any representation. Whence the impossibility of 'mourning' it" (67–68). Alternative possibilities for the development of the feminine have been lost. Because they have been excluded, we cannot fix their identity. But because something (alternative lost possibilities) may be mourned, femininity's potential scope exceeds cultural understandings of women as lack. The mourned feminine is by definition unnamable. We cannot know precisely what we mourn, what we have lost.

In *I Love to You* (1996a), Irigaray comments, "I defend the impossible. . . . But am I actually allowed to do otherwise? Is not what is offered me already within a horizon that annihilates my identity and my will?" (9). But she would go on to give a more fixed definition to annihilated femininity:

> [T]he relation between the genders [*genres*] is determined by man's needs
> with no consideration for woman's identity. . . . [O]ur tradition lacks the
> mediations enabling her to keep her identity as a woman. . . . It is from a de-
> sire for exchange that women's melancholy ensues rather than from nos-
> talgia for return. (135–36, translation modified)

In this passage, women's identity begins to seem closer to a static property. Now Irigaray associates their melancholia with a thwarted desire for
exchange rather than with the foreclosure of an unnamable, alternative
identity.

The other relevant point here is Irigaray's shift to making recommenda-
tions for institutional reform. Rather than emphasizing the necessary
failure of any appropriation or "cannibalism" of the other, Irigaray shifts
her political impetus to creating the social conditions necessary to interrupt cultural cannibalism. Irigaray's later work (as seen in her discussions
both of sexual difference and of love and friendship) underemphasizes
the inevitable resistance and excess of the other to appropriation. By contrast, this emphasis is a crucially enabling aspect of her early work. In the
shift to devising political programs, we expect Irigaray's continued emphasis on what we might call the necessary failure of successful appropriation (the other—as unnamable excess—is always the remainder to its
own cannibalism) and also, in another sense, on the necessary failure of
success. Any appropriation inevitably fails. At the same time, my successful nonappropriation of the other will also involve some extent of appropriation of the other. No political program can avoid this, and any political program must take it into consideration.

According to Irigaray's early notion of melancholic mourning, we may
theorize a mourning that does not entail a fixed identification of what one
mourns. What one mourns exceeds any particular understanding or identification we may have of it. To return to the theorization of friendship, not
only is mourning very far from entailing a fixed identification of what one
mourns, but, Derrida suggests, such an identification is impossible.[5] In Irigaray's depiction of cultural cannibalism, the other becomes "me" or
"mine," rather than remaining she or he to whom I make the address, she
or he who addresses me. Without disagreeing with this kind of point, Derrida (1989) articulates the failure and impossibility of such cannibalism. In
mourning, for example, the other lives only in us, as "image, idol, or
ideal" (6). The friend has been reduced to our interiorization of him or her.
In this sense, we must cannibalize the other. But we can not cannibalize
the other. Derrida emphasizes what he cannot know and say of his
mourned friend Paul de Man, the friendship "I wouldn't know how to cir-
cumscribe, to limit, to name (and that is as it should be)" (xvi). The other
resists my knowledge and memory of him or her:

[W]e know our friend to be gone forever, irremediably absent, annulled to the point of knowing or receiving nothing himself of what takes place in his memory. . . . [I]t would be unfaithful to delude oneself into believing that the other living *in us* is living *in himself:* because he lives *in us* and because we live this or that in his memory, in memory of him. (Derrida 1989, 21)

Invoking the concept of impossible mourning in *Memoires for Paul de Man* (1989), Derrida makes reference to how the "'normal' 'work of mourning' has often been described" since Freud: in terms of "memory and interiorization":

It entails a movement in which an interiorizing idealization takes in itself or upon itself the body and voice of the other, the other's visage and person, ideally *and* quasi-literally devouring them. (34)

Freud's work on mourning, and that of certain other psychoanalysts, produce a formulation of subjects as always already the interiorization of the other. Derrida's intervention introduces an ethical interrogation of how alterity may be theorized at the heart of this "eating of the other."

Derrida draws on post-Freudians Maria Torok and Nicolas Abraham in his evocation of the question of how to be responsible to the friend one loses.[6] If the otherness of the other is annulled in the assimilating work of "normal" mourning, it seems that "failed" mourning could be described as more faithful to the lost friend than "successful" mourning. Perhaps such failure recognizes that the other cannot be assimilated. But it is the very distinction between successful and failed mourning that Derrida will question. Can there be a successful mourning? In this context, the pertinent question is how to be faithful to the other:

What is an impossible mourning? . . . And as concerns the other in us . . . where is the most unjust betrayal? Is the most distressing, or even the most deadly infidelity that of a *possible mourning* which would interiorize within us the image, idol, or ideal of the other who is dead and lives only in us? Or is it that of the impossible mourning, which, leaving the other [the other's] alterity, respecting thus [the other's] infinite remove, either refuses to take or is incapable of taking the other within oneself, as in the tomb or the vault of some narcissism? (Derrida 1989, 6)

Of course, fidelity to the other implies that one mourns the loss of the other. Failing to mourn suggests indifference to the other. But perhaps the failed mourning of incorporation is a greater fidelity to the other? A successful mourning successfully assimilates or digests the other's presence, so that I "get over" and no longer miss him or her. But in failed mourning,

I cannot assimilate the other. Derrida converts the issue of mourning into one concerning the ethics of alterity. What is the other to me in my various modes of fidelity and mourning? In successful mourning, the other is to me digestible and assimilable. But in failed mourning, the other is to me indigestible, unassailable. Rethought from the perspective of the ethics of alterity, the successful mourning therefore fails: "[M]ourning is an unfaithful fidelity if it succeeds in interiorizing the other ideally in me, that is, in not respecting his or her infinite exteriority" (Derrida 1995a, 321). Mourning could be said to have failed if ever it renders the other assimilable.

From this perspective, there is some communication between the cannibal metaphors deployed by Derrida and Irigaray. In the case of Irigaray's ethics, nondigestion is the emblem of a greater fidelity to the other, a better recognition of the other's difference. *I Love to You* proposes alternatives to cannibal relations. Not assuming there could be such alternatives, Derrida does not move in this direction. But for both, digestion and assimilation could be said to represent infidelity toward the other. Both emphasize and place value on this nonassimilability of the other to my digestion.

What would a successful mourning be? Derrida offers a paradoxical formulation in which the success of mourning is said to be its failure, and the failure of mourning its success:

> We can only live this experience in the form of an aporia: the aporia of mourning and of prosopopoeia, where the possible remains impossible. Where *success fails*. And where faithful interiorization bears the other and constitutes [him/her] in me. . . . It makes the other a *part* of us . . . and then the other no longer quite seems to be the other, because we grieve for [him/her] and bear [him/her] *in us*. . . . And inversely, the *failure succeeds:* an aborted interiorization is at the same time a respect for the other as other, a sort of tender rejection, a movement of renunciation which leaves the other alone, outside, over there in [his/her] death, outside of us. (Derrida 1989, 35)

These themes come together in Derrida's joint declarations (1995a): "Faithful mourning of the other must fail *to succeed/by succeeding* (it fails, precisely, if it succeeds! it fails because of success!)" (321). Irigaray does not disagree that effacement of the other fails in this sense. Discussing sexual difference, she argues that its appropriation fails, and that this failure is a success for sexual difference. I will turn in a moment to the way in which she might be said to theorize the success of failure and the failure of success.

Derrida's material branches out from a discussion of literal mourning to a discussion of our status as cannibal subjects more generally. Cannibalizing the other is both inevitable and impossible. From this point on, the simultaneous failure of success and success of failure can be theorized in various ways. For example, a successful appropriation would be a failure from the perspective of an ethics of alterity. Failure would be a success from the perspective of a counterappropriative ethics. Because Irigaray's early and late philosophy is counterappropriative, successful appropriations are failures, and failed appropriations successes. Indeed there can be no successful appropriation. The other is always in excess of my appropriation of alterity. The other constitutes the subject and stage for my projections, fantasies, identifications, assumptions, preconceptions, and so on. The friend, or the woman, does not exist absolutely distinct from this relationship and is to some extent the product of it. But he or she is not entirely reducible to my projections, fantasies, identifications, assumptions, and preconceptions either.

In the early work, Irigaray assumes the excess of sexual difference to its historical and traditional depictions. In this sense, she bases her entire philosophy on the necessary failure of the cannibalization of femininity. More recently, she has devised political programs to enable mediated relations between subjects in order to interrupt cultural cannibalism (the tendency to appropriate and interiorize the other). The emphasis is placed on the need for social and political change to interrupt cannibalism. Because the cultural and political problems we face reflect the success of cultural cannibalism, Irigaray argues the need for a series of (linguistic, legal, religious, media, and economic) social reforms that would enable mediated self-other relations and facilitate less appropriative relations between individuals in contemporary life. Her argument for these programs is premised on her diagnosis of the (troubling) success of cultural cannibalism. Also, some of her presentations of her institutional forms associate them with the possibility of an absence of cannibalism. In this sense, they seem idealized as successful. Does this idealization require the response (a response that can be derived from her own earlier work) that appropriation of the other always fails—and so does any ideal of nonappropriation of the other? To return to the example I discussed, this failure is deemphasized in the depiction of an emblematic friendship in which Imbeni is transparent to Irigaray and in her reassurance that there would not be projection between them. The other is always in excess of my reductions, identifications, projections, and so on. Why have these points become deemphasized in her more recent work?

This issue allows some comparison of interventions into psychoanalytic theory by Irigaray and Derrida. The key issue in Irigaray's early interrogation of Freud is the failure to theorize sexual difference. Her criticisms of Freud in *Speculum of the Other Woman* are directed at his impoverished and phallocentric account of women and femininity. In occupying the thematic of mourning in his work, she argues that women and girls can be interpreted as mourning the impossibility of their own sexual difference (Irigaray 1985b, 66–72). Derrida occupies psychoanalytic accounts of mourning in order to destabilize our understanding of the integrity of the subject who mourns the other and the identity of the mourned other. According to Derrida, the subject may be thought in terms of a generalized structure of literal mourning. We are always already an interiorization of the other, which always exceeds that interiorization:

> Upon the death of the other we are given to memory, and thus to interiorization, since the other, outside us, is now nothing. And with the dark light of this nothing, we learn that the other resists the closure of our interiorizing memory. With the nothing of this irrevocable absence, the other appears *as* other, and as other for us, upon his death or at least in the anticipated possibility of a death, since death constitutes and makes manifest the limits of a *me* or an *us* who are obliged to harbor something that is greater or other than them; *something outside of them within them*. (Derrida 1989, 34)

We are never proper to ourselves, self-identical: "[W]e are never *ourselves*, and between us, identical to us, a 'self' is never in itself or identical to itself" (Derrida 1989, 28). True, we are always cannibal selves. In day-to-day life, we identify with the other, love and befriend the other, internalize the other as ideal ego, are influenced by others. And the other has been internalized within my boundaries in the very formation of the subject. Freud (1914) theorizes primary narcissism as a stage prior to the distinction between object-libido and ego-libido. He describes "an original libidinal cathexis of the ego . . . which fundamentally persists and is related to the object-cathexes much as the body of an amoeba is related to the pseudopodia which it puts out" (75). The oral or cannibal phase—the ego's incorporation of objects into its boundaries—is the prototype of identification (Freud 1917, 241, 249). Ego and object-libido cannot be distinguished, and what is designated the "me" or "mine" is always already the object or other.

We have seen Irigaray's condemnation of narcissistic relations. At several points in his work, Derrida questions whether we think of narcissism in sufficiently complex ways.[7] In Freud's account, the adult interconnection between identification and object love is related to primary narcissism. There can be confusion between whether I love the other as other to me, or love the other as incorporated with me, in the mode of identification. Freud distinguishes narcissistic and object-directed forms of love in adult life. Loving the other narcissistically is loving the other in terms of an economy of sameness. As Freud argues in "On Narcissism" (1914), I engage with the other insofar as she or he represents to me my idea of what I was, would like to be, or am. However, *all* forms of love and identification are also expressions of an ego constituted in the mode of primary narcissism. All forms of love involve the attachment of ego-libido to the object. Narcissism as presented by Freud is loving the other as what I identify with, want to be, and so on, in terms of an economy of sameness or ego-oriented relationality. Narcissistic love, like mourning, reflects the structure of primary narcissism in which there is no rigid self-other distinction. But from the perspective of an ethics of alterity, each of these modes—adult and primary narcissism, "failed" and "successful" mourning—can be seen as an enfolding of the other within the heart of the "self-same" that nevertheless entirely fails to annihilate otherness, is constructed around otherness, and, in failing to annihilate otherness, is paradoxically "faithful" to the other.[8]

What then of Irigaray's specific denunciation of narcissistic self-other love relations as subordinating the other to my nostalgia for unity? She writes, "The nostalgia of the one has always supplanted desire between two. This nostalgia takes different paths. It can aspire to fusion: with nature, with a divine figure, with the energy of the other, with others. At times, it corresponds to narcissistic self-love. Often, it is the equivalent to the will to be or to possess the whole. To remain between two requires the renunciation of this sort of unity: fusional, regressive, autistic, narcissistic" (2001, 57, translation modified). Here, she considers narcissism to be unethical and a failure to recognize the two. But does Irigaray suppose too quickly that narcissism is a successful subordination of the other to the self? In addition, does she suppose too quickly that narcissism can be avoided? Perhaps what is needed is an emphasis that narcissism is at once unavoidable and yet always failing, at once exclusion and incorporation of the other, infinitely complicated?

Drawing on Freud's conceptualization of narcissism, Derrida (1989) is led to the formulation that "a 'self' is never in itself or identical to itself" (28). The normal self does not possess integrity, any more than does the mourning self. We are the constant interiorization/incorporation of the other. In *Memoires* (1989), Derrida discusses interiorization in the context of narcissism. Compare with Irigaray for whom narcissism's problem is its pretension to autonomy, its ruses, mimes, and strategies. Derrida—and the early Irigaray—underline the impossibility of narcissism's autonomy. Its very appropriation of the other supposes the other and so undermines its simultaneous effacement of the difference of the other.

In chapter 5, I argued that Irigaray's ethics of nonappropriation is a difficult ethics, precisely because it occurs within the context of a theorization of the subject as always having eaten the other. Similarly, speaking of metonymical eating, Derrida (1991) reminds us, "[O]ne must begin to identify with the other, who is to be assimilated, interiorized, understood ideally" (115). One must eat, he asserts. There must be eating: our relations with the other must, inevitably, involve assimilation, identification, interiorization. Yet, and this is a tenor that receives decreasing emphasis in Irigaray's later work, we also see Derrida (1991) remind us that we *can not* eat the other: "[O]ne must begin to identify with the other, who is to be assimilated, interiorized, understood ideally (something one can never do absolutely *without addressing oneself to the other* . . .)" (115). The other *cannot* be (entirely) effaced. There can be no complete autonomy over oneself or of the other, if we have always eaten the other. Instead, the possibility of an adequate political and ethical perspective could begin only once one acknowledges that "*we* are never *ourselves,* and between us, identical to us, a 'self' is never in itself or identical to itself" (Derrida 1989, 28). How then to locate responsibility toward the other, when we have always already appropriated the other? This is the question posed in the formulation "how to eat well," to which I shall turn in a moment.

Derrida's formulations call into question traditional ideals of autonomy. In *Monolinguism of the Other* (1998b), he again points out that none of us have a proper cultural identity, a proper country, a proper language, a self-present identity as cultural. Languages are never pure of foreign elements. Cultures always contain aspects of other cultures. And just as our language and culture are not self-enclosed but always enfold the foreign, in our existence as linguistic and enculturated beings we are not self-enclosed. We acquire our own language; it does not belong intrinsically to us. It is the enfolding of the other within us, one could say. Enculturation comes to us from without, a matter of the enforcement of norms and demands, the imposition on and colonization of the neonate, not an integral possession or birthright. Sexuate identity comes to us from without. It does not, except retrospectively, reflect what we assume to be our most interior and personal self. It is not "proper"—it enfolds within it the other, as a relationship to or differentiation from norms for sex, others of the same sex, others of the opposite sex.

Irigaray's emphasis on sexuate genre can be understood as a theorization of how a subject as sexed is never identical to itself. It is an argument—just one of many possible means of theorizing a subject in such terms—for how a subject is always an infinite series of connected relations with others of his or her sexuate genre. It is also the enfolding within of one's differentiation from the opposite genre. In Irigaray's reformulation of the structure of identity, one never has self-identity as sexed. However, once she affirms sexual difference as the privileged site of difference, I will argue that she returns to an identification of difference that we might wish to see left more in suspense.

Irigaray's concern is directed at the narcissistic breakdown of boundaries. But in response, we could also ask what integrity for the self's identity I could hope to establish? Consider Irigaray's critical depiction of a widespread contemporary practice in philosophy, religion, and politics: "There is talk of the other's existence, love of the other, concern for the other, etc., without it being asked whom or what this other represents. This lack of definition of the alterity of the other has left all thought . . . in a state of paralysis" (1996a, 61). Of course, the conception of "the other" in the politics of difference is sometimes not sufficiently complex.[9] But does Irigaray's own work succeed in this regard? One response is to simultaneously put into question the integrity of the self. Theorizing the self as always already the other risks incurring Irigaray's accusations of narcissism and cultural appropriation. But the status of self and other may also be too secure in her own theory. Perhaps an adequately complex account of what the other is requires an account of how we must already be the other.[10] Think of how Irigaray worries we may think she is projecting onto her friend Imbeni. She thus disavows the necessity of this projection. The boundaries between oneself and one's friend could never be secured.

What are the implications for the relationships between those belonging to different genres? The boundaries between the sexuate genres to which they belong could similarly never be cordoned from each other. The series of infinite relations I have with those of my sexuate genre, which sex me as female or male (and as permanently incomplete as such), could not be considered as radically distinct and separable from the infinite series of relations that sex the opposite sex. These series must intertwine in every way, in relations of identification and distinction, of distancing and proximity, and in the relations of identification, love, envy, and aggression one has with those of the same and the other sex.

In "On Friendship," as we saw, Montaigne proposes that perfect friendship is more possible between two likes—such as two adult men—than between adults and children or between men and women. Montaigne supposes that we know the like and that the like occurs in homosocial friendship. In *I Love to You*, perfect friendship is depicted by Irigaray as more possible between the different, depicted above all as the couple formed by a man and a woman. Irigaray supposes that we know the privileged site of the anticipation of the different: the heterosocial friendship. I want, finally, to return to the thinking of homo and hetero relations implied in this position. Irigaray has been widely criticized for the relentless emphasis in her more recent work on a heterosocial imaginary.[11] A problem occurs with her figuring of both the hetero and the homosocial imaginary.[12] For example, she opposes those forms of homosocial politics between women that are "based on oneself," feminist politics based on egotism:

> [B]y basing their politics on themselves, on their needs and desires (real or imagined as they may be), and not on those of all women, these practitioners of direct democracy or egological feminism . . . [show] no concern for the rights all women need—including the young girls of today and tomorrow, and women of other cultures. . . . What is more, as they lack a positive definition of their gender [*genre*] and the objective qualities which give it an individual and collective content, these female minorities are very often formed in opposition to the other gender [*genre*] and from refusal of a mixed-sex culture. (1996a, 2–3)

This comment suggests that Irigaray endorses a politics of difference, resisting any subordination of the other to myself in both heterosexual and homosexual contexts. But if so, she should affirm the play of difference in the homosocial context, rather than assuming it to be the privileged location of the self-same. Irigaray's discussion of friendship and love illuminates this point. The heterosexual, even in an ideal heterosexuality, is no more a privileged site of potential difference than the homosexual is a privileged site of the self-same. If she supposes otherwise, Irigaray discounts the inevitable alterity within homosocial and homosexual relationships. Thus she reinstates the belief that the other can be stably identified and known. But it is this supposition about the other's identity that her work also resists.

In Irigaray's more recent politics, subjects particularly engage with difference at the site of sexual difference.[13] The most telling deficiency is that the inevitable *failure* of this encounter with difference is not factored into her politics, the fact that I must always be projecting onto the other, subordinating the other to my domain of anticipation, communication, and knowledge. The objection here is not that the politics is "utopian," or even that it is heterocentric, but that it is misleading. The depiction of heterosexuality is aligned with a new and questionable supposition: the transparency of sexual difference. Irigaray's own premises, and her concept of sexuate genre, allow us to question the transparency she attributes to those demarcated as different. My use of the word transparency might be questioned, since Irigaray is clear that the emblematic man and woman are transcendent, not transparent to each other. But transparency is the appropriate description for the imagining of their comfortable recognition of each other as different, for the ideal depiction of these entities as two sexed identities between whom the difference lies. These sexed selves are different from each other and secured from each other in their identity as different. This is a criticism that has long lingered in the minds of those who ask whether a deconstructive reading of Irigaray might also be important, one based on, and sympathetic with, her own premises. If so, the critical point of interrogation would be the question of whether difference returns in a figuring as "between"—between two identities, the male and the female. I argued in chapter 5 that Irigaray's concept of genre allows a theory of sexed identity as "differing/deferring." Irigaray could still situate difference between men and women, so long as she also situated it between women and women, between men and men, and at the heart of every subject, in their differing, deferring identity. But when heterosociality and heterosexuality become the privileged site of difference, and homosociality and homosexuality the privileged site of sameness, then the concept of identity as differing and deferring has collapsed. The problem is not just that Irigaray situates difference between a man and a woman, but that she situates it as part of a recognition that potentially occurs between them. Each is to say to the other: here is difference. The problem is clear when we compare the implications for those of the same sex. Could they be certain of being in the presence of sameness? It is an individual's mediation by his or her genre that provides the field of difference between one subject and another, as well as at the heart of the subject. I disagree that the result must be privileged relationship of difference between a man and a woman. I imagine relations between men and men, and between women and women, as no less potentially divided (referring here to the division that makes possible their relationship) by the relationship of each to his or her genre than would be the case in relations between men and women.

It is possible to deemphasize the exaggeratedly heterosexual imagery in Irigaray's recent work. One can see Irigaray as arguing that there can be no heterosexuality except as traversed by the homosocial, since the situation of each sex in the context of one's own sexuate genre enables relations of sexual difference.[14] In other words, one can, through the emphasis on the concept of genre, locate difference within her figuring of the homosexual and homosocial. But although the apparatus for this reading arises from Irigaray's own work, it should also be acknowledged that Irigaray does not always take the location of difference at the heart of relations between women as a political imperative.

When Irigaray's politics speak in the name of a nonappropriation of the other, we must ask what the proper boundaries of the subject would be. It is a certain assumption on this point that allows her to condemn both narcissism and projection as unethical oversteppings of those boundaries in relation to the other. The encounter between Derrida and Irigaray's work on friendship allows us to ask anew what is proper to the subject. Irigaray's condemnation of narcissism and projection subtly attempts to identify my secured boundaries and those of the other. Her politics of nonappropriation of the other (even if it is a utopia) replaces a politics that could recognize and deal more adequately with the fact that I must always have appropriated the other. For Derrida ethics begins, rather than fails, at the point of this recognition. If one must always have "eaten" the other, then, concludes Derrida, ethics begins with the question of how to eat well. For Derrida (1991), this is precisely what is deemed *the moral question*: "The moral question is thus not, nor has it ever been: should one eat or not eat . . . but since *one must* eat in any case . . . *how* for goodness sake should one *eat well (bien manger)?* And what does this imply? What is eating?" (115).

I think a Derridean ethics of eating well could combine well with an Irigaray ethics of not-eating. Could Irigaray continue to speak in the name of a politics of nonappropriation, while also acknowledging that we have always appropriated the other, inevitably? It is that very appropriation that renders it impossible that we could ever be subjects with discrete identities who meet others, the difference lying securely "between us." It is that appropriation that renders incoherent recent Irigarayan evocations of heterosexual friendship as the privileged site of anticipated difference.

Ascribing mystery to the place of sexual difference, Irigaray (2002) has written:

> The human species [*espèce*] is made up of two genders [*genres*], irreducibly different, attracted to one another by the mystery that they represent for each other, an undisclosable mystery that is a source of natural and spiritual life. (83–84)

Again we see Irigaray's dilemma. She presents the genres as irreducibly different. She depicts their relation as a mystery to them both and as that which is transcendent. But it could be counterargued that it is not the genres that are irreducibly different from each other. Relationship to genre enhances difference between subjects (and difference at the heart of subjects). But the genres are not two radically distinct, different forces. It is the subjects, mediated by their relationship to genre, who are irreducibly different from each other. This difference would not be more pronounced in male-female relations than in male-male or female-female relations.

Irigaray offers an interventionist displacement of models of alterity that assume the fundamental neutrality or generic nature of the other in relation to the subject. A model of alterity that does not specify the sex difference of the other in question fails as a model of alterity. Yet insofar as Irigaray locates alterity particularly at the site of sexual difference,[15] she assumes our capacity to identify and anticipate the site of mystery. With the supposition that homosociality and homosexuality are less privileged sites of mystery, the gambit fails. Mystery is the site of that which we cannot predict, and there can be no prior assurance that the homosocial or the homosexual will be less the source of natural or spiritual life than is the heterosocial or heterosexual. Indeed, the definition and locale of life itself must remain as much the locus of unanticipated mystery in a politics of alterity.

9

Sexed Discourse and the Language
of the Philosophers

To Be Two

> We need . . . a historiography that emphasizes . . . contingent devel-
> opments, formations that may be at odds with or convergent with
> each other.
> Wendy Brown, "The Impossibility of Women's Studies"

In this chapter, I return to Irigaray's treatment of language. Having developed a linguistic methodology to argue that language is sexed, Irigaray uses that methodology to analyze historical philosophical texts. As
in the previous chapter, I shall raise possible problems arising more
strongly in the later work than in the earlier work. I have argued that Irigaray's references to heterosexuality and homosexuality consolidate a
static notion of sexuate identity, despite her concurrent undermining of
any concept of sexuate identity as fixed. In considering her late use of linguistics to discuss historical philosophical texts, I shall also argue against
her rigidification of the notion of sexual difference.

In previous chapters, I considered the transitions in Irigaray's work on
linguistics. Her initial interest was in linguistic analysis of subjects suffering from dementia and schizophrenia. Then followed a period of interest in the status of sexual difference in contemporary culture and in
writers such as Freud, Lacan, Marx, Lévi-Strauss, and historical philosophers, in which she drew on the arguments she had developed through
her readings of the philosophers that sexual difference is excluded from
culture. Returning to linguistics, she then argued that the patterns of
speech favored by men and women bear witness to the impossible status
of sexual difference in our culture.

In her linguistic work, Irigaray applied the concept of sexual difference generated in her readings of the history of philosophy to analyze the status of sexual difference in the everyday speech of men and women. By contrast, in her 1997 book *To Be Two* Irigaray reverses the direction of influence. She brings to the analysis of Sartre, Merleau-Ponty, and Lévinas the linguistic analysis she has developed in considering the absence of sexual difference in everyday speech.

In order to assess Irigaray's importation of her linguistic research into the study of the philosophers, I want first to consider some of the noticeable aspects of the earlier work. In Irigaray's publications in the area of linguistics she quantifies differences and predominances between men's and women's language use. She does so based on the interpretation of consistently simple phrases formulated by subjects in questionnaires. Subjects might be asked to construct phrases with the words *see, her,* and *dress,* for example, or with just one word, such as *dog* or *between.* The resulting data provide short sentence structures for analysis.

Conclusions drawn by Irigaray, on the basis of extensive research with different teams of researchers working in different languages, are summarized in a number of her publications. A brief example may be found in *I Love to You* (1996a) in which she claims: "Men and women do not use these prepositions in the same way: *à* (to), *entre* (between), *avec* (with)— nor these adverbs: *ensemble* (together), *peut-être* (perhaps)" (79). Commenting on the responses given for a particular test cue, she continues, "[T]he results obtained . . . reveal the fact that women seek communication with the other, the other-man in particular, and in this they are different from men. In various ways, responses to the following cues manifest the same tendency: a desire for communication on the part of women to which men do not respond since they are concerned with other things than intersubjective exchanges" (80, translation modified). Furthermore, "men's responses indicated that the *tu* is either a woman, an anonymous person or the Other" (82).

In one analysis, a given cue is to construct a sentence using the word *entre* (between/among). Irigaray analyzes the results as follows: "65.5% of women form an utterance that puts two or more persons in relation to one another." Here, three cited examples are "There is an atmosphere of intense curiosity between us," "The distance between him and her was very slight," and "we are among friends." Masculine responses tend to give a more negative connotation to the relationship, as in "There is such coolness between you and I" and "There are problems between us." Some male responses eliminate difference, she argues. Three examples are given: "There is no difference between someone from the Netherlands and someone from Holland," "Between is within," and "Enter without knocking; there are no formalities between us." According to Irigaray, "this is not true in women's responses, where difference always expresses a space between, a space that is generally positively valorized" (1996a, 85–86, translation modified).

Irigaray tends to valorize the ethical relationship to the other that is reflected in women's language use. Her view is that women's privileging of relationality and the I-you relationship occurs not as a product of a masculine-oriented culture but despite that culture. In this regard, it is worth noting that she is quite unlike those critics who have argued that some women's privileging of care, empathy, or relationality rather than objectivity is the product of patriarchal forces at work in early familial and child-rearing relations, most notably Catharine MacKinnon in her critique of Carol Gilligan (in DuBois et al. 1985).

In this chapter I will raise some questions about Irigaray's linguistic research as it is synthesized with her analysis of the history of philosophy. I note her tendency to deemphasize inconsistency and variety of response and aberrance in the sexedness of one's discourse in her presentation of the linguistic data. How should we understand this development in Irigaray's work? It occurs concurrently with a related change in Irigaray's approach to the analysis of philosophical texts. This change can be seen most clearly in *To Be Two*, which synthesizes her linguistic research with an interpretation of philosophers such as Sartre, Merleau-Ponty, and Lévinas.

Irigaray's linguistic research focuses on the consistency of an individual subject's discourse and of the overall research findings to reinforce her argument that there is a relationship between sexual difference and sexed language use. Previously, Irigaray kept her philosophical research distinct from her linguistic research. *To Be Two* speculates on the extent to which a discursive analysis of the texts of Merleau-Ponty, Sartre, and Lévinas might support the hypothesis of a masculine relationship to language. Some degree of what Irigaray names masculinity can be located in their texts. But this analysis occurs through a deemphasis of the discursive complexity of these texts, a complexity Irigaray has been at pains to demonstrate in the methodological orientation of her earlier work on the history of philosophy.

Speculum of the Other Woman (1985b) analyzes textual instability and self-contradictory argument in accounts of women, embodiment, nature, and matter in the history of philosophy. *An Ethics of Sexual Difference* (1993a) tries to recuperate elements in the history of philosophy—in the work of Spinoza, Plato, Aristotle, Merleau-Ponty, and Lévinas—that have the potential to resist the marginalization, devaluation, or dichotomization of matter, embodiment, femininity, alterity, and flesh. Both approaches—the deconstructive and the recuperative—presuppose, and read for, the presence of multiple and polyvalent textual elements in historical philosophical texts. By contrast, in her approach to her concurrently undertaken recent linguistic research, discussed in works such as *I Love to You* (1996a), Irigaray instead highlights consistency in an individual subject's discourse and in her overall research findings. She reinforces her claim that men and women manifest different structures of language use by avoiding discussion of exceptions to or ambiguities in the patterns of discourse she analyzes.

In *To Be Two*, Irigaray situates herself—as she already did in *I Love to You* (1996a)—as a philosopher of eros and of the ethics of alterity, who should be situated in the context of the phenomenological philosophy of Sartre, Merleau-Ponty, Heidegger and Lévinas; and as a feminist who offers alternatives to the tradition of French phenomenology. Unlike many Beauvoir scholars,[1] and although she has occasionally made reference to Simone de Beauvoir (Irigaray 1993b, 9–14), Irigaray does not include Beauvoir as a member of the above historical series.[2] In this work, Irigaray contends that masculine and feminine voices in philosophy are akin to the literal differences in masculine and feminine language use that can be quantified through linguistic analysis.[3] In the following passage, notice how she runs together the issue of sexed language use, on the one hand, and the question of whether there is evidence of masculine and feminine discourse in philosophical texts, on the other:

> Both my experience as a woman, and my analysis of the language of women and men [here a footnote refers us to *Sexes et genres à travers les langues* and to *I Love to You*], have taught me that the feminine subject almost always privileges the relationship between subjects, the relationship with the other gender [*genre*], the relationship between two [*la relation à deux*]. . . .
>
> In the place of the intersubjective relationship, desired by women . . . with men, one finds the subject-object relationship. . . . There is another difference: the relationship with the object, with the other, with the world, is realized through an instrument that can be the hand, sex, and even a tool. . . . Moreover, instead of a relationship between two, omnipresent in the feminine universe, man prefers a relationship between the one and the many, between the I-masculine subject and others: people, society, understood as *them* and not as *you*. . . .
>
> These differences between the being and speaking of woman and man can help us to interpret the way in which certain male philosophers—such as Jean-Paul Sartre, Maurice Merleau-Ponty, and Emmanuel Lévinas—have conceived carnal love, and can make apparent the feminine character

of my remarks concerning loving relations, particularly on the caress. (2001, 17, translation modified)

Irigaray takes for granted the methodological viability of moving between a linguistic analysis of language samples from tested speakers and a less technically linguistic analysis of the discourse favored in the French phenomenological tradition. This proves to be, according to the interpretation I am proposing, the crucial passage in *To Be Two.*

Irigaray's commentators have been faced with the difficulty of reconciling her linguistic research with her early work in texts such as *Speculum.* Several of her recent books have included chapters on historical philosophers and also included separate chapters discussing her linguistic research; *I Love to You* is the most recent example.[4] By contrast, *To Be Two* is the first work by Irigaray to attempt a synthesis of this material. She argues that men privilege the subject-object relation, rather than the *être deux,* by reference both to her linguistic data and to philosophers such as Sartre and Merleau-Ponty. Their writing, she says, manifests what she has defined as a masculine form of discourse.

In no other discussion of her linguistic data has Irigaray ever appealed so specifically to philosophical texts to support this notion of masculine and feminine sexed language use. Instead, as I have noted, the findings have been based on surveys in which participants are asked to construct simple phrases using individual word elements. It could be said that Irigaray always had a huge sample of linguistic constructions from the history of philosophy available for analysis. Rather than drawing on this resource, she tested participants through questionnaires. She does not discuss the methodological decision to turn to a parallel analysis of philosophical writing. The approach is novel because her linguistic analyses are not elsewhere integrated with her readings of historical philosophers.

I mentioned that one of the curiosities of *To Be Two* is the absence of Beauvoir from the series: Sartre, Merleau-Ponty, and Lévinas. The absence is not unrelated to a concept of sexed consistency in the work of the philosophers Irigaray does consider. It is not clear how Irigaray would have dealt with Beauvoir in these terms, had she included her. Debra Bergoffen has argued that Simone de Beauvoir's philosophy of eros contains some points of proximity with contemporary philosophy of difference. The argument relies on her proposal that Beauvoir's work contains muted voices, in addition to its dominant, conflicting arguments and themes (Bergoffen 1997, 3).[5] To recognize Beauvoir as a philosopher of eros, perhaps Irigaray, similarly, would first have been obliged to recognize, distinguish, and engage with what Bergoffen takes to be Beauvoir's multiple textual voices, the dominant and the minor. Bergoffen uses the concept of the muted voice in philosophical writing by a woman to bring to light suppressed and undeveloped moments that may be richer, more subversive, or more innovative than the text's dominant thematics. This is not a methodology deployed by Irigaray in relation to a woman philosopher. Only rarely has Irigaray analyzed the work of women theorists.[6] These rare instances have not demonstrated close analysis of texts understood by her to be complex and polyvocal.

This failure to read the work of women theorists is all the more interesting because Irigaray's earlier work does offer analyses of what might be called the polyvocal multiplicity of voice of historical male philosophers (Descartes, Lévinas, Kant, Hegel, and so on). There are substantial differences between Bergoffen's suppositions about multiple voice and those of the early Irigaray. Bergoffen uses her technique to reclaim Beauvoir as a stronger and more original woman philosopher than might otherwise be perceived. By contrast, Irigaray's technique, which identifies inconsistent and unstable, multiple, mutually undermining refrains in a philosophical text, is not used to reclaim the philosopher in question. Whereas Bergoffen's interest is to recuperate what she evaluates as the best moments of Beauvoir, Irigaray's project is to expose and undermine a male philosopher's phallocentrism as constitutively unstable.

The move made by Irigaray in *To Be Two* provokes the question of how we might relate the analysis of historical philosophical texts to her linguistic analysis of sentence samples from men and women. Lacking from Irigaray's more recent linguistic work is anything that might approximate a concept of multiple voice, partly because she works from the analysis of very simple word units.

The examples considered above are indicative in this regard. In the study discussed, 65 percent of women are said to have responded with utterances that place subjects in a positive relation to each other. We are not provided with examples of the remaining 35 percent, whose difference might be of interest. Also, we are offered only two or three examples of responses from the 65 percent pool. A useful comparison can be made between *To Be Two* and *Le langage des déments* (1973) and *Sexes et genres à travers les langues* (1990), both of which offer more complex detail on varieties of responses from participants, often listing all responses in appendices. A review of one such appendix to a chapter of *Sexes et genres* (1990, 67–82), which lists every response in a particular study, suggests the ambiguity of many responses from both men and women concerning the kind of relationality they favor and whether they do so positively or negatively. Even the brief examples Irigaray cites in works such as *I Love to You* call for more complexity of analysis. For instance, how readily should we accept the claim that the response "Between is within" "eliminates difference" and so should be seen as an exemplary response from a male participant?

Irigaray's drive to find homogeneity of voice in men and women by examining simple sentence formulations does not reflect a simple disciplinary difference between linguistics and philosophical commentary. Earlier linguistic work such as *Parler n'est jamais neutre* (1985a) and *Le langage des déments* (1973) reflects greater interest in complex and polyvalent language use by masculine and feminine speakers. There is a discrepancy between most of Irigaray's early work on the philosophers and her recent work on language use. *To Be Two* is an attempt to integrate these domains. Certainly in the early work that analyzes philosophical voice, Irigaray locates the contradictory, extremely unstable, self-undermining, and zigzagging discourse—a kind of inconsistency or ambiguity of voice—which occurs in a philosopher who both acknowledges and excludes the possibility of sexual difference.[7] By contrast, in her recent analysis of language use, Irigaray looks to locate consistency and univocity of masculine and feminine discourse in her interpretation of her findings.

To Be Two presents Lévinas, Merleau-Ponty, and Sartre as exemplars of masculine styles of linguistic usage that privilege the relationship between humans understood as same, an appropriative relationship to the world and to the other, the relation between self and a generalized other rather than the "I-you," and norms and universal principles that apply to all rather than to the specificity of the other. Irigaray criticizes Husserl and Hegel for positing an asexuate subject in their discussions of the transcendental reduction and absolute spirit. She criticizes Lévinas for reducing relations with the other to the moral dimension of life and "passing through a God in order to respect the other" (2001, 104, 109). She criticizes Jean-Paul Sartre for his description of desire as conflictual and as an impossible attempt to possess the other's consciousness through possession of his or her body:

> Thus, I can "possess" the other, and according to Sartre, there is no fulfillment of desire without such possession: the fact that the other is also a body possessed of a consciousness determines the desire to possess it. This male philosopher represents the impossible ideal of desire in the following way: the transcendence of the other is to be possessed as pure transcendence, inaccessible to sensible experience, but nevertheless as body. (2001, 18, translation modified)

She groups Merleau-Ponty among those philosophers who depict the existent's attempt to possess the consciousness of the other in the relation of desire (2001, 21).

By contrast, argues Irigaray, we can conceive of the *"tu"* as being a *"tu"* only because we cannot possess him or her. The aim of possession loses its sense. Rather than equating the for-itself with consciousness, and the in-itself with embodiment, Irigaray proposes reconceiving the for-itself as that which I am insofar as I belong to sexuate genre. Embodiment is not simple facticity, she argues, but already consciousness (31). She describes the primordial relation with the parental other, particularly the mother, as the basis for all self-other relations. Where Sartre sees the other's consciousness as conflicting with mine, Irigaray argues that he overlooks the fact that I am a consciousness only because of and through this primary relationality with the other (31–32). Her formulation also calls for a reconsideration of the role of the body. In the original relation with the (m)other, my embodiment is an intentionality in relation with the other that is animated by the other's conscious and unconscious existence.

The account of Lévinas as privileging relations with an other figured as "same" is particularly surprising. Irigaray criticizes him for articulating a masculine-centered engagement with alterity and with divinity, through the path of his engagement with the feminine, while failing to articulate an equivalent spiritual path specific to women. An apparent philosophy of alterity fails as such by subordinating the feminine. Lévinas, she says, appropriates the relation to the other as a means of the subject's communion with God. By contrast, Irigaray explains that she favors a more genuine displacement of the language of inappropriability, mystery, and invisibility, or the via negativa, away from God or the Other considered as substitute for God, to our relations with the other: "you *(tu)*." She presents what she takes to be an alternative whose ethical stakes are the interruption of appropriative relations with the other. Structures of mediation and irreducible mystery are resituated between self and other (as *tu* / you) (110, 189).[8]

Barring some moments of sympathy with elements of Lévinas and Sartre,[9] Irigaray sets them up oppositionally in contrast to her own approach. To sustain this distinction between the masculine and feminine philosophical subject, she excludes the textual moments in the work of these philosophers that would undermine this clear-cut distinction. She groups together Hegel's, Heidegger's, Merleau-Ponty's, and Sartre's depiction of conflictual relations between those conceptualized as same (113 ff.), as if the strong differences among their accounts of self-other relations and embodiment are not of importance to a feminist reading. For example, commentators have noted that while Sartre offers a primarily conflictual account of self-other relations, Merleau-Ponty does not.[10] Irigaray deemphasizes these distinctions, establishing these philosophers' homogeneity as a group and homogeneity within the discourse of each.

In Irigaray's discussion of linguistic samples we do not hear of male speakers whose privileging of relationality is ambiguous. Similarly she has no will to locate in Sartre's text conflicting tenors that undermine her own account of his argument. By contrast, one can imagine the Irigaray of *Speculum* locating contradictory refrains in Sartre's work that suggest that subjectivity is not just threatened by, but is also constituted by, the engagement with the other. Irigaray might have located those aspects of his account that undermine his metaphorical association of the in-itself with embodiment and materiality and the for-itself with consciousness and interpretation. Even in the light of his own work, such associations are as untenable as the gendered connotations attributed to the for-itself and the in-itself.[11] She could have located in his text elements indicating that the difference and alterity of the other undermine its representation as a parallel though competing consciousness impinging on me. We do not hear about the significant differences between Sartre and Merleau-Ponty with regard to their depictions of the other, facticity and freedom, and the body (see Whitford 1982). We also do not hear about the extent to which my relation to divinity or the "Most High" is shifted from my relation to God toward my relation with the Other in Lévinas's work. Instead, Irigaray opposes herself to Lévinas on this and other points on which they share some affiliation.

Clearly, the phenomenology Irigaray articulates as her own is more indebted to Merleau-Ponty, Lévinas, and others than is avowed by her. Appropriation, insertion of the feminine voice, mimicry of and borrowing from the philosophers are too much a part of Irigaray's project for us to raise the issue of an economy of intellectual property rights. But we can ask how masculine and feminine speaking positions can be distinguished by Irigaray.

Her conceptual apparatus deems masculine the suppression of difference and feminine the privileging of relationality. But in many of Irigaray's own linguistic analyses the examples from test participants are ambiguous as regards their figuring of relationality. Irigaray's attempt to stabilize the examples by sorting them into discrete categories seems the least interesting approach to take to their ambiguity. Moreover, her lack of attention to examples not according with consistently sexed discourse provokes our curiosity. How might she analyze the 35 percent of masculine responses in a given sample whose discourse apparently requires more complexity of interpretation? More complex reading of Sartre, Lévinas, and Merleau-Ponty is excluded by an analysis uninterested in the ambiguity of their depictions of relationality. Why is Irigaray so uninterested in the ambiguities of sexed discourse in male and female philosophers and subjects?

In the publication preceding *To Be Two, Le souffle des femmes* (1996b, 231), Irigaray criticizes those of her critics who in her view favor the deconstructive over the constructive and have not received well her more recent work. Her critics applauded her for dismantling masculine culture but, she argues, retained only the deconstructive aspect of her work, not following the more constructive aspects. Women, she insists, need construction more than they need deconstruction (1996b, 232). This opposition between the deconstructive and the constructive should be resisted. The reasons we should resist it become clear in *To Be Two*. Here, Irigaray offers a critique of philosophers whose phallocentrism she earlier either did deconstruct, as in the case of Merleau-Ponty and Lévinas (see 1991b and 1993a), or might well have deconstructed, as in the case of Sartre, and whose work, particularly in the case of Lévinas, she has also been influenced by.[12]

Irigaray's most recent work on linguistics constitutes a period in which she is more committed to supposing discursive univocity. When the interpretations of male and female language conjoin with interpretations of French phenomenological philosophy in *To Be Two*, Irigaray treats Merleau-Ponty, Sartre, and Lévinas as if their voice were univocal. Is this a more constructive, rather than deconstructive, politics? How constructive is a history of philosophy recounted as a history of the univocal masculine voice? According to such a history male philosophers have opposed the for-itself to the in-itself and consciousness to the threat from the other.

Irigaray is hardly the first to comment on the unsatisfactory nature of Sartre's description of desire as conflictual and as an impossible attempt to possess the other's consciousness through possession of his or her body.[13] But it is also true that on Sartre's account (1958) we aim to possess something of the other's specificity (for example, his or her perception of me, or the other's perspective, which inevitably escapes our possession):

> This being which I am preserves a certain indetermination, a certain unpredictability. And these new characteristics do not come only from the fact that I can not *know* the Other; they stem also and especially from the fact that the Other is free. . . . [T]he Other's freedom is revealed to me across the disquieting [*inquiétante*] indetermination of the being which I am for [her/ him]. Thus this being is . . . the limit of my freedom . . . given to me as a burden which I carry without ever being able to turn back to know it. (262, translation modified)

Irigaray argues, against Sartre, that I can conceive of the other as such only at the point at which I cannot possess him or her. This is asserted as an argument contra Sartre, an argument against his economy of appropriation and possession. More complicated is that this economy already breaks down in Sartre's own work.

It does so partly for paradoxical reasons discussed by Sartre himself— the very thing he argues we want (to master the other's consciousness) is impossible. This is an argument made against Sartre by Irigaray, but it is also an argument made by Sartre against his own view of desire's project. Irigaray argues contra Sartre that the aim of Sartrian desire loses all sense, but Sartre has already argued that the aim of desire as he conceives it loses all sense. Furthermore, the anxieties I express about the other as that subjectivity which escapes my limits and around which the world organizes itself indicate a greater implicit recognition of the other's difference than Sartre recognizes.

Feminists writing about Sartre have sometimes focused on the overtly sexist examples Sartre uses in his accounts of freedom and bad faith, such as a "frigid" woman (Sartre 1958, 54) and a woman on a date who is unable to admit to being attracted to a man's desire, the naked expression of which would also horrify her (Sartre 1958, 55).[14] But it is indicative of Irigaray's response to Sartre in *To Be Two* that she is not interested in these examples or the sexist aspects of his anecdotal argument. She proposes that a feminist approach might instead interrogate the quality of Sartre's depiction of self-other relations the quality of his depiction of embodiment. Having moved through several different stages since the publication of *Speculum of the Other Woman* (1985b) and *This Sex Which Is Not One* (1985c), Irigaray now has as her prime concern to generate a positive, alternative philosophical account of the basis of self-other relations and of corporeality. Rather than focusing on the overt comments about women and femininity in Sartre's work, Irigaray therefore offers a framework intended to substitute for his approach to such points as the relationship between facticity and transcendence. She brings to her engagement with Sartre a model of embodiment and of otherness according to which my encounter with the other exceeds and disrupts the subject-object dyad.

Irigaray's most fundamental objection to the Sartrian account is not the sex bias of his examples, anecdotes, and imagery, but their fundamental sex neutrality as seen in his account of self-other relations and embodiment. There is, she would agree with Moira Gatens, "no neutral body, there are at least two kinds of bodies, the male body and the female body" (Gatens 1996, 8). Sartre assumes the fundamental likeness of subjects. That the other is in this sense my alter ego is most obvious in his assumption that our aims are fundamentally similar, as when he writes, "Everything which may be said of me in my relations with the Other applies to the Other as well. While I attempt to free myself from the hold [*emprise*] of the Other, the Other is trying to free [her/him] self from mine; while I seek to enslave the Other, the Other seeks to enslave me" (Sartre 1958, 364, translation modified).

On Irigaray's countermodel, we are constantly aware that we may not know the aims of the other, we may wrongly infer those aims, and we may not be engaged in a pursuit of the same aims. On Sartre's model subjects are fundamentally similar in their desire to objectify rather than be objectified, to appropriate rather than be appropriated, to know rather than be known or, if necessary, to be known in the most ideal version of themselves by an other consciousness whose perspective one would appropriate if possible. In that sense, the other holds no mystery for me insofar as I assume that I know his or her aims. The other also holds no mystery because the fundamental question I direct toward him or her, however impossibly, is a question about my own identity: Who am I? How do I seem? Who am I for you? Can I appropriate your understanding of me?

Attempting to distinguish the sex of the subject is for Irigaray a first step in establishing difference between the subject and the other. Emphasizing the potential for sexual difference between self and other represents Irigaray's emphasis on the other's difference more generally. Imagine that I am interested in the other, not because of what the other can potentially tell me about myself, but because I am intrigued by and engaged with a potentially different subjectivity. Sexual difference is the question that grounds Irigaray's philosophical project. But this interest coincides with a second: to formulate a philosophical paradigm based not on one generic subject, homologous to others (as in the Sartrian model), but on diverse subjects, fundamentally different from each other, starting with the potential difference between the male and female.

As we have seen, the most common and important critical response is to ask why she particularly privileges sexual difference. Irigaray's intervention works best as a displacement of a paradigm such as Sartre's. It does effectively highlight his fundamental assumption that the subject is one, same, generic, and sex neutral. Irigaray asks how his framework would accommodate two subjects considered as sexually different and perhaps as ontologically different as such.

The emphasis on difference also leads Irigaray to ask how Sartre's model would be altered by a focus on other forms of difference between subjects. She proposes a reconsideration of his model in terms of the alterity of intergenerationality. How might Sartre accommodate a model according to which there is a self-other encounter between those of different ages? The model she considers is that between parent and child. Sartre factors the child only once into his philosophical framework, describing the primacy of the body as it is for me over the body-for-others. For example, he writes, the child knows how to grasp, push away, or pull objects toward itself, long before it looks at its hand as an object. The hand and the body that the child learns to integrate spatially with its lived body is the Other's body, the body seen rather than the body lived (Sartre 1958, 358). Irigaray is alert to Sartre's underemphasis of the fact that this process occurs only in the context of the child's relationship with an other, often a parent. As such, and in its most primordial variants, the relationship is not necessarily conflictual. Nor is it best modeled as a master-slave type struggle. According to Sartre's imagery, an autonomous child teaches itself to reconcile the lived with the seen body. The child he depicts is a lone child, not a child engaging with others in the world.

One could compare Sartre's account to Merleau-Ponty's description (1964) of the child's relations with others in a state of syncretic sociability in which we mimic and confuse our bodily boundaries with those of parents and children around us, until there is a gradual acquisition of bodily boundaries. We do not originate in a state of autonomy from the world, subsequently engaging with it. Instead, we originate in a state of integration with the world, and only subsequently learn to disentangle ourselves from it. Merleau-Ponty would have us originally plural and dispersed in the other. On Sartre's model we are originally solo. Irigaray proposes the alternative model of the originary two.

Partly because Sartre associates my object-body with my reduction to a being-for-others, Irigaray's rethinking of his account of embodiment also rethinks his account of self-other relations. She rebukes Sartre for forgetting that the first body we encounter in our life is the body of the mother, a body that fills us with its intentionality. This is already a break with Sartre's model according to which the other is either body and therefore object of my perception, or subject and therefore source of a possible perspective on me. The relation to the mother's body must be different, an Irigarayan model suggests. It does not conform to a model binarized between objectifying and being objectified.

It is many months before the neonate can distinguish the mother as a fundamentally separate entity, or as the objectified object of its perceptions. It is many months again before it learns to be self-conscious or embarrassed. It is Sartre who raises the issue—albeit in one example only—of data from child development psychology that might support his account of adult embodiment. The door is opened to Irigaray's intervention. What is our original relationship to the mother's body? she asks. It is one of nonseparation, the child carrying a corporeal sense of the mother's voice, touch, movements, gestures, and comportment. This sense of the other's body animates us, before we develop a sense of a discrete subjectivity and differentiation from others, and it continues to animate us through that development. Quite apart from the adult awareness I have of the other as body-object, or myself as body-object in his or her eyes, I also have an awareness of the other as a physical entity, and I have a bodily responsiveness to his or her movement and gait, gestures and attitudes. In this sense, "my body is inhabited by a consciousness which begins with its first relationship with the parental other, with the mother in particular" (Irigaray 2001, 31).[15]

To some extent, Irigaray brings to Sartre's model an alternative that breaks with, and bears little relationship to, his own. This is seen when she offers an alternative account of facticity. For Sartre, our facticity amounts to the material facts about us, historical, bodily, or contextual, which we surpass or transcend or "choose" in our freedom. For Sartre, sexual difference, while not discussed, would certainly amount to a facticity surpassed or negated by human freedom. For Irigaray, on the other hand, sexual difference is more centrally crucial to subjectivity. More generally, she opposes Sartre's model of a for-itself perpetually transcending—fleeing, in his metaphorics—the body. She proposes an alternative concept of becoming: "[T]he becoming which I propose is different. In so far as I belong to a gender *[genre]*, my body—my in-itself, as Sartre would say—already involves a for-itself. It is not simple factuality or 'facticity,' but is already consciousness. This cannot be reduced to a flight forward. . . . It must be a return towards me, a return in me, to cultivate that being which I am: a sexuate body, a body potentially animated by a consciousness which is my own" (2001, 31, translation modified).

Irigaray responds to *Being and Nothingness* with a philosophical account of cultivating an understanding of myself as a sexed body. But her response is generated out of her critical relationship with Sartre's account. Within the context of his own work, Irigaray finds unacceptable and nonsensical a reference to a neutral subject.

On the one hand, Irigaray understands herself as external to Sartre's work, presenting an alternative model. But on the other hand, Irigaray presents herself in a more intimate relationship to Sartre. She adds her perspective to the French phenomenological tradition, amending his framework. In this regard, she writes, "These differences between feminine and masculine speaking and being [*l'être et le parler féminins ou masculins*] can help us to interpret the way in which certain male philosophers—such as Jean-Paul Sartre, Maurice Merleau-Ponty, and Emmanuel Lévinas—have conceived carnal love and can make apparent the feminine character of my words on loving relations, particularly on the caress" (2001, 17, translation modified). Irigaray does not present her philosophical framework as unable to communicate with the Sartrian model. To the contrary, she explains those points of communication. Her problematic relationship to Sartre is heightened by an additional element, her attribution of a masculine discursive structure to his work.

Insofar as Irigaray diagnoses the masculinity of Sartre's philosophy, *Être deux* synthesizes her previous linguistic research with her analysis of philosophical discourse. Irigaray is not thinking of the overt sexism of Sartre's language, the references to women, frigidity, slimes and holes, sexual penetration, female embodiment, feminine passivity, and so on. Instead, she assesses the quality of the structure of his relation to the other as linguistically manifest in his writing. Appropriative relations with the other, in which I relate to the other as object or as property, she takes as examples of masculinism. Sartre's account of an appropriative relation to both the world and the other is relentless, and it is easy to consider his writing an instance of masculinist discourse in this sense.

However, I suggested that diagnoses of this kind see Irigaray as departing from the earlier patterns in her work. *Speculum of the Other Woman* and *Marine Lover* emphasize the unstable, self-contradictory, and paradoxical language of historical male philosophers. These philosophers exclude sexual difference and mythologize the sex-neutral subject. But they fail in these attempts, and their discourse simultaneously undermines these representations. Informing this work on historical philosophy is Irigaray's notion that discourse is not univocal or homogeneous. The subject's phallocentric intentions discursively undermine themselves.

The concept of discourse informing Irigaray's work in the area of linguistics has a different emphasis. She emphasizes the extent to which language is consistently masculine or feminine. Masculine discourse takes an appropriative relation to the other and tends to formulate a subject-object relation rather than a relation between two different subjects. She presents linguistic study evidence so as to deemphasize the importance of the exceptions. We do not hear about tendencies toward both masculinity and femininity (as Irigaray defines these) in a particular subject's discourse. Irigaray would surely acknowledge that a given subject's discourse might sometimes manifest both masculine and feminine tendencies. Exceptions to the norm can doubtless be located in men and women. But these are not the focus of her interest.

This same change in orientation is seen in Irigaray's approach to the philosophers, personified in the figure of Sartre. She considers Sartre as an example of masculine discourse, and we hear about the extent to which Sartre's philosophical writing in *Being and Nothingness* accords with the masculine discursive type. We do not hear about elements in Sartre's work that undermine this tenor, or about the potential ambivalence or unstable nature of his masculinism. His philosophical language is presented as consistently and homogeneously masculine. Yet perhaps the strongest feminist reading is one that exposes the extent to which his masculinism undermines itself. And when the alternative perspective of *To Be Two* locates the possibility of resistance to Sartre's masculinism, it establishes secure boundaries between Sartre and Irigaray. Apparently Sartre and Irigaray offer two radically different, alternative discourses. Irigaray would bear no debt to Sartre, or Sartre to Irigaray, in the Irigarayan reading of Sartre.

And yet another feminist reading of Sartre is possible, one more indebted to the reading approach of an earlier Irigaray. One of the most consistent criticisms Irigaray makes of Sartre relates to his failure to depict the other as different from me rather than as an equivalent, competing consciousness. But what if Sartre's text is also traversed by its implicit recognition of the difference of the other? He deems the other to be my parallel insofar as we are assumed to be engaged in the same struggle not be objectified. The other I objectify represents the constant risk of objectifying me and also represents the risk of the unknown quantity:

> In fact if I start with the Other's body, I apprehend it as an instrument and in so far as I myself make use of it as an instrument. I can *utilize* it in order to arrive at ends which I could not attain alone; I *command* its acts through orders or supplications; I can also provoke its acts by my own acts. At the same time I must take precautions with respect to a tool which is particularly delicate and dangerous to handle. (Sartre 1958, 321, translation modified)

For Sartre, this is the risk of a perspective turned toward me about which I know nothing and over which I have no control. The moment the question of the other is posed in these terms, I am the object of the other's potential perspective on me. But the description is also an implicit avowal that the other is a source of mystery that escapes my control.

In addition to the vicissitudes of my self-other relations, I have always also internalized the other. If not, I could not be a being-for-others if another person was not present or if the other's subjectivity did not coincide with my inferences about it:

> [W]hat *most often* manifests a look is the convergence of two ocular globes in my direction. But the look will be given just as well on occasions such as a rustling of branches, or the sound of a footstep followed by silence, or the slight opening of a shutter, or a light movement of a curtain. (Sartre 1958, 257, translation modified)
> [T]o apprehend a look is not to apprehend a look-as-object . . . it is to be conscious of *being looked at*. The look which the *eyes* manifest . . . is a pure

reference to myself. . . . What I apprehend . . . is that I am vulnerable, that I have a body which can be hurt. (Sartre 1958, 258–59)

I may become a being-for-others alone and in the privacy of my home. I am a being-for-others when I look in the mirror, and when I become embarrassed that an other would consider me vain. Though Sartre presents the phenomenon of being-for-others as evidence of the existence of others, his examples demonstrate that my being-for-others becomes detached from the actions of and engagement with a particular other at a particular time. For example, though I may become transformed into a peep in the eyes of a potential other if I am spying through a keyhole and hear footsteps in the hall, the same transformation in my being will occur even if I am mistaken that I hear footsteps. These examples suggest that my encounters with the other are paranoid about, but in fact indifferent to, the actual subjectivity of another subject.

However, one can reconsider Sartre's work from the perspective of Irigaray's concerns. We must, she emphasizes, have internalized the other in a primary way, in order to have subsequent relations with the other of any kind. The inevitability of this conclusion can also be read into Sartre's work. How can we explain the fact that I become a being-for-others, traversed by the potential responses, assessment, and perspective of the other, in the absence of a particular other, except via such an account? While Sartre does not belabor this internalization, his text calls, against his explicit commentary, for such an articulation. Irigaray opposes to Sartre's master-slave dialectic a subject who has always already incorporated the other. But Sartre's master-slave dialectic is not itself coherent or viable except with an account of a subject who has always already internalized the other. Irigaray is able to pit her account against that of Sartre, but she can also (although she does not) lift its necessity out of Sartre's work.

Sartre defines language as originally being-for-others. Language "presupposes an original relation to another subject." Language is the recognition of the Other "in the intersubjectivity of the for-others" (Sartre 1958, 372). These formulations occur in the midst of a chapter that begins with a definition of the original relation to the other as one of conflict: "Conflict is the original meaning of being-for-others" (Sartre 1958, 364). Yet how may the account of language as originally being-for-others be reconciled with the account of being-for-others as fundamentally conflictual? Sartre describes the original upsurge of the Other into our world as the arising of language as the "condition of my being" (373). However, he also describes the advent of language as the advent of the look. Irigaray's critical response would challenge the depiction of the advent of language and the Other as an alienating look. Yet Sartre's own account of language also disrupts his account of alienation. He does not describe the advent of language as a conflictual battle with the Other. Apparently his account implicitly calls for a theorization of an original being-with-the-other that disrupts the dyad between objectifying and being objectified, the opposition between looker and object looked at.

At one point, Irigaray's reading is appreciative of fragments in Sartre's text that do move in the direction of depicting nonconflictual being-with-the-other. She describes positively his discussion of the "we-subject." Sartre describes occasions when I consider myself as interchangeable with the others who are or could be undertaking the same banal projects as myself—making a train connection, for example. As Sartre describes the we-subject, we do not realize particularity in this kind of self-conception: "My immediate ends are the ends of the "They," and I apprehend myself as interchangeable with any one of my neighbors. In this sense we lose our real individuality" (Sartre 1958, 424, discussed Irigaray 2001, 38–39). Irigaray introduces an ethical stance missing in Sartre's discussion. She argues that one should not reduce oneself to an undifferentiated "great human stream." With a rigorous approach to my subjectivity and that of the other, this reduction may be resisted. As she emphasizes, "I am not reduced to an 'anybody' in the corridor of the subway station at La Motte-Picquet-Grenelle if I walk towards you. My interiority, my intention remain my own, and immediate, in spite of the crowd. This interiority safeguards my mystery, as your interiority makes you a mystery for me" (Irigaray 2001, 39, translation modified).

While she values Sartre's vivid depiction of the "we-subject," she is critical, as he is not, of this mode of being-with-others. It is inadequate in not recognizing the other's specificity. An account of being-with-the-other is unsatisfactory if it understands all subjects as equivalent or akin in their undifferentiated transcendence. Sartre's account of this phenomenon therefore becomes the context for Irigaray's critique. But opposing the Sartrian account, again Irigaray downplays the extent to which his account of an undifferentiated we-subject undermines his own model of self-other conflict as the fundamental basis of self-other relations. Each instance of nonconflictual relation to the other is assumed by Sartre to be marginal, incidental, or extraneous to primary conflict. Yet much of the discussion of *Being and Nothingness* can be read against Sartre's own representation of what is primary: alienation and conflict.

Irigaray finds no greater value in a Sartrian model of undifferentiated transcendence than in a model of alienation in conflictual struggle. Her discussion of Sartre is subordinated to her own presentation of an alternative account of embodiment and alterity. But concerned to present an alternative model and explain its points of difference from the Sartrian model, Irigaray forgoes the opportunity to consider the ways in which his account of undifferentiated transcendence might undermine his model of appropriation of the other in a conflictual struggle. Again this is an issue of homogeneity versus plurality of voice. Does Irigaray want to emphasize the Sartre who is conflicted on the question of alterity, or the Sartre whose appropriative or phallocentric discourse is in this regard entirely stable and consistent?

Sartre's account of being-with-the-other in language is interestingly inconsistent with an account of being-with-others as a form of undifferentiated transcendence. How can language operate as the advent of the other into our world, except insofar as it operates as the advent of the difference of the other? The advent of language, according to the tenor of his own discussion (although he does not make the point), is not inherently conflictual, nor does language enable me to merge with an indiscriminate and nondistinct other.

Irigaray criticizes Sartre's depiction of subjects as striving always to master the other. She redefines the "you," the *"tu,"* as that force which resists my appropriative drive. Having so redefined the "you," she then deems the will to appropriate the other incoherent. Instead, the "you" is precisely that which cannot be expropriated (Irigaray 2001, 18–19). But even without this redefinition of the status of the other, the incoherence of the will to possess the other does emerge from Sartre's text. As he acknowledges, it is an impossible desire. A consciousness I appropriate is no longer the consciousness I hoped to appropriate. My relation to the other is prone to collapse at each moment, as I dissolve into awareness of another potential consciousness. To attempt to physically appropriate the other, as occurs in love and desire according to the Sartrian model, risks collapse into embodiment. Sartre does not define the other as that which, by definition, could not be appropriated. However, he does define appropriation as an impossible and doomed project. Irigaray's ethics condemns the human will to appropriate. She proposes an alternate philosophical basis for conceiving the self-other relation where Sartre encourages the subject's affirmation of its inevitable freedom.

Certainly, Irigaray's affirmation of sexual difference as irreducible in the self-other relation is a radical alternative to Sartre's philosophy. But there is a cost to her deemphasizing those admittedly infrequent moments of Sartre's text that come closest to Irigaray's interpretation,[16] or that disrupt those elements of his text to which she most objects. In the light of Irigaray's own earlier work, must she mount an alternative, Irigarayan phenomenology at the expense of an interpretation that would continue to highlight the failures and troubles, the inconstancy and inconsistency of a discourse understood as masculine?

I am not arguing that Sartre positively conceptualizes the other in terms of difference and alterity. Readers will agree with many of Irigaray's comments about him. He does not succeed in offering positive accounts of the encounter with alterity, nor does he figure the encounter with the other in terms of reciprocity. It is interesting, as Irigaray suggests, to ask how Sartre's work might have to be altered by the recognition that "the first other which I encounter is the body of the mother" (Irigaray 2001, 30); and indeed, to reflect on how this encounter may occur differently depending on whether it is that of boy or girl to the mother. But I am arguing that a reading consistent with Irigaray's earlier approach might consider the worst aspects of Sartre's own text as destabilized by some of its own content: those very narratives of anxiety, paranoia, and dread of the other, for example. Some recognition occurs of an alterity that would need to be conceptualized in terms that exceed Sartre's. Tenors and strains in Sartre's work lean, for all his paranoia, in this direction.[17]

To consider one final example, we have seen Irigaray's questioning of Sartre's equation of the for-itself with consciousness, and the in-itself with embodiment. But again there are conflicting aspects of *Being and Nothingness*. The in-itself is inseparable from the for-itself, embodiment always within the domain of interpretation, response, attitude, "consciousness":

> [I]t is impossible to determine in each particular case what comes from freedom and what comes from the brute being of the for-itself. . . . [I]t is impossible to decree *a priori* what comes from the brute existent and what from freedom. (Sartre 1958, 488)

Thus is it Irigaray or Sartre who, while equating the for-itself with consciousness and the in-itself with embodiment, also wants to argue that embodiment "is not simple factuality or 'facticity' but is already consciousness" (Irigaray 2001, 31)? Is Irigaray against or with Sartre here, or do these boundaries blur? What significance might their blurring have for the sexedness of the language of each, in her view?

Irigaray proposes reconceiving the for-itself as what I am insofar as I belong to sexuate genre. This change would transform the Sartrian approach. To situate the interpreting and attitudinal domain of human existence as always sexed is a new contribution to the tradition of (French) phenomenology. But there is no need to depict Sartre, Merleau-Ponty, and Lévinas as monodiscursive texts privileging (as the case may be) subject over other, consciousness over embodiment, or sameness over alterity. It remains open to Irigaray to read these philosophers for the strains and tenors in their work that lean more in her direction, often against their professed terms of analysis.[18] This is what we see in *An Ethics of Sexual Difference.*

Irigaray has moved from appropriating some of the multiple voices she exposes in the texts of philosophers such as Freud, Nietzsche, and Merleau-Ponty, to not reading for those multiple voices. Against a Sartre, Merleau-Ponty, or a Lévinas whose texts she has stabilized as masculine, she is able to pit an alternative she designates both as her own and—presumably, although she does not say so—as feminine. The issue is whether, as feminist philosophers, we should prefer narratives consolidating the view that the male voices of the history of philosophy have been (by Irigaray's definition of the term) consistently, stably, and homogeneously masculine. This myth is consolidated when Irigaray synthesizes her recent linguistic research with her approach to the history of philosophy in her most recent work.[19]

What are the results of this synthesis for her philosophical analysis? The linguistic research, which serves as the fundamental point of reference in *To Be Two,* presents research findings from extensive surveys that suggest that there are differing structures of language use, deemed masculine and feminine. The work in philosophy then brings to light those aspects of a philosopher, such as Sartre in *Being and Nothingness,* that manifest similar discursive structures: the tendency to privilege a relationship to a generalized other rather than a specific *"tu,"* the tendency to assume that a neutral interlocutor is specifically male, the tendency to take an appropriative relationship toward the other, and so on. Where the work on language tends not to focus on inconsistency and ambivalence in speech, Irigaray's philosophical work then seems to manifest a greater tendency to downplay these same aspects in a philosopher's discourse. The result is the generation of findings, in the discussion of both everyday speech samples and a historical text such as *Being and Nothingness,* that suggest that masculine and feminine discursive positions are both internally consistent and entrenched.

I began this chapter with an epigraph from Wendy Brown. She argues that we need analyses of the power formations that produce subjects. These analyses require "careful histories, psychoanalysis [and] political economy." We also need analysis of cultural, political, and legal discourse. But, argues Brown (1997), in constructing genealogies of subjectivity, we should not presume "coherence in the formation of particular kinds of subjects," for we need to emphasize instead "formations that may be at odds with or convergent with each other" (94). How might this recommendation affect our methodologies for interpreting the history of philosophical discourse? One of the best contributions made by Irigaray's early work is her recognition that a phallocentric discourse is not inevitably a coherent discursive formation—to the contrary. The instability of such texts may not lessen their phallocentrism. But it does provide the possibility of more enabling readings, which open to the new through the inconsistencies and divergences of discourses that exclude alterity, difference, and sexual difference. Something is lost when Merleau-Ponty, Sartre, and Lévinas are grouped as a consistent and an internally coherent group of texts forming part of a genealogy of conceptions of subjectivity dominated by the metaphysics of sameness.

10

Effacement Redoubled?

Between East and West

To the extent that Irigaray is suggesting that each of us should be a horizon of significance for the other, it is clear that this claim does not and should not apply only to relationships between the sexes. If we can extend this claim to characterize same-sex relations as well as relations between individuals of different races, ages, and social classes, her position becomes much more appealing and much more powerful.

Gail Weiss, *Body Images*

Given the history of U.S. feminism and U.S. race relations, it is imperative to set aside as a now-obvious falsity [Irigaray's] assumption that gender suffices to ground multiculturalism.

Patricia J. Huntington, *Ecstatic Subjects*

We have seen that Irigaray attributes primacy to sexual difference as the most universal difference running through all cultures. "The most universal and irreducible difference . . . is the one that exists between the genders [*genres*]" (2002), she writes in her 1999 work *Entre orient et occident*, just as she claimed in *An Ethics of Sexual Difference* more than a decade earlier. But should we suppose that sexual difference means the same thing throughout cultures, at least sufficiently so that we could say that "it" does permeate them all? The claim is possible only insofar as we assume that we know what sexual difference is. We assume that the term we already have in mind permeates all cultures. It must be, at least to the extent that enables its identification, "our" sexual difference that we imagine permeating all cultures. Yet Irigaray is at her best when she is not assuming that we already know what sexual difference is. I want now to consider the status of cultural difference in Irigaray's work. Irigaray is obliged to assume that her own understanding of the status of sexual difference is sufficiently widespread throughout all cultures to justify her claim about primacy.

This returns us to the theme discussed in the introduction. What is the status of cultural difference in Irigaray's work? Should cultural difference occupy a status of impossibility, as does sexual difference? If not, does Irigaray address the reasons? In this chapter, I want to ask whether Irigaray's politics of impossible difference addresses, or offers the potential to address, the thinking of cultural difference.

Irigaray's most recent work revisits the earlier position to which she has been strongly committed, that sexual difference is the primary difference. I have mentioned that Irigaray does persist with this view in *Between East and West*. However, up until the publication of this work the primary emblematic ideal for her was the qualitatively improved structural relation between a woman and a man.[1] In *Between East and West* Irigaray argues that a culture of sexual difference would facilitate qualitatively improved structural relations between those of different cultures, races, and traditions. Whereas recent work might have responded to the question "Why must we cultivate differences of and among women?" with the answer "So as to facilitate a culture of sexual difference," the 1999 work effectively answers the question of why we must cultivate relations of sexual difference with the answer that they will better facilitate multiculturalism (as Irigaray understands this). We have seen many commentators argue that Irigaray's recent, more simple formulations concerning legal reform must be understood in the context of the early, complex Irigarayan concept of sexual difference. But what about Irigaray's recent formulations concerning cultural difference? Are we to understand cultural difference in Irigaray's work as based on an aporia of recognition, as are her formulations on sexual difference?

Irigaray's concern for issues of cultural difference is apparent in many of her writings. In "Femmes et hommes: une identité relationelle différente" (1995), she contributes to a volume of debate and discussion surrounding the fourth international conference on the status of women held at Peking. To impose a normalized model of equality on those of different cultures is, she writes, already a failure to respect or ensure equality:

> For example, to impose on a white woman, or a black man, or those who worship Mahomet, the model of the white, adult, western, competent, property-owning man of the Judeo-Christian tradition. In the name of what authority does this white man choose himself, or come to be chosen, as the measure against which all, men and women, have the right or the duty to be equal? (137)

When a norm is imposed on those deemed marginal, even in the name of equality politics, the possibility of real equality is excluded, she argues. This holds as much for the imposition of phallocentric norms as for those of capitalism or indeed of Christianity. Irigaray's early work contests the assessment of women's equality, sameness, or difference in terms of a benchmark of value associated with masculinity. In the passage cited here, she makes a similar point in the context of cultural, racial, and religious difference. To this extent, her politics of cultural and sexual difference take on, at least at first glance, a similar appearance. In fact, I will argue that in contrast to her politics of sexual difference, her concept of cultural difference is not founded on a politics of impossibility. Irigaray's inconsistent approaches seem to suggest her implicit supposition that thinking sexual difference and thinking cultural difference are not similarly impossible.

Between East and West stages the conjunction of old and in many ways new Irigarayan concerns. Irigaray's ongoing critique of western forms of divinity, which dates back to *Speculum of the Other Woman*, is married with a newer attention to issues of multiculturalism. But those readers who have questioned Irigaray's frequent silence or glibness on this issue may not be greatly reassured. The two themes coincide insofar as Irigaray, dissatisfied with western religious traditions, writes of her turn toward eastern traditions, including Buddhism and the practice of yoga. Irigaray speaks of the importance of an improved and more respectful relationship to breath and nature in addition to embodiment. The religious practices of eastern cultures, particularly those of India, serve as the context for a discussion of the limitations of the West, with its pollution, noise, technology, and ecological failures. A strong degree of idealization is manifested in her reluctance to consider the possible problems of pollution, noise, technology, and ecological failure in what she deems the orient. Furthermore, a problem she does not raise is the very problem of comparison, discussed by one of Irigaray's interlocutors, Rada Iveković, in her work *Orients* (1992). As Iveković writes, "[S]peaking of two different traditions does not take place without a minimum of comparison, even if this is not avowed. . . . Thus one is left with the awkward problem that the 'common denominator' . . . has not been chosen on the basis of some common agreement between the parties concerned" (28).[2] The moment I engage in the project of comparison, subordination of the other to my own regime of comparison has occurred, and "the comparative method is itself western" (10). "Comparison itself is not a neutral operation. Neutral comparison does not exist. This is because it is obliged to adopt a mode of thinking and terminology that are, in this case, occidental. And they *make capital*, in the words of Jacques Derrida, for western thought" (28). Irigaray makes capital, by definition, from the comparative project—capital for her denunciation of the western tradition.

The ethics of capitalizing on the figure of the "East" is not problematized by Irigaray. Whether or not women are deemed equal or different, Irigaray's point is that subordination has occurred to the extent that women are assessed according to a masculine viewpoint. Whether the orient is seen as similar or different, a similar problem inevitably occurs. Irigaray finds points of similarity to or difference from a western standpoint, whether the latter is valued or depreciated by her. There is no attunement to this issue in her work.

Entre orient et occident (1999) followed the 1997 publication of *Être deux*. Both works echo the need to cultivate a qualitative relationship *"entre deux"*—between two.[3] The themes evoked include the irreducibility of the other to me, an irreducibility said to protect my own existence (1997, 22). The relation between self and other in the *"être deux"* is a relation regulated by mediation: the work of the *"entre,"* the between. Irigaray proposes breath and matter as examples of the possible *entre* (the between). The idealized relation is as follows:

> Only love consents to a night in which I will never know you. Between those who love each other there is a veil. . . . Does such a night correspond to blind faith or to respect for the one I will never know? Is it not this unknown which allows us to remain two? The existence of a mystery safeguards each of us. In blindness we remain distinct, one towards the other. . . . Leaving both of us to be—you and me, me and you—never reducing the other to a mere meaning, to my meaning, we listen always and anew to each other, so that the irreducible can remain. (2001, 9)

While a complex reconstruction of Irigaray's concept of mediation is necessary to understand what makes possible the *entre deux*,[4] the values it represents are clear: nonappropriation of the other, irreducibility of the one to the other, valuing the possibility of mystery between self and other, respect for what we cannot know.[5] Those factors that do or might protect such a relationship are valued by Irigaray, though readers might differ in their views about the social programs or philosophical values that could ensure the possibility of such a relationship between subjects.

The theme of the *entre deux* is reprised in *Between East and West*. A criticism directed at Christian and particularly Catholic religions is their failure to place a female subject in the relation of the *entre deux*. Irigaray argues that the biblical representation of Mary as addressed by the intermediary of an angel ("And the angel said to her, 'Do not be afraid, Mary, for you have found favor with God. And behold, you will conceive in your womb and bear a son, and you shall call his name Jesus," Luke 1, 30–31) excludes the possibility of a preliminary question that might have been directed to Mary: Does she want to be the mother of a savior? She is left as the "simple vehicle at the service of giving birth to the son of God-the-Father" (2002, 53). Irigaray notes the difference between certain religions that favor forms such as the hymn, the song, and poetic discourse, and forms of address more typical of Judeo-Christian mythology. The imperative mode is prevalent in the latter. An adult is repeatedly represented as subject to the authority of an absent God. In such contexts, "there are no longer two persons" (*"il n'y a plus deux personnes"*) (2002, 53). The suggestion is that some eastern religions might fare favorably by comparison, despite her subsequent acknowledgment of exasperation with hierarchical structures of authority in relation to the teaching of yoga, at the least.

So the reader must interrogate the title *Entre orient et occident* and the kind of relationship—the ideal for an *"entre"* and *"être" deux*—indicated by it. Insofar as Irigaray expresses concern about a subject positioned as passive recipient of another's authoritative discourse, how might this concern carry over to the representation of the east ["*orient*"]? This is an obvious question, one prompted by Irigaray's own title. The book asks it at times, but often indirectly. When, in "Femmes et hommes" (1995), Irigaray turns to demarcate the defaults of the west, the figure of the east is deployed to assist this argument. Her concern is less to question representations of India and Asia. In fact, she rarely engages in such criticism, and thus is not led to self-criticism on this point. Arguing that the west is culturally impoverished, her work contributes to an idealized depiction of the east serving the denunciation of western culture. Her discussions of Christian religion are particularly indicative in this regard. In writings included in the anthology *Le souffle des femmes,* Irigaray offers a critical reading of the western tradition of representing the feminine as mediator between Jesus and God. Her interpretation is also recuperative and interventionist. She believes that biblical stories can be read otherwise, so as to offer the possibility of the invention of a new imaginary. For example, she proposes that Jesus' birth be retold as a story of how Mary participated in and consented to the conception. The advent of the angels is to be seen not as an announcement but as an interrogation of Mary's aspirations.

Irigaray tells us repeatedly that it is her experience of the east that enables her to turn both a critical and a reconstructive eye on the Catholic tradition to which she belongs. Here, and in similar writings included in *I Love to You* and *Le souffle des femmes,* Irigaray's depiction of a culture deemed oriental is nothing but positive: "It is not true that 'every representation and everything written is dominated by traditional representations of sexual difference.' Go examine Hinduism, for example. There, you will discover other representations than those coded to suit the patriarchal imaginary" (1996b, 242).

Some time must elapse in Irigaray's corpus before she comes to ask if Hinduism might not also be subjected to her deconstructive-reconstructive analysis, rather than held up as a model assisting her depreciation of the west. She does not question whether it is appropriate, on the strength of visits to India and a practice of yoga, to use Asia to enlighten a western feminist about her objections to Catholicism and western Christianity. Consider, for example, her claim that "resituated in the horizon of other traditions—those of the Indian extreme orient, for example—the Christian tradition offers us the means of opening up a new era for the advent of divinity" (1996b, 208). Place this claim in the light of her personal narrative: "In this way, I returned to my own tradition more awakened [*éveillée*], more autonomous as a woman, and having acquired something of the culture of the Far East [*et avec un peu de culture extrême-orientale*], which has given me perspective on my own beliefs" (1996b, 186). In both contexts, the Indian is valued for its utility in the intellectual transformation of a western, feminist intellectual.

An appreciation of this most obvious point is missing from Irigaray's work. While she is more than aware that Asia has been appropriated and disregarded in the western tradition, she does not incorporate into her writing an appreciation of the way in which her own writing is part of the western tradition of which she is critical. This failure may be considered in the light of an overall feature of Irigaray's writings—its reluctance to analyze its own position as potentially appropriative. Her writing argues that women's impoverished position renders them all the more prone to appropriate the other. An analysis of Irigaray's own inevitable implication in such tendencies should follow from this point. But it does not. In many ways, this is because of the unique rhetorical position she adopts. Though she sometimes denies that her writing is utopian, her own figuring of her subjective position in her writing is extremely so. Her writing does not figure its own engagement in practices of appropriation, violence, and indifference, because it tries to perform the utopian gesture of a possibly nonappropriative, nonviolent subjective position attentive to possible difference. The seeming cultural indifference of her writing should be interpreted in these terms. Her writing does not mean to be culturally indifferent, of course, but to occupy an ideal or utopian position in which a discussion of India by a western woman need not be appropriative. But again I would make a point suggested in chapter 8. Even if we imagine that there are brackets around "cultural difference" so as to anticipate its

maximally broad possibilities, the idea of transparency (for example between Irigaray and Asia) can hardly be accepted as an ideal. She should be
telling us that there could never be any such transparency.

So we can interpret Irigaray's gesture according to the previous analysis
of sexuate rights. Imagine a culture, she might be saying, in which, with
adequate mediation between us, my discussions of other women need not
be neglectful, my discussions of other cultures need not be self-serving or
appropriative. The declaration of sexual rights emphasizes their impossibility given the widespread rhetorical commitment to equal rights. Can
the same be said of Irigaray's utopia for relations of cultural difference?
Irigaray does not declare a politics opposing appropriation of the east or
different access to speaking positions for eastern and western voices. This
omission causes trouble for her attempt to perform a utopian nonappropriative discourse in relation to another culture. When this attempt is contrasted with her attempt to evoke a potentially nonappropriative discourse between men and women (in the opening chapter of *To Be Two*, for
example), a critical difference is evident. The latter is bolstered by a concurrent politics of close analysis of the history of phallocentric discourse
and bolstered also by an elaborate politics addressing the transformative
and wide-ranging social and political reform that would be necessary for
a qualitatively improved culture of sexual difference. By contrast, a parallel politics is lacking from Irigaray's approach to race and cultural difference. There is also no equivalent to the declaration of sexuate rights, no
declaration of the rights of cultural difference. Some principles are offered
in *Between East and West*. She considers that the family unit has already
been undergoing transformation. It is no longer faithful to one law and
one set of customs, one kind of ancestral custom. The "nomadic and multicultural" family, lacking economic and localized stability, is the emblem
of contemporary intercultural life. Irigaray points out that our political institutions seem to be lagging behind these developments. To some extent,
then, an Irigarayan multicultural politics seems to be expressed as a call
for institutional reform that must catch up to the reality of how we exist in
our pluriracial and multicultural lives (2002, 133–34): "While public au-
thorities will look into the difficult problem of integration, new families
will have initiated the young generations into a multiracial, multicultural,
etc., cohabitation. . . . Curiously, what has become an imperative for our
era, at all levels, is still being frustrated by administrative, legal, and political habits" (2002, 134–35, translation modified). Irigaray does go on to
call for the necessary revolution in thought, but an equivalent to the bill of
sexuate rights is not offered for multiculturalism. Also, these passages
seem to revert more squarely to the politics of recognition. In addition, her
work has not offered sustained critical analysis of eurocentric discourse,

leaving her writing all the more prone to consolidating, rather than deconstructing, eurocentrism.

Certainly, we are left with the question of whether hers is the right utopia. Some might argue that relationality is fundamental to us and yet implicates us in the inevitability of violence, aggression, and appropriation, in addition to love, friendship, and respect. Perhaps there can be no possibility of love, friendship, or respect without our ongoing negotiation with the presence of violence, aggression, and appropriation. Irigaray's utopia envisions and declares the possibility of love and friendship without aggression. This is not, as Margaret Whitford (1994) has written, because she is oblivious to the workings of the death drive. To the contrary, her constructive philosophy attempts to redress the subject's governance by the death drive.[6] Nevertheless, as a result, and because of the visualization of her utopia for human relations, Irigaray downplays the tendency to appropriate the other in one's own-self interest. Nowhere are the limitations of this approach more apparent than in the Irigarayan writings on cultural difference, where she draws upon the east as the figure that serves as ground to depict the limitations of the west, and the utopian aspect of the depiction of the east precludes an engagement with the inevitably appropriative stance underlying that depiction.[7]

For all its problems, Irigaray's treatments of cultural difference in *Between East and West* do represent an important modification in her work. In the last chapter of the work Irigaray discusses the contradictions grounding assimilationist policies in Europe, endorses multiculturalist politics, and takes as the emblematic loving relationship that between a black man and a white woman: "Thus, a couple formed by a white woman and a black man can, from the fact of its being multiracial, become a site of civic education" (2002, 135). Here, sexual difference is not, per se, our cultural goal. Instead, our goal is a culture that values and lives well with difference. I suggested that sexual difference takes on the status of the means to this end. We need not see it as the most important difference, and not necessarily the ultimate goal to which we are working. It is the most important difference only if it is the difference that might better facilitate all other differences in our culture. The passage cited above, which begins with the claim that "sexual duality runs through all races, cultures, and traditions," continues as follows: "It is therefore possible to organize a society starting from this difference. It presents the double advantage of being globally shared and of being able to join together the most elemental aspect of the natural with the most spiritual aspects of the cultural" (2002, 136). Now sexual difference is presented in terms of its utility. While it is the most useful difference, it is not designated a goal in itself in such passages. While difference and in particular cultural difference is now a "capital G Good" (to return to David Krell's formulation), sexual difference interestingly is not—except as means to an end.

The moment that this occurs, much of the framework begins to open itself up to a more radical rethinking. Opening toward a more general privileging of a culture of difference, Irigaray steps back, intermittently, from her focus on sexual difference. "In fact," she writes, "all attraction is founded on a difference, an 'unknown' of the desiring subject" (136). An Irigarayan philosophy of difference becomes a philosophy of our fundamental encounter with the unknown, mystery, or surprise. True, this philosophy is given leaden boots by the passage that follows it: "attraction beginning with what pushes the boy and the girl, the man and the woman toward each other" (136). But there are other ways to put this point. We might argue that sexual difference is, or is potentially, a particularly intense and significant experience of childhood and adult formation. If so, we might say that our experience of sexual difference, given its heavily invested social importance, may restructure and remap our various experiences of the unknown, offering a context of the reinterpretation of this experience. Perhaps our fundamental encounter with a sense of the unknown comes to be resignified as "sexual difference" in a way that importantly structures our identity. But our experience of difference need not be reduced to sexual difference. This is a more plausible interpretation than that which deems original our encounter with sexual difference. Irigaray presents sexual difference as a formal structure of respect for the unknown, as the difference that is the most demarcated in all societies. Once Irigarayan sexual difference becomes a conceptual means or device to realize a culture of respect for the unknown, there is less motivation for the reduction in her own work.

Just as Irigaray has argued previously in her work for the cultivation of a culture of sexual difference, she now argues that a culture of cultural difference needs to be cultivated: "[W]e still lack a culture of between-sexes, a culture of between-races, a culture of between-traditions" (139). Relationships between sexes, races, and traditions constitute the fundamental character of our life, she argues, but this is insufficiently valued. We need to cultivate an ethical framework for the negotiation of these relationships. While we praise multiculturalism, we devote insufficient ingenuity to cultivating the ethical, legal, and economic means for the negotiation of relationships between sexes, races, and traditions.

Affirming multiculturalism does not necessarily allow the complex cultural work necessary to develop structures that address and help individuals live with its complexities. To return to the debate discussed in chapter 3, usually white Australian support for reconciliation with the Aboriginal population has lacked the serious commitment and particularly the institutional commitment to negotiating structures allowing an adequate exchange between Aboriginal and white Australian legal structures. Indigenous Australian land rights claims are subordinated to a British-originated legal structure of land ownership, wrongful theft, and compensation. Financial compensation has been inadequate, and there has been a failure to grapple with the problems involved in the interaction of different understandings of law, land occupation and ownership, responsibilities and rights, identity and hospitality, forms of compensation and forgiveness.[8] Irigaray is right that a culture of cultural difference is lacking in such contexts. A culture of cultural difference is not reducible to the affirmation of multiculturalism. It is a will to meet the conceptual and practical challenges faced by those engaged in cultural co-habitation and, according to Irigaray's argument "the complexity of human identity, the multiplicity of its subjective facets, its relational aspirations and difficulties, its need for objective contexts in order to develop individually and to live together in peace" (2002, 139). While a politics of recognition might call for the acknowledgment of cultural difference, an Irigarayan politics imagines institutional structures of mediation justified by their fostering of identity transformation toward maximal diversity. She asserts the inadequacy of any institutional politics of recognition that will not think along these lines.

To some extent, Irigaray repeats her model for a thinking of sexual difference in thinking about cultural difference. In order to have a strong *entre deux* in relations of cultural difference, she argues that there need to be rules, norms, ethics, and the cultivation of traditions. "The modifications to carry out are, moreover, multiple and complex," she writes. "It is a question therefore of defining an objective framework thanks to such transmutations can be realized without destructuring civil community" (137). For example, she continues, while the state has much to say about property rights, "the law has not been very explicit about its role as regards the defence of the identity and the dignity of citizens, of their access to the symbolic world, of the relations between them." The state operates more on the level of having than being, she notes (138).

Yet Irigaray's work seems unable to formulate this argument without idealizing eastern cultures, partly because of its interconnection with Irigaray's denunciation of the West: "Unfortunately, most patriarchal philosophical and religious traditions are like this: they have replaced life with speech without assuring the necessary connections between them" (2002, 53, translation modified).[9] In brief, she does tend to pit east against west and to credit eastern cultures with a better relationship to everything from breath to silence. For this reason, an important shift occurs where Irigaray finally turns to discuss limitations, as she understands these, in her vision of eastern cultures (2002, 49), after several highly utopian depictions of the east in *I Love to You*. This shift does temper, to some extent, our sense that the orient is merely serving as a screen for an idealizing projection facilitating Irigaray's analysis of western culture.

The point is not that Irigaray is any better placed to offer critical judgment of the hierarchical structures surrounding practices such as yoga than to revere those practices. But her reverence suggests a failure of attentiveness, a construction of an Irigarayan imaginary of the east with which she should have as little sympathy as she does with idealized images of the eternal feminine. For this reason her acknowledgment that prostitution, violence, and murder against women occur in India is important—not, of course, because we would turn to Irigaray's writings to learn about India, but because it suggests some willingness on her part to think in more complicated ways about her own imaginary ideal. Eventually, she offers a strong critique of contemporary practices of yoga, both western and Indian. She opposes representations of yoga that seem to promote the cessation of thought. We need, she writes, to relearn how to think, not to promote a nonintellectual embodiment in exchange for a disembodied intellectuality. She criticizes the hierarchical nature of yoga's traditional master-student structure and the tendency to avoid a thorough philosophical exchange of ideas in association with the practice. Yoga instructors are as prone as other teachers to exclude certain questionings of their practice as unwelcome or inappropriate. She questions the marginal role of women in relation to the traditions of yoga. Women tend not to be represented as teachers with a valuable knowledge to impart (2002. 67), and stereotypes about the role of women are often consolidated. "I expect," she writes, "yoga to help develop this horizon of sexual difference, through taking account of our body and our psyche as women and as men. I fear that yoga practitioners are moving more in the direction of sexual difference's neutralization" (69, translation modifed).

Irigaray is surely right to sacrifice the cordon she occasionally erects in her work between phallocentric western culture and an idealized eastern culture more respectful of sexual difference. However, her attempt to criticize the thinking of sexual difference attributed to Buddhism and yoga incurs its own problems. The situation is not greatly improved as long as Irigaray assumes that "west" and "east" require the same kind of deconstruction. The reasons one might question a neutralization of sexual difference, and the meanings such a neutralization might have, are not necessarily similar within western and eastern traditions. There is no recognition on Irigaray's part of the inevitably different cultural stakes involved in the thinking or the foreclosure of sexual difference in these different contexts. Insofar as this is the case, the traditions and meanings associated with the thinkings of sexual difference, and those associated with the failures to think of sexual difference, begin to be reduced to each other on a global scale. Her failure to engage in this kind of speculation does lead to an overall impression that she has homogenized these traditions.

So what of the arguments made by many of Irigaray's commentators, beginning with Margaret Whitford, that Irigaray's later, simpler work needs to be interpreted in the context of her earlier formulations of sexual difference? What does this mean for the later work on cultural difference, for which it might be said that we are not provided early, more complex formulations? We need to consider what an Irigarayan philosophy of cultural difference could be. As I asked, are we to understand cultural difference in Irigaray's work as based on an aporia of recognition, as are her formulations on sexual difference?

While some may wish to consider whether an Irigarayan model of the aporia of recognition has a contribution to make to debates about post-coloniality and multiculturalism (and I would not want to deny this possibility), it is evident that Irigaray does not consider cultural difference to be entirely analogous to her thinking of sexual difference. Consider, for example, her remarks on the difference between the mystery and the secret of the other. In "Le souffle des femmes" (1996b, 199), she interrogates the question of possible relations between women. Women should, she writes, respect the singularity, the specific history, and the "secret" of the other woman. But she goes on to qualify that the secret of the other woman is not the same as the "mystery" of the other gender (*genre*).[10] Differences among women of different cultures and races, generations, classes, and contexts are thereby qualified as the domain of the secret. By contrast, Irigaray qualifies as the domain of mystery the relationship of irreducibility she attributes to relations between the sexes. She does not apply the same notions of difference (those of mystery and those of the secret) to sexual difference and to relations of cultural and race difference.

This distinction between the secret and the mysterious could be given both a positive and a negative interpretation. Perhaps it avoids a problematic conflation of sexual and cultural difference. While the thinking of their disjunction is inevitably inadequate, the gesture might nevertheless act to counteract the assumption that they are to be thought as same, and opens the text more to the acknowledgment that they are not the same. On the negative side, it might be said that Irigaray reconsolidates here a hierarchy she discussed in previous chapters, that between different kinds of difference. The secret is subordinated to the domain of the mysterious in the passage cited above.

This returns us to the fundamental paradox of a politics of the impossible. Irigaray uses the language of mystery and the unknown to describe

176 A Politics of Impossible Difference

the sexually different other. But her prose has often demonstrated the tendency to think it does know and can indicate the other. At the very least, it might be said that her writing is insufficiently traversed by an engagement with this problem. Have we not already made our assumptions when we designate alterity in terms of the other of sexual difference? How can we identify the other sex, while retaining the signification of mystery, for example? These are not easy criticisms of Irigaray. She does deem sexual difference a mystery, and does have to name it to say so. But a strong philosophy of mystery must negotiate with its own aporia. One of the fundamental problems of a philosophy of mystery must be its inevitable tendency to assume the knowledge and recognition it wishes to counteract. How is this problem to be addressed? This is a serious problem, as Irigaray has sometimes acknowledged in her philosophy of sexual difference, but one she has wished less to address in her recent work.

Perhaps cultural difference is not sufficiently theorized by Irigaray as impossible? True, Irigaray does speak in the name of the possibilities for the identities and ethical relations relating to cultural difference that would arise from intersubjective reform. But she also refers to multicultural life as if it were the simple reality with which our social and political institutions have not yet caught up. Also her work has been repeatedly grounded in the unproblematic assumption of her knowledge of other cultures, implying a belief in the possibility of transparency also seen in some of her comments on friendship discussed in chapter 8.

Irigaray's claim that sexual difference traverses all cultures[11] and is the primary difference presupposes the translatability of sexual difference from one culture to another and their transparency to Irigaray. The tendency to suppose transparency has intensified as Irigaray has come to write more extensively about her experiences of Indian culture and philosophy. Though her work on sexual difference was notorious for its apparent naming of women and sexual difference, it also contained the qualification that Irigaray was resistant to such a naming and in fact deemed it impossible. Perhaps one might greet with more sympathy Irigaray's desire to depict her positive experience of Indian culture if it too operated in tandem with the recognition that the depiction is impossible. Irigaray's finely constructed work in the philosophy of sexual difference—its attention to the point that we must name sexual difference, and that we cannot name sexual difference—is not reiterated in her approach to race. We can only speculate what an Irigarayan politics of race that maintained this politics of negotiation between inevitable and contradictory positions—both politically critical—might look like.[12]

Like Ellen Armour and many others, Pheng Cheah considers that the status of sexual difference changes in Irigaray's later work. "Is the same notion of sexual difference still operative after *An Ethics of Sexual Difference?*" He continues, "It seems to me that there, Irigaray's idea of sexual difference changes dramatically, and it is formulated as a generative interval that exists between the two sexes" (Butler and Cornell 1998, 27). The concept of sexual difference as the interval has given rise to concern generally because it seems to posit difference as lying between two subjects, rather than at the heart of subjects. Does Irigaray consider that sexual difference does or would lie between men and women, and if so, has she reinstated the subjects between whom difference lies as self-present identities?

Irigaray conceives of genre as a sensible transcendental in which a relationship and continuity with the infinite is enfolded within us at our heart. Think of a woman as constituted as a woman only by the differences from all other women and as a man as constituted only by the differences from all other men. This is genre, thought of as a vertical relation. Then imagine a relation between a man and a woman or between a woman and a woman. An interval lies between them, which consists of the fact that each is situated and situates him or herself among the infinite series that is their sexuate genre. This is the difference of genre, thought of as a horizontal relation between two subjects, each of whom also operates as part of a vertical axis of relations. The encounter between two women still takes place in the context of the situation of each among the infinite series of women, and the relationship is still mediated by the interval of genre, in this sense. Irigaray is clear that relations between women require mediation, just as do those between men, and between men and women. She theorizes one's relation to sexuate genre as providing the possible domain of mediation. An interval of difference between two subjects (provided by the fact that each, in encountering the other, simultaneously situates him or herself in the context of the infinite series that is his or her sexuate genre) does not mean that either of the subjects should be understood as an identity. The fact that difference lies between does not mean that it must be understood as lying between two identities.

The infinite is not for Irigaray an ideal, divine realm from which we are severed. We enfold the infinite within us at our heart, in our relationship to and *in our situation* in the context of genre. This means that as a relation to genre, sexuate identity is not fixed, not a stable entity, nor that in which we are reflected. It is an infinite series to which we bear an avowedly deferring, rather than fixed, relation. An interval exists, not between two subjects but between provisional points in series, each of which is the site of a ceaseless deferral of sexuate identity, rather than its static presence. In arguing that we are mediated by genre, Irigaray imagines that sexuate identity is always deferred but in a way we can both avow and affirm.

Rather than identifying with static identificatory ideals from which we are severed, we can affirm deferral as an alternative, positively unstable location of sexed subjectivity. Cheah proposes that it is the fact that there must be two sexes that amounts to the "trace of the other in us, the constitutive trace of sexual alterity" (Butler and Cornell 1998, 28). I think this emphasis in Irigaray's work can be questioned, within the terms of her own argument. In fact, the trace of the other in me as a woman situating myself in the context of *sexuate* genre is, on Irigaray's account, the trace of other women. I have questioned the intermittent tendency to situate wonder between the genres. An alternative conclusion to draw from her work is that wonder occurs between subjects who are mediated and distanced by their different relationships to and situations within genre. In the light of this chapter, an additional disadvantage of Irigaray's tendency to situate wonder between the genres (given that she limits these to two sexuate genres) is that not discussing wonder between those who locate themselves as belonging to different cultural backgrounds or races seems negligent. Whether or not wonder is the most useful thematic in these contexts, Irigaray's privileged restriction of wonder to the domain of sexual difference can still be questioned. And the failure to consider that one's relationship to race and cultural identity might serve a mediating and differentiating function analogous to that of genre must similarly be questioned.

This book began with the juxtaposition of two 1999 publications: Okin's *Is Multiculturalism Bad for Women?* and Irigaray's *Between East and West*. It closes by adding to this pair a third work from the same year, Gayatri Chakravorty Spivak's *A Critique of Postcolonial Reason*. Spivak has long posed questions about Jean-François Lyotard's "pagan," Roland Barthes's "Japan," Michel Foucault's "Maoist," Julia Kristeva's "Chinese Woman," Hélène Cixous's "Indonesian" and "Indian." What might be Spivak's response to the "India" presented in Irigaray's recent publications?

In a discussion of Irigaray, Kristeva, and Cixous in her well-known early essay "French Feminism in an International Frame," Spivak had argued against supposing the relevance of French feminism to third world contexts. ("I am suggesting, then, that a *deliberate* application of the doctrines of French High 'Feminism' to a different situation might misfire" [Spivak 1988b, 141]). But the essay's conclusion, and her later "French Feminism Revisited," also question the presumption that Irigaray's philosophy is irrelevant to non–Western European contexts. She writes of the possibility of "exchange between metropolitan and decolonized feminisms" (1993b, 144). Simply to deem "metropolitan feminism" as "white feminism" is to forget that migrants and diasporics also engage in "deconstructive subversion" (160) and "want to inhabit the national subject by displacing it" (145). Is one not fetishizing the figure of the Other if one expects Algerian feminist Marie-Aimée Hélie-Lucas "only to listen to purely 'traditional' Algerian things?" (157).

In "French Feminism in an International Frame," Spivak had emphasized the relevance of reflections on the excess of the clitoris and female pleasure in third world contexts where poor women are defined as mere reproductive subjects, both the constituents and the producers of the "cheap labour that the multi-national corporations employ" (1988b, 153). Again, in "French Feminism Revisited," Spivak also reminds us of the possibility that a non–Western European woman might find a use for the Irigaray who rereads Lévinas or Plato, for example when her country's "domestic/international political claims" deploy a "teleological talk" that "turns into unacknowledged, often travestied, articulations of the Plato of *The Republic* or *Laws*" (1993b, 171).

In *A Critique of Postcolonial Reason,* Spivak's few references to Irigaray, and to her project of sexuate rights, remain sympathetic in tone (Spivak 1999, 247). We can assume that Spivak finds more of use in Irigaray's reflections on sexuate rights than in her depictions of India. It is easy enough to note Irigaray's reliance on an East/West opposition. She is to be added to those French intellectuals who can be characterized thus: "French theorists such as Derrida, Lyotard, Deleuze and the like have at one time or another been interested in reaching out to all that is not the West because they have, in one way or another, questioned the millennially cherished excellences of Western metaphysics. . . . In spite of their occasional interest in touching the other of the West, of metaphysics, of capitalism, their repeated question is obsessively self-centered" (Spivak 1988b, 136–37)

Surely, Irigaray's recent writings about India must be added to this group. But it may be hard to do so in a way that adds either to our appreciation of the useful aspects of her work, or to the field of postcolonial and race studies. At one point in her second essay on French feminism, Spivak (1993b) cites Irigaray's comment, "[W]ho or what the other is, I never know. But this unknowable other is that which differs sexually from me" (165). Again, Spivak reads Irigaray generously, finding the ways in which she works best. Irigaray's emphasis on the unknowable, sexually different other can be deployed, Spivak notes, as an intervention into Lévinas's supposition that the erotic does not accede to ethical signification. To be sure, Spivak notes the Christian inflections of Irigaray's discourse. She interrogates the latter, "Is this a new regulative narrative?" and answers: "Perhaps so. It is hard for me to enter this garden." (169). But again Spivak puts Irigaray to work, not presupposing the irrelevance of French feminism to the non–Western European reader. Spivak reminds us that whatever her own response, there should be no romanticizing assumption that Hélie-Lucas does not wish to enter Irigaray's garden.

Still, we can imagine how Irigaray's work could be enriched by questions prompted by Spivak. Just as Spivak (1999) has analyzed the dependence of European philosophy on the figure of the "native informant," one could argue that some of Irigaray's recent directions have become increasingly dependent on her figuring of the East. Spivak has asked western philosophers from Kant to Marx a question that we can in turn ask of Irigaray's discussions of India: Who is Irigaray's native informant? To follow another theme from Spivak's work, we might suspect that the subaltern is doubly displaced in Irigaray's work. First, Irigaray seems to suppose India's transparence to her interpretation. Second, the subaltern woman seems particularly silent in these Irigarayan readings of Indian culture. While we would doubtless be concerned to see her suppose that contemporary Indian feminist writing could be taken to represent a collective, generalized subject ("women in India"), it is startling to see her make feminist criticisms of the status of sexual difference in some aspects of Indian culture without reference to local activism and feminist writers, about which Spivak's *A Critique of Postcolonial Reason* provides some guide and suggestions for reading. One might conclude of Irigaray's work on India that "[w]ithin the effaced itinerary of the subaltern subject, the track of sexual difference is doubly effaced. . . . If, in the contest of colonial production the subaltern has no history and cannot speak, the subaltern as female is even more deeply in shadow" (Spivak 1999, 274). Spivak's work prompts questions of the form: Who is the other woman who disappears from Irigaray's work?

But Spivak's work does not only offer the means with which to interrogate these aspects of Irigaray's work critically. She also offers some possibilities for their interpretation otherwise. For example, I have questioned Irigaray's apparent supposition that a politics of impossibility might have a different status in the politics of race than in the politics of sex. I suggested that Irigaray would also err in supposing an equivalent status. Spivak emphasizes that the marginalization of race has not followed the same trajectory in the history of philosophy as the marginalization of sex. Philosophers have offered eloquent, extended arguments for the exclusion of women. This is not true of the central position attributed to the white European: "[T]he discontinuity between sex- and race-differentiation is one of the arguments of this book. When the Woman is put outside of Philosophy by the Master Subject, she is argued into that dismissal, not foreclosed as a casual rhetorical gesture. The ruses against the racial other are different" (Spivak 1999, 30). Perhaps, therefore, the counterruses are also appropriately different.

What if we return to Irigaray's countering of the history of philosophy's marginalization of women? Rereading the history of philosophy, Irigaray asks what notions of woman and femininity are intolerable in particular contexts. This project is viable because philosophical arguments have repeatedly been put about women's appropriately marginal role. What, I asked, if the history of philosophy is reread from the perspective of its othering of race, following the lines of Spivak's 1999 project? What if Irigaray were to interrogate the notions of race and cultural difference, the figures of the savage, the native, and the colonized, which seem to be most tolerable and most intolerable in particular philosophical contexts? What if her interrogations of the place of women occurred in this context? Spivak has argued that the most absent subject would then emerge as the subaltern rural woman, the poorest woman. And in the light of Spivak's powerful work, it is hard not to conclude that Irigaray simply fails to see the poorest rural subaltern woman as the most impossible subjectivity in the canon she rereads.

But this is not to say that Irigaray could simply "extend" to a reading of race exactly the same configuration she has offered for her reading of sex. Spivak prompts our reflection on the possibility that these projects do not work in the same way. Irigaray is able to diagnose the elaborate arguments made about the status of women because philosophers have formulated those arguments extensively. Through close readings, she is able to imagine them otherwise. Spivak's point is that elaborate arguments have not been made to the same extent about the status of natives, savages, colonized subjects. Instead, one tends to see "casual rhetorical gestures" (Spivak 1999, 30) of dismissal. It may be that these exclusions do not allow the same kind of elaborate rereading and diagnosis proposed by Irigaray, the same chasing of zigzagging logic. Furthermore, could one imagine positive, invented, hypothetical notions of race difference, reinserted into these texts, so as to serve displacing, disruptive, and creative functions? Despite Spivak's reiterated interest in Irigaray's work (including, most recently, Irigaray's writing on sexuate rights), and the affiliations between their methodology seen in their interpretations of what it is impossible to say about the woman or the native informant in particular cultural and textual contexts, Spivak has had no interest in reproducing the more controversial aspect of Irigaray's project. At the risk of putting the point coarsely, it is hard to imagine Spivak formulating a bill of native informants' rights. Perhaps Irigaray is right to have refrained from extending her approach to sexuate rights to her discussion of multiculturalism and cultural difference? At the least, Spivak's work can help our reflections about why Irigaray, particularly as she has turned to consider what she terms "multiculturalism," has not offered equivalent strategies for her politics of sex and cultural and race difference.

Finally, their different use of the terms "secret" and "trace" help clarify the light Spivak's work sheds on Irigaray's recent project. In closing, I return first to the figure of the "secret" as discussed by Irigaray. As we saw, she distinguishes the "mystery" between women and men from the "secret" of cultural difference, the latter located in the relationship we might see between two women of different races or cultural backgrounds ("Il importe de respecter la singularité de l'autre femme, son histoire, son 'secret,' même si celui-ci n'équivaut pas au 'mystère' existant dans la relation à l'autre genre" [Irigaray 1996b, 199]). In *A Critique of Postcolonial Reason,* we also see Gayatri Spivak use the term "secret" to refer to a relationship with the other woman, the woman of another racial or cultural context. But in Spivak's case, this other woman is the subaltern woman, and "I"— the I of this relationship—am the metropolitan feminist. Spivak's reflections on the secret are more extensive. The secret, she elaborates, is "not what we wouldn't tell, but what we would, desperately tell" in the context of some impossibility of communication or representation (Spivak 1999, 384). Communication is always at the limit, impossible, because there is never the fully self-present, self-transparent consciousness who communicates his or her intention to a receiver who receives it with equally transparent understanding. But Spivak's use of the term "secret" marks the special impossibility that may arise in a postcolonial situation. The intentions of a subject and the context in which those intentions form are overdetermined by a history that is both colonial and patriarchal. Transparency of understanding will not be achieved with good intentions and attentive listening. It is better to be attentive to the necessary limits of understanding, achieved through respect for the "secret" that must escape the best efforts of the well-intentioned. Responsibility, suggests Spivak (1999), might be seen in this question: "how to *earn* the 'secret encounter' with the contemporary hill women of Sirmur'" (273, my emphasis).

When Spivak discusses the secret, this other woman is not someone belonging to another cultural background, with whom I enter into negotiating dialogue. There is much more preventing the possibility of this dialogue than Irigaray wishes to consider when she depicts Indian culture. Even if we earned each other's trust, we could never rely on transparency of communication. Spivak asks both how the metropolitan feminist may earn trust, and also how she can respect this necessary excess. Spivak's reflections occur in the context of the crucial question formulated in "French Feminism in an International Frame" (1988b): How can the metropolitan feminist "learn from and speak to the millions of illiterate rural and urban Indian women?" (135). This is to query the other woman and the native informant imagined by Irigaray when she depicts "India."

We can also query the identity of the woman (and the man) imagined by Irigaray in the multicultural couple. How shall we understand Irigaray's supposition that the secret between women of different cultures is not at the level of the mystery between sexuate genres? I think the reason Irigaray makes this supposition is that she confines the parameters of the "multicultural" to those sharing a metropolitan, western context. In Spivak's work, the secret is not similarly curtailed in its scope. Nor is it compared to (or distinguished from) the mystery between men and women. One of the best questions Spivak's work is able to direct at Irigaray relates, therefore, to the status of the secret.

This book ends, then, with two figures of relational difference. On the one hand, the allegory of mystery between a metropolitan man and woman that I have diagnosed in Irigaray's work as a "transparent" mystery: Luce Irigaray and Renzo Imbeni. On the other, the allegory of the nontransparent secret between Spivak, the metropolitan feminist intellectual, and the "contemporary hill women of Sirmur" counted among the poorest women. It does not occur to Irigaray to ask the kind of questions formulated by Spivak, such as "how to earn the 'secret encounter' with the contemporary hill women of Sirmur.'" Irigaray's texts do not acknowledge that this is the encounter she would need to earn. And the deeply complex analyses offered by Spivak for which the term "secret" stands in—analyses of the reasons why the speech of subaltern woman and the contexts in which she is heard may be so overdetermined by a history of colonization and patriarchy that it may be naïve to assume she can "speak" to the metropolitan feminist or that the latter can hear her—do not appear on Irigaray's horizon. But surely they should, in a contemporary French intellectual's reflections on India.

We saw that for Irigaray, the "constitutive trace of sexual alterity" is the "trace of the other in us" (Cheah in Butler and Cornell 1998, 28). I have asked who must be absent so that Irigaray's multicultural man and woman can form their couple. If we are dealing with a metropolitan couple, they are the product of a history of immigration and/or coloniality. Who must be absent so that this couple can be present? Perhaps it is the ancestors or the family, or those poorer, less mobile? What sustains the multicultural encounters of those in the western metropolis? This man and woman are certainly sustained (economically, if not historically and culturally) by the third world workforce sustaining a first world economy. The day-to-day existence of the multicultural couple, and their place at the forefront of Irigaray's politics, are possible because of invisible others, elsewhere. The metropolitan multicultural couple bears the trace of those others, elsewhere.

While Spivak identifies the trace of the impossible, absent other who makes possible this western multicultural subject, Irigaray identifies the trace of impossible sexual difference that makes possible their relation. An analysis of these traces—that we might clumsily name "Irigarayan" and "Spivakian"—should be intertwined. If not, the former becomes the trace of the latter. We have seen that sexual difference should entail the differential relation with all the other women (or men) belonging to one's genre—those of different races, nationalities, cultures, classes. But in the practice of Irigaray's writing, the scope of subjects remembered and discussed by her, particularly as she reflects on multiculturalism, is limited. It is in the difference between the thinking of these traces—those articulated by Irigaray and those articulated by Spivak—that we can locate one of the imperative questions for Irigaray's later work.

Conclusion

Luce Irigaray generates a feminist politics through the affirmation of a concept of sexual difference as both possible and impossible, without and (in the form of its own exclusion) within culture. Her recommendation is that political and public policy for which difference is a value not be restricted to the politics of recognition. Social reforms might be understood as positive and legitimate in terms of their possible contribution to the reimagination and reinvention of difference. Such a politics need not be grounded in an empty affirmation of any and every kind of difference. Irigaray's work suggests that we should attend most to those differences that hegemonic cultural forces are most invested in excluding. These are not, of course, confined to sexual difference, and this is a point Irigaray has come to recognize increasingly in her most recent work. An Irigarayan politics committed to the invention of difference invents not arbitrarily, or out of "thin air," but on the basis of overinvested exclusions identified in a specific cultural context.

I have discussed how Irigaray's project conjoins a politics concerned about the exclusion of alternative possible formations of difference in the texts of the history of philosophy with a politics concerned about the one-to-one relations between friends and lovers. In both contexts, Irigaray is concerned about the appropriative nature of our treatment of difference. A masculine-oriented history interprets the feminine in self-serving ways, appropriating alternative, excluded possibilities for the feminine. A self-oriented subject interprets the friend and lover in self-serving ways, appropriating alternative, excluded possibilities for the friend or lover. In chapter 8, I asked if all our encounters with friends and lovers are inevitably narcissistic and self-serving. Irigaray offers an ideal image of a mediated, peaceful, loving, differentiated, and nonhierarchical relationship between self and other. Certainly, we can interpret this ideal in many ways. For example, it can be seen as emphasizing the impossibility of such a relationship. Perhaps it acts to provoke us to reflect on the reasons for this impossibility. We may also wish to ask whether it is the right ideal. Perhaps an emphasis on the inevitability of aggression, appropriation, and narcissism and the need for us to avow and negotiate these forces would be more appropriate? Certainly, insofar as Irigaray understands sexual difference, friendship, and love to be appropriative, she also imagines that our figurings of women, friends, and lovers bear the trace of exclusion of their broader possibilities, which are simultaneously acknowledged and disavowed by us.

Irigaray imagines a couple able to encounter each other as different. She does not imagine that the identities of participants in the emblematic "two" would ever be static, accomplished, or complete. The relationship of a woman or man to their genre leaves each mediated by an infinitely displaced and deferred series of relational differences. Yet that differentiating, relational field does envelop and sediment around subjective points: subjects or selves. Irigaray will then value their capacity for self-love rather than—for example—for a self-loathing that seeks compensation from the other. These sedimented subjects are produced by difference, but they are produced. Irigaray does not imagine a static, accomplished subject. Neither does she imagine a radically decentered, entirely disseminated and fractured nonsubject. Identity is produced by infinite, never accomplished differential relations, but it is thereby produced. Positively valued and institutionally reinforced, identity is imagined by Irigaray as a structure for which we would not be perpetually seeking furtive compensation. As we have seen, she understands this model of identity to be an important alternative to identification, which leaves us too dependent on orthopedic props from which we are severed, and for which we make subordinated others pay the price.

What of genre? The field of genre is so infinitely displaced and deferred that one must ask whether it makes sense to imagine two series of differentiated, displaced genres, "two" separate genres. What would secure the boundaries of these genres as "two." Why two? One answer is that "two" corrects the supposition of "one" genre, a sex-neutral genre of humanity. Instead, we imagine two subjects encountering each other, each mediated by his or her belonging to the infinity of dual never-accomplished sexuate genres. Kelly Oliver (2001) has pointed out that the "two" is significant as an alternative to Hegel: "[T]hese two are . . . not equivalent; their differences cannot be sublimated in a Hegelian dialectic. . . . Recognition requires that we are two different beings, inaccessible to each other, and yet able to communicate because of what is between us" (208). Oliver offers a positive account of this model of sexual difference as irreducible, but suggests that "it is just a strategic opening onto other irreducible differences. . . . [H]er emphasis on *two* sexes [is] a strategic move to open up multiplicity. . . . [I]n order to get multiplicity we first must have two" (209). Irigaray does situate relation to multiplicity at the heart of each genre. Still, she seems very resistant to conceptualizing multiple (rather than two) genres. This reluctance has important implications for her understanding of cultural difference. Cultural difference and race difference are not analogous to sexual difference, in her thinking. In this sense, Irigarayan sexual difference both does and does not offer a strategic opening onto other irreducible differences. It does in two senses. First, genre embodies the multiplicity of women and supposedly acknowledges their differences. Second, a positive (and institutionally reinforced) relation to genre would supposedly promote less appropriative relations with others. My relations to other women are less likely to be narcissistic and identificatory, less subordinate to the fields of sameness, more open to the possibilities of difference if I have a positive relation to genre. But Irigarayan sexual difference does not offer a strategic opening onto other irreducible differences, since she does not conceptualize multiple cultural and racial genres as succeeding an initial period of situating oneself in the field of sexuate genre. This is very clear in Irigaray's comments on multiculturalism in *Between East and West.* Sexuate genres would allow for more multiplicity, more difference, less racism, even a multicultural culture— but sexuate genres would not lead to the advent of cultural genres. I have questioned this aspect of Irigaray's work.

Irigaray imagines two sexed entities, each relating to his or her sexuate genre, who might encounter each other nonhierarchically as different and new. They need not be a man and a woman. However, it is the relationality of each to his or her sexuate genre and their mediation by that relationality that allows each to be more receptive to the other as new. We have heard passages from Irigaray's work that emphasize the importance of relating to the other as unfamiliar. At times, Irigaray argues that because they are situated in two different genres, a man and a woman have a more privileged relation to alterity and the new than do two men or two women. But in *Between East and West,* Irigaray also clarifies that the relationality of each to his or her sexuate genre and their mediation by that relationality allows each to be more receptive to the other's newness. That is, she clarifies, as much the case between subjects of the same sex as between a differently sexed couple. Crucially, she also considers it to be the case for subjects of different races and cultures.

Debating the politics of recognition, Kelly Oliver and Judith Butler have discussed as a problem how a subject encounters the new. As Oliver (2001) has written, "The tension between recognizing the familiar in order to confirm what we already know and listening for the unfamiliar that disrupts what we already know is at the heart of contemporary theories of recognition. How is it possible to recognize the unfamiliar and disruptive? If it is unfamiliar, how can we perceive it or know it or recognize it? These questions are related to the question of how we experience anything new or different. Conceptually, these questions seem to lead to paradoxes or aporias that can leave us with the belief that we experience newness only through what we already know and therefore that we cannot experience newness at all." And yet, Oliver asserts, "we do experience newness and difference. How could we possibly become functioning adults if we didn't? If we always experienced the world only in terms of what we already knew, then we couldn't learn anything at all. We would remain infants unable to make distinctions and therefore unable to function" (2).

Oliver notes that the paradox emerges partly from the conception of the subject who is taken to encounter difference. The subject is positioned prior to that encounter with difference, as if it is a stable and self-identical, discrete identity. It is considered a sameness machine, able to encounter the other only through the subordinating lens of its own machinery. Difference is taken to be subordinate to an identity or at least a cognitive field of the self, posited as original. Identity is then opposed to difference. An alternative, Oliver and Butler emphasize, is to see the subject as always already mediated by difference. As Butler (1998) writes, casting "alterity beyond the domain of the thinkable . . . reconstitute[s] the radically alien character of 'the other,' and continue[s] to cover over the ways in which the 'other' may well be more properly a constitutive part of the self than first appears" (43).

What does Irigaray have to contribute to this debate? Up until her most recent work, we have seen that she conceptualizes openness to two kinds of newness. She discusses one kind in terms of sexual difference. Our history has excluded alternative possibilities for sexual difference and disavows these greater, excluded possibilities. She discusses the other kind in terms of relations with friends and lovers. We exclude alternative possibilities for friends and lovers, just as we exclude alternative possibilities for sexual difference. Our relations with lovers, friends, those of the same and the other sex are traced by the exclusion of these possibilities. Irigaray does not conceive alterity as alien. She does not consider the subject a machine subordinating all to sameness, in such a way that difference and alterity must be alien to it. On her model the subject disavows and excludes alternative possibilities for difference. It is precisely for this reason that the subject is not alien to but intimate with the possibility of alterity. I think this model is consistent with very abstract conceptualizations such as that suggested in chapter 7 of excluded alternatives of sexual difference. Elizabeth Grosz proposes in *Volatile Bodies* (1994b) the model of a body inverted outside in, whose "outside turns over on itself to become the inside" (160). Irigaray's work suggests that this image can be used to imagine subjects who, because their constitution is premised on the exclusion of alternative possibilities for what they recognize, enfold that infinity within their parameters as excluded (im)possibility.

Irigaray also offers a therapeutic concept of identity. She proposes the idea of relation to genre as potentially therapeutic because it would not commit us to excluding particularly overdetermined alternative possibilities. For example, the exclusion of alternative possibilities for sexual difference is particularly overdetermined by the identification with ideals for masculinity. A subject mediated by its relation to genre *resists being enclosed upon its own identity, or situating alterity as foreign.* Mediation by genre would be mediation by foreignness. In addition, Irigaray hypothesizes, relation to genre would allow a better openness to foreignness. Commenting on political ideals of transformational dialogue, Butler (1998) writes: "[F]or there to be dialogue, does there not have to be a certain notion of 'distance.' . . . [T]o speak and to hear you [is] a chance that may be as much conditioned by what separates us as by any common set of presuppositions we might have. Is it not the case that what divides two interlocutors may be as necessary to the possibility of conversation as what implicitly binds them together?" (46). Irigaray's position is in some ways consistent with this view. We know to what extent she privileges the possibility of conversation between two. The conversation whose possibility she imagines is one in which I listen to you "as to another who transcends me" (Irigaray 1996a, 116). Many would argue that difference always, inevitably, lies between us. What divides us is necessary to the possibility of our conversation. Situating Irigaray in this debate, we see she takes a different position. She thinks conversations have not been taking place. We have not been listening to the other "as to another who transcends me." We have been reducing the other to our dimensions of sameness, self-understanding, and presuppositions. Irigaray argues that in our apparent dialogues there has been an absence of communication. She agrees that we need division for communication, but disagrees that we have sufficient psychic, subjective, and institutional structures to allow adequate division. She imagines how our mediation by our relationship to genre could promote sufficient division between us to foster the distance between myself and another subject that would allow for qualitative communication, both between those of the same sex and those of the opposite sex.

Once the most positive aspects of the Irigarayan project have been identified in these terms, Irigaray's work also opens itself up to criticism. It does not always sustain its own concept of difference as impossible. Irigaray's work is stronger, I have argued, insofar as it acknowledges its lack of foundations and theorizes sexual difference as the "to come" of which our culture bears the possible/impossible trace. Sexual difference lacks identity, fixity, and foundation. This kind of conceptual instability is philosophically valuable. I take one of the most useful aspects of Irigarayan philosophy to be her theorization of sexual difference in terms of a constant swinging movement between impossibility and possibility.

However, at times Irigaray does refer to sexual differences as a self-identity in a way that breaks with and potentially paralyzes that swinging motion. Many readers of her work have had the experience of finding this rather paralyzed notion of sexual difference amidst an inventive philosophical project with which they are highly sympathetic. The reader may feel that sexual difference should not be paralyzed in this way and that the Irigarayan text teeters unstably between its own commitment to an unstable sexual difference (swinging between possibility and impossibility) and its references to a stable sexual difference frozen in possibility and the "there is."

Is such paralysis inappropriate or infelicitous, some kind of erring on the part of the author? If we think so, we erect an imaginary, ideal Irigaray who need not and should not paralyze sexual difference. I think this is a common response to her writing. Do we hope to save the author from the most troubling, unstable moments of her own arguments? To what extent is the instability between the swinging (which I take to be philosophically crucial) and the paralysis itself critical to Irigaray's philosophy? One tends to think that Irigaray's philosophy works despite, not because of, its own occasional moments of paralysis. But perhaps the better reading of Irigaray's work might sympathetically attend to its tendency to paralyze a notion of sexual difference that should be perpetually swinging between possibility and impossibility. One assumes that Irigaray sometimes falls short of the best deployment of her own best concept. But why suppose that the concept of impossible sexual difference that one might value as coherent and operative can be abstracted from, and exists independently of, the moments of paralysis to which, in Irigaray's work, it seems to be regularly attached? The intermittent paralysis in Irigaray's work may serve as a crucial reminder that self-undermining, rigidity, and appeals to identity inevitably haunt such politics. While philosophical texts are not unmodifiable or fixed structures, it may not always make sense to interpret them as abstractions from their own internal trouble. Should we tactfully isolate the warring elements? Can one abstract a notion of impossible Irigarayan difference (which I value) from its own self-undermining and moments of paralysis? Could one not defend a notion of difference while recognizing its tendency to paralysis, and negotiate with that tendency?

I have questioned the approach taken by Irigaray to Sartre and Merleau-Ponty in *To Be Two*. She considers their exclusion of alterity and sexual difference, but not (as she does in her early work) how such failures themselves fail, thereby opening themselves up to the advent of the new: the possibility of an alternative thinking of sexual difference. Reading for inevitable failure can open up the possibilities apparently closed down by a text's own norms and declarations. One of the most productive aspects of Irigaray's work is the analysis of the double, impossible movements by which philosophical and social texts foresee as a possibility what they exclude. I have argued that one of the most valuable aspects of Irigaray's philosophy of sexual difference is its association with the development of this methodology. And I have also suggested a reading of Irigaray's work that is consistent with this methodology and inspired by it. An appropriate and constructive reading of Irigaray must listen for her failures, her exclusions, and so the trace and advent of the new in her own work. This may be the most positive reading we can offer of the status of race and cultural difference in both her earlier and more recent work. It offers a means to think about the contribution of an Irigarayan philosophy of sexual difference to a philosophy of race and cultural difference that goes beyond the actual comments about multiculturalism made in the late work.

Many feminist readings have agreed with Irigaray's diagnosis that Merleau-Ponty relies in his work on the depiction of a sex-neutral body. Nonetheless, many commentators (Young 1990; Diprose 1994; Olkowski 1999) have also emphasized that Merleau-Ponty's theory of embodiment is useful to feminism. It emphasizes that we interpret from an embodied position. We are not psychic forces interpreting the world, objects and others. We are bodies inhabited by bodies and interpreting bodies. We are social interpreting bodies mediated by social meanings and possibilities for our embodied existence. It is in such terms that Iris Young (1990, 146) has explained the way many girls experience their bodies more in terms of the "cannot" than of the "can," as in the phenomenon of "throwing like a girl" discussed in chapter 7.

One might speak of the different relationships to mobility, agility, and embodiment of boys and girls, men and women. In this book, I have considered an alternative approach to sexual difference. Throwing a ball and all other kinds of spatial comportment bear the trace and enfold the exclusion of alternative possibilities for embodiment. Irigaray's philosophy of sexual difference is not based in claims about the differences between men and women: for example, how do they use language differently, or manifest a specific motility and agility. While she does sometimes discuss such data, Irigaray considers them to be illustrative of the absence, not the presence, of sexual difference.

What is the relationship between embodiment and impossible sexual difference? Irigaray understands lived embodiment to express the absence of sexual difference and to be traced by that absence. Lived feminine embodiment, as Dorothea Olkowski has emphasized, is the limitation of or impingement on alternative possibilities forestalled in advance. The sense of awkwardness or feeling that one "cannot" manifests negative meanings for one's embodiment. It also manifests the exclusion of alternatives and a sense that the range of alternatives has been impinged upon. One lives a bodily knowledge that broader ranges of activity will easily place one in the categories of the implausible, the nonsensical, the unintelligible, or the ridiculous.

Anticipating the future otherwise is not something we do as minds or neutral bodies. We do it as bodies mediated by lived social meanings. This is one of the reasons Irigaray places considerable importance in her early and later work on imagining alternative meanings for the feminine body (including the two lips sexuality, the placenta as mediation, the inviolable status of virginity). Can we open up new political and social possibilities without refiguring the body? she asks. The suggestion is that new futures, political and social, are maximally anticipated by bodies whose diversity of possibility is least impinged on.

Until very recently Irigaray's work has offered a fairly exclusive focus on sexual difference. Her work has seemed inattentive to questions of race, racism, and cultural difference. Addressing women's own racism, misogyny, and forms of appropriation of the other (such as narcissism, jealousy, and violence), Irigaray has suggested that they might be related to women's poor relation to identity. Crudely put, she argues that if women had a less impoverished relation to gender identity, they might be less impelled toward racism, sexism, and the marginalization and exploitation of other women. Race relations would not, by this explanation, be marginalized in a philosophy of sexual difference, but would be addressed by it. She seems to think that a culture of sexual difference might allow better race relations. In *Between East and West*, a philosophy of sexual difference is depicted as already a philosophy of multiculturalism. But it is clear that a philosophy of race or cultural difference is not given the status in her work of a philosophy of sexual difference. Irigaray does not add to her interest in sexuate genre an interest in the development of diverse cultural or racial genres. In other ways also, Irigaray has continued to be a philosopher who emphasizes sexual difference most strongly throughout her corpus. Her analyses of historical philosophers have asked what notions of sexual difference seem to be excluded from their writings. She has never offered readings of Nietzsche, Plato, Hegel, or Kant that ask what notions of race or cultural difference are excluded from their texts. Clearly such a project would be possible along the lines of her methodology. But she never undertakes it. In this sense among others, it is clear that sexual difference has the priority in her work.

It is intriguing to consider the possibility of an Irigarayan approach to race and cultural difference inflected by the terms of her approach to sexual difference. In the essay "No-One's Land," Genevieve Lloyd adds to her earlier study of the gendered connotations of reason a discussion of the raced connotations of reason and property. How must we retell the history of philosophy from this perspective? For Emmanuel Kant and John Locke the indigenous represents "a lesser stage of human development." Think of how "the Lockean analysis of property and the Kantian temporalization of reason come together to rationalize European presence as embodying the most fully human way of relating to the land" (Lloyd 2000, 33, 34). Bhikhu Parekh (1999) adds that the belief that nonliberal communities should be coerced to assimilate to liberalism "informed J. S. Mill's attitudes to the native peoples, the Basques, the Bretons, the Scots, and the Francophones in Quebec, and formed the basis of his justification of British colonialism in India and elsewhere. Alexis de Tocqueville shared his view" (69). Charles Mills (1997, 64) has analyzed the extent to which the social contract as discussed in the work of Hobbes, Locke, Rousseau, and Kant was implicitly a racial contract. And Gayatri Chakravorty Spivak (1999) recounts how the figure of the native is needed "in Kant . . . as the example for the heteronomy of the determinant, to set off the autonomy of the reflexive judgement, which allows freedom for the rational will; in Hegel as evidence for the spirit's movement from the unconscious to the consciousness; in Marx as that which bestows normativity upon the narrative of the modes of production" (6). Spivak suggests we think of the native informant as both needed and simultaneously foreclosed in the history of these philosophical texts.

We can reconstruct how the history of philosophy has represented race and associated reason and property with the European white rational man. Irigaray would encourage us to ask, in tandem with such a reconstruction, how the history of philosophy has not represented the indigenous, cultural difference, the stranger, the colonized, and the immigrant.

What modes of indigenous identity are excluded by the available options of sameness versus difference? How have we always not been thinking cultural difference? An Irigarayan approach would propose a genealogy not just of what has been said about race and cultural difference throughout the history of philosophy, but of what that history has not wanted to say about race and cultural difference. Such a genealogy would ask what notions of difference have been possible (both racist and egalitarian) in the history of philosophy, and also what notions of difference have not been possible. Such a project will not follow exactly the same pattern as Irigaray's analysis of the impossibility of sexual difference. But a genealogy of the unsaid about race and cultural difference in philosophers from Plato to Merleau-Ponty and Lévinas and later, about the stranger and the racially different other, is no less timely than Irigaray's work on sexual difference, and I take it to be the unsaid of her work.

Notes

Chapter 1. Sexual Difference as a Basis of Equality

1. In the late nineteenth and early twentieth centuries, there had, however, been a sustained and sometimes militant campaign for women's rights (in particular the right to vote) in which well-known feminist intellectuals and activists such as Louise Weiss and Madeleine Peletier had participated.

2. Beauvoir herself did not identify as a feminist until the 1970s, by which time feminist organizations including the MLF (Mouvement de libération des femmes, or Women's Liberation Movement) had proliferated in France. Beauvoir then publicly allied herself with them (Schwartzer 1984, 32). This was a period when feminist political activity in France spanned reformist movements and radical separatist feminisms; the publication of a range of journals (including *Choisir, Nouvelles féministes, Le quotidien des femmes, Questions féministes, Sorcières, Revue d'en face, des femmes en mouvements, Le torchon brûle,* and *Cahiers du GRIF*); the activities of at least two feminist publishing houses (Editions des femmes and Tierce); the agitation for women's rights, economic, professional and social equality, legalized abortion and other legal reform; and the literary output of a diverse range of well-known feminist intellectuals such as Hélène Cixous and Luce Irigaray. An overview of developments in French feminism over the twentieth century can be found in the two introductions to Elaine Marks and Isabelle de Courtivron's anthology *New French Feminisms* (1981). For a history of pre- and early-twentieth-century activity, see Scott 1996 and Offen 2000. Important from the 1970s onward are a series of post-Marxist and postexistentialist feminist theorists and writers influenced by psychoanalysis and poststructuralism and interested in avant-garde literary practices. One of the genres of feminist intellectual activity that developed at this time is sometimes termed *"écriture féminine"* or "feminisms of difference." Many writings that represent this genre are included in *New French Feminisms,* which introduced translations of work by late-twentieth-century French feminist intellectuals such as Cixous, Kristeva, and Irigaray to an English-speaking audience. Other anthologies have since appeared. These include Claire Duchen's *French Connections* (1987) and her overview *Feminism in France* (1986), both of which seek to temper the excessive weight that Duchen argues is attributed in *New French Feminisms* to those radical French feminisms "preoccupied with questions of psychoanalysis and language" (Duchen 1987, 12).

3. For a discussion of her feminist activism, see the interviews with Beauvoir included in Schwartzer 1984 and in particular the discussion at 32–33.

4. Again, see the anthology of this name edited by Marks and Courtivron (1981).

5. This said, some commentators have noted exceptions to that aim within Beauvoir's work. For an interpretation that brings to light alternative themes in Beauvoir's work, see Bergoffen 1997.

6. Chanter (1995) provides an extremely clear discussion of the relationship between Beauvoir's and Irigaray's work.

7. Throughout this work I draw frequently on Irigaray's identification of her politics as impossible. I refer the reader to Ewa Ziarek's focus on the importance of impossibility as an Irigarayan thematic in her *An Ethics of Dissensus* (2001). Ziarek associates impossibility with "contradictions, conflicts, incompleteness— in the formation of all identities" (153). Sexual difference is the actualization of the negative in the subject, but in this rereading of a Hegelian model, the negative does not lead to a more accomplished spirituality (164). On Ziarek's reading, sexual difference is impossible partly because it can never be identified in positive terms (152). By contrast, she points out that in a psychoanalytic context one might say that sexual difference is impossible insofar as it is "what is excluded from the domain of symbolization" (154). Ziarek goes on to offer a complex analysis that synthesizes both concepts of impossibility (164), also noting the paradox that "the impossible of the sexual difference is fundamentally linked to the *possibility* of becoming, to the affirmation of the future, transcending present limitations" (154), and thus linked with "the disruptive temporality of history" (157).

8. For her discussion of whether or not "feminism is back in France," see Le Doeuff 2000a.

9. Again, Michèle Le Doeuff has been a particularly acute analyst of the relationship between France's role in European and international politics and its fickle expressions of "state supported feminism." See Le Doeuff 1991, 1995, and 2000a.

10. In the Bibliothèque Marguerite Durand, Paris, the archived dossier on Michèle Le Doeuff contains an unpublished long version of a letter of 1 July 1992 sent to the newspaper *Le Monde* in which she objects to the reference in the Maastricht treaty to the *"droits de l'homme"* agreed by European convention in 1950, when divorce, contraception, and abortion were illegal in many European countries. She writes, "Maastricht is not a step forward for the construction of European political union. It is an arresting of the gradual integration of women's rights into the concept of the rights of the person. European women merit better than an old-fashioned convention that protects the rights of Man, and that dates back to the period preceding the proliferation of women in the political space." Le Doeuff goes on to protest the fact that the Maastricht treaty does not address local and customs restrictions on contraception dissemination and abortion within the treaty countries.

11. The 1974 Veil law is widely believed to have legalized abortion in France, and is referred to in *New French Feminisms* as the "repeal of the law forbidding abortions" (Marks and Courtivron 1981, 26). But as Le Doeuff explains in *Hipparchia's Choice* (1991), "[U]nder the law passed in 1920, which has not been repealed, and still constitutes article 317 of the Penal Code [*code pénal*], abortion, information on abortion and propaganda—meaning advertising—for contraceptive products are still offenses under the law. Two family planning activists were charged with them in January 1988, for giving out addresses of foreign

clinics. The Neuwirth law, which permits the prescription of contraceptives and their sale in chemists, and the Veil law which permits abortion in certain circumstances, are simply dispensations, and quite restricted at that, in relation to the law of 1920" (247, translation modified).

12. A recent issue of the journal *differences* is devoted to translations and debates from the French parity movement. See "Special Section on Parité in France," ed. Joan Scott, *differences* 9 (2) (1997): 69–142.

13. See Le Doeuff 2000b.

14. But the story is not so simple, and this tradition has always been grounded in a "self-evident contradiction" (Scott 1996, 3). As Scott points out, "From the Revolution of 1789 until 1944, citizens were men" (ix). The very tradition on which France's egalitarian principles were founded excluded in its eighteenth-century origins women from participation as citizens owing to "the weaknesses of their bodies and minds, to physical divisions of labor which made women fit only for reproduction and domesticity, and to emotional susceptibilities" (ix). Accordingly, as Scott narrates, "[i]n the age of democratic revolutions, 'women' came into being as political outsiders through the discourse of sexual difference" (3). Since the eighteenth century, women philosophers such as Olympe de Gouges have had to contend with women's exclusion from citizenship "legitimated by reference to the different biologies of women and men [and] 'sexual difference' . . . established not only as a natural fact, but also as an ontological basis for social and political differentiation" (3). Scott goes on to argue that this thinking grounded feminist discourse of the day in paradox: "Feminism was a protest against women's political exclusion; its goal was to eliminate 'sexual difference' in politics. . . . To the extent that it acted for 'women,' feminism produced the 'sexual difference' it sought to eliminate" (3). Charles Mills (1997) offers a close analysis of the founding of eighteenth-century egalitarian discourses in the exclusion of non-Europeans. He reminds us that the exclusion of other races and cultures provides the historical condition of equality between European white males.

15. However, it is worth citing Margaret Whitford's reserve (1991a) regarding Irigaray's attempted "greater accessibility": "[H]er later work is in some ways as difficult to understand as her earlier work, for the simplified statements cannot simply be taken at face value. Their meaning depends on the complex analysis and infrastructure of the earlier work" (11–12). More recently Tamsin Lorraine (1999, 92–93) has strongly endorsed this argument.

16. On this point see Bono and Kemp 1991, 12–13 and 109.

17. Subsequent chapters will raise the problem of whether such politics are too instrumental, assuming that desired social change would follow from proposed linguistic or legal modifications.

18. Take, as an example, Irigaray's proposal that there should be a proliferation in the public and private sphere of positive images of women. This leads to her suggestion at one point that domestic households and public spaces should display positive images of mothers and daughters, or of biblical women such as Anne, Mary, Ruth, and Naomi (see Irigaray 1996b, 198), or important and inspiring women represented in an interconnected genealogy. What significance should we derive from the fact that Irigaray's suggestion for "putting up public images of mothers and daughters to counter negative publicity surrounding this

relationship" (Lorraine 1999, 92) seems to us somewhat simplistic? Some of Irigaray's proposals work best turned on their head. True, the suggestion seems weak if we are to suppose that the simple display of such images will lead inevitably to positive social change, particularly of the radical kind sought by Irigaray. This said, what significance is to be derived from the fact that western societies are particularly impoverished in their public display of positive intergenerational images of women?

19. Rosalyn Diprose's *The Bodies of Women* (1994) problematizes models of women's subjectivity and embodiment formulated in these terms.

20. For a positive and sympathetic interpretation of the social and feminist efficacy of the Dworkin-MacKinnon ordinance, see Lacey 1998, 89–92.

21. Drucilla Cornell (1995, 235) cautions that we should not be overconfident about the capacity of the law to ensure social change.

22. This said, many forms of injunction and prohibition can also be seen as contributing to the construction of new identities, or opening up such possibilities.

23. This supposition would be the Irigarayan equivalent of Carole Pateman's argument that the social contract is implicitly a sexual contract. Margaret Whitford and Eva Ziarek have both drawn attention to similarities between points made in this regard by Carole Pateman and Irigaray. See Pateman 1988; Whitford 1991b, 174–75; and Ziarek 2001, 173.

Chapter 2. Irigaray on Language

1. This said, it is not that Irigaray considers subjects who do not suffer from dementia to be fully functioning as subjects of enunciation, entirely in control of their statements. She agrees that we are all of us spoken by language as much as we speak language.

2. The results of this research, first published in 1967, are included in Irigaray 1985a, 35–53, 81–116, 189–221.

3. A smaller version of a similar approach is seen in *Parler n'est jamais neutre*, when all responses of schizophrenic subjects in a particular study are listed. See Irigaray 1985a, 92–103.

4. For a definition of phallocentrism as the representation of women in terms of the same, the opposite, or the complement, see Grosz 1989, xx. The chapters on Irigaray in this book offer further elaboration and an excellent introduction to her early and middle period work.

5. For an analysis of different forms of scientific writing in particular, see "Is the Subject of Science Sexed?" Irigaray 1989a.

6. Irigaray's focus on the self-contradictory and unstable nature of traditional representations of sexual difference is further discussed in Deutscher 1997, 75–86.

7. This point has been thoroughly debated in Irigaray commentary, often in the context of argument about Irigaray's essentialism. A widely recognized essay on this problem is Naomi Schor's "This Essentialism Which Is Not One" (1994).

8. For a comprehensive discussion of Irigaray's interpretations of these philosophers, see Chanter 1995. For a discussion of Irigaray's treatment of Nietzsche

and Heidegger, see Lorraine 1999 and Mortensen 1994. A discussion of Irigaray's interpretation of Merleau-Ponty is to be found in Vasseleu 1998 and Olkowski 1999. Vasseleu (1998), Chanter (1995), and Stella Sandford (1998) are among those who have written of her interpretation of Lévinas. A discussion of Irigaray on Plato is to be found in Butler 1993 and also in Walker 1998.

9. Ironically, this leaves her a potentially stronger supporter of parity than Michèle Le Doeuff (see Le Doeuff 1995 and 2000a).

10. [Evidemment, le langage ne se présente pas immédiatement sous cette forme.]

11. For a discussion of this material, see Schwab 1998.

Chapter 3. Rethinking the Politics of Recognition

1. For example, Margaret Whitford (1991b, 170) has argued that Irigaray's project could usefully be framed by Rousseau's account of the political pact, since, like Carole Pateman (1988), Irigaray analyzes women's exclusion from the social contract between male citizens. Bono and Kemp (1991) point out that one of the distinctive features of the "Italian 'reading' of Irigaray is that she is not regarded as an abstract theorist at all, but as a deeply *political* thinker, whose work . . . is extremely concrete and attentive to the actual contexts of women's lives" (12–13).

2. Again see Bono and Kemp (1991) on the Italian interest in Irigaray's work: "Her attitude is understood as it is reflected in her images of multiplication and openness, in her call for all women to give voice to their difference, and differences, in dialogue" (13).

3. See for example, Brown 1995, 19: "According to objects relations theorists (Nancy Chodorow), feminist developmental psychologists (Carol Gilligan), feminist economists (Julie Nelson), some French feminists (Luce Irigaray), and some North American cultural feminists, women inhabit a different moral, psychological, cultural or nascently political universe than men, with different sensibilities and concerns."

4. In *Witnessing: Beyond Recognition* (2001), Kelly Oliver also offers a critical reading of the politics of recognition. The language of recognition can act as a "symptom of the pathology of oppression" when the victims of oppression crave recognition by their oppressors (9). She also asks whether the politics of recognition is inadequate to the experience of that which is beyond recognition. In other sections of her book, Oliver writes extensively of bearing witness to the Holocaust, in which it may be as important to recognize that its horrors are beyond recognition as to recognize them. In his essay "Race, Multiculturalism, and Democracy" (1998), Robert Gooding-Williams also argues for a modification of our understanding of the politics of recognition. He resists the model according to which the one is dominated, the other dominating, with recognition bestowed by the former on the latter. Gooding-Williams criticizes Charles Taylor's model for a separation of cultures, which insufficiently acknowledges that a dominating culture is already mediated and constituted by a dominated culture. He calls for new modes of self-recognition by marginalized cultures. Irigaray's work bears some relation to these reflections. She argues that male culture is mediated

by femininity in a variety of ways. She would sympathize with those who reject the separation of cultures implied in some versions of the politics of recognition. And, as will later be seen in her concept of "genre," she also calls for new forms of self-recognition, connected to a concept of transformation of sexuate identity. She also argues that sexual difference cannot be recognized, although she sometimes calls for its (paradoxical) recognition. In this sense, she argues for recognition of the nonrecognizability of sexual difference. However, the reason is not that sexual difference is beyond representability. Instead, it is because of the anticipatory structure of sexual difference. In *Witnessing* (2001), Oliver discusses Irigaray's *I Love to You* in these terms, arguing that recognition in Irigarayan sexual difference is a recognition of that which is beyond recognition.

5. The author of *In a Different Voice* (1982), Carol Gilligan is well known for her controversial findings that in situations of moral reasoning, women tend more toward a contextualizing and "care"-based approach, where men tend more toward the application of abstract principles. Gilligan does not investigate the question of how these differences might be explained, or how approaches to moral reasoning or sexuate identity might be reinvented or reshaped. She argues that subjects should not be subjected to a sex-neutral evaluation of the adequacy of moral reasoning, which privileges abstract-principle-based reasoning as a more advanced form of moral development, and according to which women's care-oriented tendencies might systematically (if indirectly) appear as inferior.

6. Taylor takes this issue up further in *The Ethics of Authenticity* (1991). Because identity depends on my relations with others rather than being inwardly generated, Taylor sees the equal capacity to develop one's own identity as an important component of equality. Recognizing difference, he suggests, is really recognizing the equal value of different ways of being (51). In this sense, "authenticity" involves creation and construction as well as discovery (66).

7. In addition to Carol Gilligan and the ethics of care, feminist theory discussed by Tully (1995) includes Lugones and Spelman's notion of differentiated difference (1990) (which he describes as a notion of criss-crossing, overlapping cultural differences); a postmodern disintegrative notion of difference referenced to a discussion by Linda Alcoff (1988, 49); and the work of Genevieve Lloyd (1984, 50).

8. Fraser (1997) examines the way in which a politics of recognition has come to compete with a politics that emphases the primary importance of issues of redistribution. She argues against the bifurcation of these issues, since justice "requires *both* redistribution *and* recognition" (12).

9. "Every colonized people—in other words, every people in whom an inferiority complex has been created by the death and burial of its local cultural originality—finds itself face to face with the language of the civilizing nation; that is, with the culture of the mother country. The colonized is elevated above his jungle status in proportion to his adoption of the mother country's cultural standards. He becomes whiter as he renounces his blackness, his jungle" (Fanon 1970, 14).

10. The ruling of *Mabo v. Queensland* [No. 2] (*Commonwealth Law Reports*, vol. 175, 1992, p. 1) was formulated as follows: "Native title has its origin in and is given content by the traditional laws acknowledged by and the traditional customs observed by the indigenous inhabitants of a territory. . . . Where a clan or

group has continued to acknowledge the laws and (so far as practicable) to observe the customs based on the traditions of that clan or group, whereby their traditional connexion to the land has been substantially maintained, the traditional community title of that clan or group can be said to remain in existence" (Chesterman and Galligan 1999, 261).

11. While Reconciliation Sheet 10 (Native Title) at *www.austlii.edu.au/au/ special/rsjproject/rsjlibrary/car/infosheets/Inf_sht10.html* acknowledges that "native title is held by Aboriginal and Torres Strait Islander peoples who have maintained a continuing connection with lands or waters, in accordance with their traditions," it reminds in full, "Connection may involve responsibilities for the land in ways not envisaged by western systems of land ownership. Connection may be maintained in cultural or spiritual ways other than physical association."

12. To give just one example of this inadequacy from an extensive literature on the subject, Iris Young (2000) points out, "Before the British began to conquer the islands now called New Zealand . . . there was no group anyone thought of as Maori. The people who lived on those islands saw themselves as belonging to dozens or hundreds of groups with different lineage and relation to natural resources" (90). Young goes on to argue that only with the advent of colonization could the similarities among these groups become newly significant in their opposition to the English. In this sense, identities understood as "Maori" that arose after colonization may represent transformation as much as conservation of identity, but they are no less the crucial locus of rights activism.

13. Many speeches given under the auspices of the Council for Aboriginal Reconciliation have espoused the language of recognition and respect for cultural difference, equity, and social justice issues. Nevertheless, reinvention is also affirmed as a good. Patrick Dodson (2000, 271), for example, affirms the right to develop distinct indigenous "characteristics and identities" as well as the right to maintain them and see them recognized and respected. Raymond Gaita (2000) has suggested that the "vagueness" of the concept of self-determination is critical since it gestures "toward an outcome whose full conceptual character is unforeseeable" (285–86).

14. Consider, in this regard, one of his early speeches: "I contend that the Malays are the original and indigenous people of Malay and the only people who can claim Malaya as their one and own country. . . . Settlers willing to conform to the characteristics of the definitive citizen will in fact become definitive citizens. . . . But these rights and privileges do not include changing the characteristics of the definitive race" (Mahathir, cited Teik 1995, 27).

15. For a comprehensive study of this point, see Langlois 1999.

16. See Langlois 1999, and also, for an anthology of essays which debate the issue, Bauer and Bell 1999. Teik (1995) argues that Dr. Mahathir scorned efforts by overseas labor organizations to "instigate [workers] to demand high wages and better working conditions" in the name of his opposition to "infringement on the sovereignty of small nations" (64).

17. For an interpretation of her discussion of female embodiment in these terms, see Gallop 1988, 94–99. Commentators commonly emphasize the mimetic nature of Irigaray political project. A good discussion of Irigaray's politics of mimesis is to be found in Whitford 1991b, 71–72, and in Schor 1994, 66–67.

18. As Nancy Fraser (1997, 11) has pointed out, many theorists worry that issues of identity and recognition have taken the place of concern about redistributive justice. But these concerns are, as she points out, interlinked, and the one domain cannot be pursued without impact on the other.

19. Irigaray emphasizes the uniqueness of the mother-fetus relation in terms of a specifically ethical relation whose emblem is the placenta. On this, see Irigaray 1993b, 38–44, and for a discussion of this material, see Weinbaum 1994.

Chapter 4. Irigarayan Performativity

1. For an account, in the context of feminist philosophy, of the difference between performatives thought of as illocutionary and as perlocutionary, see Butler 1997, and also Langton 1993, discussed by Butler.

2. For example, Lacey (1998) points out, "What is distinctive about projects such as those of Irigaray and Cornell is that they operate first and foremost at an imaginative and rhetorical level. . . . [T]hese kinds of projects are primarily interested in the shape and dynamics of the institution of language" (234). And then, "rhetorical strategies . . . presuppose an understanding of how . . . discursive and material practices and changes interact, of how power flows through the social body. [Their legitimacy] . . . depends upon the development of institutionally oriented social theoretic insights. Without this, . . . they [cannot] attain any understanding of what their effects may be" (237).

3. See in particular hooks 1992; Phelan 1993; and Butler 1993.

4. This is the position taken by hooks (1992) on Livingston's 1991 documentary about New York–based drag balls at which largely African American and Latino competitors performed in highly varied and specific categories (business executives, soldiers, models, high school prep types, and so on) aiming to achieve the effect of "realness." For some critics, including Peggy Phelan in her essay "The Golden Apple" (in Phelan 1993), spectators of the film experienced a denaturing of categories of realness when viewing the juxtaposition of shots of the drag "walkers" enacting categories such as "the business executive" and shots of "real" executives in the street also relying on artifice and posture. For further critical discussion of the film in relation to issues of subversion and performance, see Butler 1993, and for her very critical reading, see hooks's essay "Is Paris Burning?" (in hooks 1992).

5. For example, it lacks extensive discussion of other contemporary feminist theorists both in France and elsewhere, and also lacks discussion of theorists of race, cultural difference, and postcolonialism.

6. In *Excitable Speech,* Butler is not discussing Irigarayan sexuate rights but the issue more generally of performativity and revolutionary change.

7. Many have resisted this interpretation of deconstruction, finding that its value is precisely in its complication of politics, its questioning of the desire for political certainty. For a particularly helpful discussion of these different figurings of the politics of deconstruction, see Grosz 1997.

8. Where Cornell insists on Derrida's analysis of law as "feigning presence" (Cornell 1992b, 157), I am arguing here that Irigaray sometimes formulates her sexuate rights so as not to "feign presence." This is the difference between an ar-

gument that *exposes* law as grounded in mystical foundations and one that *affirms* Irigarayan rights as similarly grounded.

9. Lynne Huffer (1995, 27) criticizes feminist theorists of performativity, particularly Judith Butler, for eliding the "key ethical questions." She contrasts this material with the work of Luce Irigaray: "Unlike Butler, Irigaray places ethical questions at the center of her consideration of epistemological problems of identity and truth" (21). Others, for example Krell, discussed above, have suggested that the problem with this kind of politics is precisely that it presupposes a capital G Good, which presupposes its own justification. What justifies a politics of sexual difference? I disagree with Huffer's pitting of Irigaray against Butler in terms of their commitment to ethics. In this chapter, I suggest that Butler's analysis of the politics of performativity can be helpful in thinking about the status of Irigaray's sexuate rights, precisely because it helps to displace a reading of them as simply justified by the truth of sexual difference.

10. "While the intended liberatory aims of feminist and queer performativity are laudable, performative theory tends to be flawed by its disregard for ethical questions." Huffer 1995, 21.

11. "A politics which denies the relevance of its own effects may fairly be accused of some degree of irresponsibility," suggests Lacey (1998, 237).

Chapter 5. Sexuate *Genre*

1. In French grammatical contexts, the term *genre* can be used to express adherence to the masculine, or the feminine, or the neutral category of things. Thus the *genre* of *la table* in French is feminine. Alternatively, *genre* is artistic style or type, as in *genres* of poetry. Or it can refer to a category, a class, or a subdivision. The first meanings given by the *Petit Robert* dictionary are those of race and the ensemble: thus, *le genre humain* is the ensemble of the human race. Irigaray's use of the word *genre* is usually rendered in English translations by "gender." The translation is misleading in one respect. The distinction between sex and gender is not significant in French as it is in English.

2. In English *genre* is translated by at least two terms: "genre" as used in English for a kind or style of art or literature, and "gender." While the first meaning given for gender by the *Oxford English Dictionary* is "Kind, sort, class; also, genus as opposed to species," and the second is grammatical gender, the *O.E.D.* goes on to specify, "In mod. (esp. feminist) use, a euphemism for the sex of a human being, often intended to emphasize the social and cultural, as opposed to the biological, distinctions between the sexes." This euphemistic use does not exist in French partly because the connotations of the English "gender" do not align with those of the French *genre*. More recently, however, French feminist contexts have begun to adopt the term *genre* to translate the English feminist usage of "gender." The cause may be the absence of a better French equivalent. Alternatively, the term has been adopted following English usage to refer to a distinction between sex and gender. A recent comment from Elisabeth Roudinesco is telling in this regard: "les uns pensent que l'homosexualité est une culture, à la manière d'un genre *(gender)*, une identité construite, les autres affirment qu'elle est innée, voire génétique, instinctuelle" (Derrida and Roudinesco 2001, 72). The insertion

of the term "gender" is Roudinesco's, not my own. Although Roudinesco is referring to a French debate, she explains that by *genre,* she means the English term "gender." The important point is that Irigaray's use of the term *genre* predated the recent French adoption of the term seen in Roudinesco's comment. Irigaray is not adhering to a sex/gender distinction, and she does not select *genre* as the best option to render "gender." Some attention needs to be paid to the variety of connotations the term has had in French to understand the linguistic play she intends in using the term. Given that the English term supposes a theoretical distinction between sex and gender not supposed in Irigaray's French usage, *genre* as used by Irigaray is best left untranslated.

3. Compare with Judith Butler (1998), who emphasizes the following concept of identification: "If efforts to make such identifications are never fully successful, is the failure to identify that results from every such effort a significant one? In other words, does the failure to achieve the norm of identity not expose the incommensurability between the norm and any of its embodiments, and does the exposure of that incommensurability not open up possibilities for a rearticulation of the norm itself?" (45). Butler takes the very fragility of identification to open up possibilities for a rearticulation of norms. Irigaray seems to agree with this kind of point, but pursues it through arguing for the need for alternative identity structures.

4. Despite its potential as a critical intervention into models that depict the girl's inevitable turning from the mother to the father, Gail Weiss criticizes Irigaray's depiction of the mother-daughter relation. Surely, she argues, Irigaray overlooks the way in which the mother-daughter and mother-fetus relation is itself always already mediated "before, during, and after the pregnancy" (Weiss 1999, 123). Irigaray herself may well agree, turning as she does to an emphasis on the placenta as figure of the mediation between mother and fetus in *je, tu, nous* (1993b, 37–44). See also Weinbaum 1994: "Irigaray suggests that women stop thinking of . . . the mother/daughter relationship as one of pathological fusion. What is so significant about her renarrativization of this relationship is that it effectively sees the maternal body as a relational situation . . . the mother as a site that instantiates the possibility of an ethical relationship between two subjects" (109).

5. On this point, see in particular Whitford 1991a, 71. Margaret Whitford offers a definitive presentation of Irigaray's relationship to psychoanalytic theory.

6. As Jacqueline Rose reminds us, "Lacan is careful to stress, however, that his point is not restricted to the field of the visible alone: 'the idea of the mirror should be understood as an object which reflects—not just the visible, but also what is heard, touched and willed by the subject'" (Rose 1986, 53, citing Lacan 1949, 567).

7. See Lacan 1953 and "The Mirror Phase as Formative of the Function of the I" in Lacan 1977. Just as Irigaray's reworking of Freud involves a reworking of the oedipal narrative, Irigaray's reworking of Lacan includes a reworking of the mirror phase. For example, Irigaray also presents her own version of a mirror phase: the specular economy. In Irigaray's narrative, *negative* mirror images—reflections of what we are not—represented by the other are crucial to identity. She argues that the negative reflection constituted by femininity-as-atrophy is one of the crucial supports of masculine identity. The masculine subject looks into a

converse mirror that affirms masculine identity through a negative contrast with that feminine other which it is not.

8. Still, as Ewa Ziarek (2001) points out, "if Irigaray's work must be criticized for its inability to address antagonisms" among women, other theorists—she gives the example of Chantal Mouffe—would have to be reproached for "an equally problematic privileging of war and conflict" (175).

9. Irigaray's is a difficult and tenuous ethics because, in Jacques Derrida's words (1991), "one eats [the other] regardless and lets oneself be eaten" (114–15). Irigaray's could never amount to an ethics of nonappropriation of the other. For Irigaray, as for Jacques Derrida, "this carrying of the mortal other 'in me outside me' instructs or institutes my 'self' [*mon 'moi'*] and my relation to myself [*mon rapport à 'moi'*]" (Derrida 1995a, 321). Merleau-Ponty also reflects on such questions. Despite our tendency toward empathy, Merleau-Ponty (1962) is careful to remind us that "insofar as I can, by some friendly gesture, participate in [*participer à*] that grief and or that anger, they still remain the grief and anger of my friend Paul: Paul suffers because he has lost his wife, or is angry because his watch has been stolen, whereas I suffer because Paul is grieved, or I am angry because he is angry, and our situations cannot be superimposed on each other. If, moreover, we undertake some project in common, this common project is not one single project, it does not appear in the selfsame light to both of us, we are not both equally enthusiastic about it, or at any rate, not in quite the same way, simply because Paul is Paul, and I am myself" (356, translation modified). Thus, it might be said that in a more ethical relationship I empathize with Paul while not forgetting that Paul's pain is not my pain, nor is the idea he provokes in me entirely my own.

10. For Lacan's discussion of ego psychology, see Lacan 1988, 24–25, and for a clear overview of the deconstruction of the metaphysics of identity, and the reasons why this seems to call into question a feminist politics of identity, see Elam 1994, 70–77.

11. For a presentation and discussion of identity politics, see Fuss 1989, 99–105.

12. Irigaray could be thought of as offering a response to Elizabeth Spelman's concern in *Inessential Woman* (1988) with the possible development of a conceptual basis for understanding women as a group whose common self-identity is not presupposed: "[I]f we acknowledge that some women are Black, some are white, some are rich, some are poor, if we insist that nevertheless they all are the same as women, that differences among women reside in some non-woman part of them, then these differences will never have made a difference for feminism. For it's the 'woman' part of any woman that counts, and if differences among women can't lodge there, then differences among women finally don't really matter" (166). According to Irigaray, in belonging to a sexuate genre, one belongs to the spectrum of differences among women that reside at the heart of one's belonging to female identity.

13. Irigaray does not ask whether all women are equally in a position to contribute to sexuate genre. Is it a matter of the extent of one's access to the public sphere, media, or speaking position that can be heard? How do less visible subjects contribute equally to sexuate genre? These are specifics into which Irigaray does not venture.

Chapter 6. Anticipating Sexual Difference

1. As Ellen Armour (1999, 131) and Elizabeth Grosz (1989, 152–55) have pointed out, Irigaray is influenced in this regard by Feuerbach's account of God as a projected ideal image of man.

2. For a further discussion of Irigaray in these terms, see Deutscher 1997.

3. Saint Augustine's writing is interpreted in these terms in Deutscher 1997.

4. Among those Christian thinkers who held this view, Pagels (1988) mentions Minucius Felix (52) and Clement of Alexandria (51).

5. See Tertullian's *De Culto Feminarum* 1, 12, cited Pagels 1988, 63.

6. Horizontality is also sometimes defined as the role of ground or matter that woman plays for man in his relation with God (see Irigaray 1993a, 109).

7. See also Irigaray's "Questions to Emmanuel Lévinas" (1991b), in which she states: "It is possible to live and simultaneously create sexual love. Here would lie the way out from the fall, for in this case, love can become spiritual and divine. . . . The two genealogies must be divinized in each of the two sexes and for the two sexes: mother and father, woman and man, for it to be possible for female and male lovers *[amante et amant]* to love each other" (186).

8. I am referring to a discussion in which Caputo (2000) makes reference only to Cornell's positive reading of Irigaray. Cornell's more critical reading may have postdated his reflections.

9. Caputo (1997) refers often to this emblematic story in his reading of Derrida's work as "religion without religion."

10. See Derrida 1994, 28, and Caputo 1997, 122–24.

11. This accords with Derrida's argument about waiting for the new democracy. See Derrida 1995b, 54, and Caputo 1997, 54.

Chapter 7. Interrogating an Unasked Question

1. Irigaray's reading of Plato and her questioning of the form/matter distinction are discussed in Butler's *Bodies That Matter* (1993, 35–55). As Butler points out, Irigaray's aim is not to critique the form/matter distinction but to "show that those binary oppositions are formulated through the exclusion of a field of disruptive possibilities" (Butler 1993, 35). The feminine is thereby produced "as that which must be excluded for that economy to operate" (36). On Irigaray's reading, therefore, there is, as Butler reminds us, "a matter that exceeds matter" (47). But, as Butler concludes, "there are good reasons . . . to reject the notion that the feminine monopolizes the sphere of the excluded here" (48). "If the feminine is not the only or primary kind of being that is excluded from the economy of masculinist reason, what and who is excluded in the course of Irigaray's analysis?" (49). An interpretation of Irigaray on Plato is also offered in Walker 1998.

2. Irigaray's interpretation of the unsatisfactory treatment of sexual difference by Nietzsche is offered in *Marine Lover* (1991a). This interpretation is discussed further in Oliver 1995, Lorraine 1999, Deutscher 2000, and elsewhere.

3. For a further discussion of the status of this question in Irigaray's work, see Chanter 1995.

4. In her *Between East and West* (2002), discussed further in chapter 10, Irigaray argues that eastern philosophies have not forgotten sexual difference as has the West. However, she goes on to raise questions, also, with regard to the status of sexual difference in some contexts identified by her as eastern.

5. But what would allow us, as Derrida wrote of Foucault's discussion of madness in *Madness and Civilization*, to deem sexual difference the same essential object persisting through time? Perhaps, to pick up the terms of that discussion, this effort from Irigaray to recount the history of the exclusion of sexual difference is "the maddest aspect" of her project (see Derrida 1978a, 34)?

6. Chanter (1995) offers a close reading of Irigaray's interpretation of Aristotle in *An Ethics of Sexual Difference*.

7. For their summaries of this debate, see Schor 1994; Whitford 1991b, 14.

8. Irigaray (1993a) focuses on Diotima's discussion of love as intermediary in the *Symposium* (24), Aristotle's discussion of place as the container of the contained body in *Physics* IV (50), Descartes's discussion of wonder at the new in *The Passions of the Soul* (73–75), Spinoza's discussion of divinity as the envelope in the *Ethics*, among other readings.

9. On this point, see Duroux 1992.

10. This is a strange and interesting move on Irigaray's part because in later work, particularly in *To Be Two*, she considers a mistaken reading of the mirror phase to be one that understands it as an original subjective relation of sameness. Rather, she writes, the encounter with the other as same is also an encounter with surprise or wonder, which embodies an implicit recognition of difference. For a similar reading of the mirror phrase interpreted through the optic of Lévinas, see Vasseleu 1991.

11. I am thinking here of Caputo's emphasis (2000, 139) on the affirmative *"viens, oui, oui"* in Derrida's recent work, also discussed in conjunction with feminist theory.

Chapter 8. The Impossible Friend

1. What is also needed here is a more complex interrogation of projection, since an Irigarayan projection, like appropriation, both recognizes and fails to recognize the other.

2. Insofar as Irigaray supposes that the different occurs especially in the heterosocial friendship, she supposes that we know, locate, and name the different. By contrast, her earlier work refused to name and fix the different, except insofar as it has been excluded from culture as a possibility.

3. Irigaray is giving an "impossible" interpretation of the relationship between herself and Imbeni as emblematic man and woman. When she writes of the mutual unknowability of those belonging to different genres, she is not assuming that we do already exist in a culture of sexual difference. If this was her supposition, Irigaray would have traveled full circle, no longer situating sexual difference as the "to come," but as the here and now.

4. For a discussion of this tradition, see Derrida 2000.

5. Derrida discusses the Montaigne essay at greater length in the chapter "He Who Accompanies Me" in *The Politics of Friendship* (1997d).

6. Abraham and Torok build a complex theory around Freud's comments on "abnormal" forms of mourning such as melancholia. Freud suggests that in melancholia a part of the ego splits and identifies with the lost object. Torok and Abraham (1984) propose that this split be renamed a process of encryptment, one's psychic encryptment of the other within oneself in a "vault" carved out within the ego. As they write, in "endocryptic identification," one "exchang[es] one's own identity for a phantasmic identification with the 'life'—beyond the grave—of an object lost" (5). The lost other persists literally incorporated within my ego, such that I will often give the responses, feelings, or manifest the attributes associated with the other. As Derrida (1985) elaborates in one of several discussions of Torok and Abraham, "The incorporated dead . . . continues to lodge there like something other and to ventrilocate through the 'living.' . . . I lose a loved one, I fail to do what Freud calls the normal work of mourning, with the result that the dead person continues to inhabit me, but as a stranger" (57–58). For Derrida "the term 'incorporated' signal[s] precisely that it could not be entirely digested or assimilated" (57, translation modified). In "normal" or "successful" mourning, the dead object or other is "taken back inside the self, digested, assimilated" (57). The dead other "is taken into me: I kill it and remember it. . . . I interiorize it totally and it is no longer other" (58). But in the case of what Torok and Abraham call unsuccessful mourning, an interiorizing memorization *(Erinnerung)* "goes only so far and then stops" (58).

7. "[T]here is not narcissism and non-narcissism; there are narcissisms that are more or less comprehensive, generous, open, extended. What is called non-narcissism is in general but the economy of a much more welcoming, hospitable narcissism, one that is much more open to the experience of the other as other. I believe that without a movement of narcissistic reappropriation, the relation to the other would be absolutely destroyed, it would be destroyed in advance" (Derrida 1995c, 199).

8. Accordingly, in *Memoires* (1989), Derrida discusses interiorization in the context of narcissism. Discussing the living of the other in us in memory, Derrida suggests that this being "in us" of the other can not be "the simple inclusion of a narcissistic fantasy in a subjectivity that is closed upon itself or even identical to itself. If it were indeed a question of narcissism, its structure would remain too complex to allow the other, dead or living, to be reduced to this same structure. Already installed in the narcissistic structure, the other so marks the self of the relationship to self, so conditions it that the being 'in us' of bereaved memory becomes the *coming* of the other" (22). And again, later in the text, Derrida returns to the question of narcissism: "All that we say of the friend, then, and even what we say *to him*, to call or recall him, . . . all that remains hopelessly *in* us or *between* us the living, without ever crossing the mirror of a certain speculation" (32).

9. On this point, see chapter 4, which discusses forms of philosophy of difference governed by the politics of recognition.

10. This is an approach to Irigaray indebted to Vicki Kirby's analysis (1997, 151) of cultural and theoretical accounts of human subjects that attempt to offer "prophylactics against contagion" by that which is posited as other, whether that other be posited as machine, nature, technology, and so on. Among many other theoretical discussions of the implications of an account of the subject as already the other, see Butler 1998, discussed further in the conclusion.

11. Citing some of Irigaray's strongest comments in this regard (such as "I think that man and woman is the most mysterious and creative couple," Irigaray 1983, 199–201) Grosz (1994a) has offered a careful explanation of Irigaray's position. She points out that a refiguring of the "hostility and contempt with which women's bodies and desires are held in patriarchy" is at issue in the reshaping of cultural formations of both homosexuality and heterosexuality (347). Though acknowledging that Irigaray's work "has provoked justified anxiety on the part of gay and lesbian theorists for its refusal to accord a place to gay and lesbian relations, as it were, beyond the phallus," Grosz nevertheless proposes that Irigaray's work is not irrelevant to gay and lesbian politics (348).

12. For a useful discussion of this problematic in her work, see Jagose 1994. Jagose describes the "tendency encountered in Irigaray's work to promote but then abandon the notion of a female homosexuality in preference to that 'difficult and complex' heterosexuality, that 'most mysterious and creative couple'" (26).

13. Butler, Cornell, Cheah, and Grosz debate this question at some length in "The Future of Sexual Difference" (Butler and Cornell 1998, 28–30).

14. One could argue that on this interpretation, the heteropolitics between men and women is subordinate to a homopolitics. Precisely what mediates relations between men and women is the "homo" between women and between men: my situation within genre is what allows a relation of difference between men and women. This makes sense of Irigaray's comment "I believe that you can love the difference but only if you're also able to love those who are the same as yourself" (1983, 199–201, cited Grosz 1994a, 347–48). But this argument still locates the male-female relation as the privileged site of difference, and the same sex as the privileged site of sameness.

15. Another reading would see Irigaray as more positively rewriting the (very conventionally characterized) feminine in Lévinas's early work as the site of alterity (Lévinas 1987, 35–36).

Chapter 9. Sexed Discourse and the Language of the Philosophers

1. See, for example, among many others, Bergoffen 1997; Lundgren-Gothlin 1996; Mackenzie 1986; Weiss 1999.

2. She thereby misses the opportunity, taken up by Beauvoir scholars such as Debra Bergoffen (1997), to consider the relationship between herself and Beauvoir as feminist philosophers intervening in the phenomenological tradition as philosophers of eros. No mere oversight, this missed opportunity is, I shall argue, crucial to the composition of *To Be Two*.

3. See Irigaray 1996a, 69–95; Irigaray et al. 1987, 5–8, 81–123; Irigaray 1990. This remains one of the least discussed themes in debate and commentary about Irigaray's work; however, it receives attention in Schwab 1998.

4. Also, see Irigaray 1993c, 167–84. There are also some broader reflections on linguistics in chapters 3 and 8 of *je, tu, nous* (1993b) and in *An Ethics of Sexual Difference* (1993a, 133–40).

5. "Though her language of transcendence and immanence seems to repeat the errors of Cartesian dualism and seems to encourage patriarchy's degradation of the female body, we discover the difference between Beauvoir's thought and

traditional dualisms once we place Beauvoir's discussions of transcendence and immanence within the context of her concept of ambiguity and once we listen for the persistent, though muted, voices of her texts. Listening to/for those voices, we discover that . . . there is also the ethic of the erotic. This ethic, grounded in Beauvoir's phenomenology of the original intentional desire, acknowledges the paradigm of reciprocity as it points to another moral paradigm—the gift" (Bergoffen 1997, 185). Bergoffen's concept of the muted voice in the text is discussed further in Deutscher 1997.

6. Judith Butler comments, "I've never seen her read a woman, and I wonder what that would look like." Grosz (in Butler and Cornell 1998a, 38) replies that Irigaray does engage positively, if briefly, with Beauvoir in work prior to *To Be Two*, adding that "[s]he does have a number of texts that do address women writers: there's a text on the placenta where she is reading a woman biologist. She also reads the feminist theologian Elisabeth Schüssler Fiorenza [see "Equal to Whom?" in Irigaray 1993b]." The short preface on Beauvoir in *je, tu, nous* to which Grosz refers is particularly interesting in the light of Beauvoir's subsequent omission from *To Be Two*. Irigaray has considerable respect for the Beauvoir she sees as a foremother of feminism, but apparently does not consider her as part of the tradition of French phenomenological philosophy.

7. "All this leaves our gentlemen perplexed in their discussion of the criteria of sexual difference. But the text goes on. . . . Apparently without a problem, a rupture. Yet on this occasion as on so many others, particularly when it is a question of woman, the text will have surreptitiously broken the thread of its reasoning, its logic. Striking off on another path that will no doubt intersect with the previous one, will in some way take up where it had left off, but in a zigzag fashion that defies all resumption of a linear discourse and all forms of rigor as measured in terms of the law of excluded middle" (Irigaray 1985b, 17).

8. While Irigaray's comments here are not extensive, she draws on a point also noted by Derrida in *Adieu to Emmanuel Lévinas* (1999a). Lévinas's early work, particularly *Time and the Other* (1987, 84–85), presents femininity as the Other. By contrast, in *Totality and Infinity*, Lévinas distinguishes between the relationship with the feminine other, as the relation with eros, and alterity formulated in terms of the language of the Most High, in French the "you" as *vous*. In arguing that the most significant ethical relationship be understood as occurring between the I and the you *(tu)*, Irigaray is proposing an alternative to this step in Lévinas's work (see Lévinas 1969 and Derrida 1999a, 36–39).

9. Irigaray's philosophical debt to Lévinas is stronger than she acknowledges either here or in Irigaray 1991b. Also, she draws on some elements of Sartre's work—for example, his discussion of the generalized "we" subject (Irigaray 2001, 38–39).

10. On this, see for example Whitford 1982.

11. On this question, see among other commentators Collins and Pierce 1976 and Gatens 1991, 48–59.

12. Irigaray has never before, to my knowledge, offered an analysis of Sartre's work, with the exception of a seminar she gave at the Collège Internationale de Philosophie, Paris, prior to the publication of *To Be Two*. Her previous work on Merleau-Ponty and Lévinas appears in *The Ethics of Sexual Difference* (1993a) and in "Questions to Emmanuel Lévinas" (1991b). For a discussion of Irigaray's

reading of Merleau-Ponty in *Ethics,* see Vasseleu 1998, and see Chanter's *Ethics of Eros* for an analysis of the earlier interpretations of Lévinas. Chanter (1995, 170–224) offers an extremely helpful account of the strong influence of Lévinas in Irigaray's work.

13. For a particularly good analysis of Sartre's sexual economy of desire and sadism, see Lingis 1985, 1–39.

14. See Le Doeuff 1991, 62–75.

15. See Walker (1998, 170–75) for an analysis of Irigaray's discussion of the maternal body.

16. In other words, on just a few points an oppositional relationship between Sartre and Irigaray is misleading. Both analyze the impossibility of appropriation of the other. Both describe the other (in terms of the structure of our potential relation with the other in Sartre's case, in terms of its ontology in Irigaray's case) as fundamentally that which resists appropriation and renders it impossible.

17. Perhaps Irigaray's less agonistic, more recuperative readings of Merleau-Ponty and Lévinas in *An Ethics of Sexual Difference* reflect greater interpretative ingenuity in this regard. While these are critical readings, Irigaray's project in this work is to locate the possibility of sexual difference in these texts. For example, Irigaray interprets Merleau-Ponty's description of ideas as the "other" side of language, haunting my interior speech, remaining beyond words, "not in the sense that under the light of another sun hidden from us they would shine forth but because they are that certain divergence, that never-finished differentiation, that openness ever to be opened between the sign and the sign." Irigaray (1993a) proposes, "This never-finished differentiation might be the symptom, the secret recollection of a sexual difference that has never been achieved in language. Something that would always sing 'behind' words, like the trace of a resistance of an other that is irreducible to myself" (167).

18. These questions are reminiscent of an early debate between Irigaray and Sarah Kofman concerning the former's reading of Freud. Irigaray allows us to hear in *Speculum* the elements of Freud that undermine his own exclusion of sexual difference. But Kofman's well-known critique of Irigaray in *The Enigma of Woman* (1985) is that she took this to be entirely her work, as if the mastery of her own reading gave her mastery over the autodestabilizing elements of Freud's writing. This debate implicitly questions the boundary line between Irigaray's property and Freud's: to whom should those autodestabilizing elements of Freud be attributed? This is discussed further in Deutscher 2000.

19. Sarah Kofman, relentless in her tracking of the play of unstable masculine and feminine sexual identifications in the philosophers, would have resisted these recent Irigarayan readings most vigorously. See again Kofman 1985.

Chapter 10. Effacement Redoubled?

1. This despite the importance that is also attributed by Irigaray to relationships between women.

2. Iveković's interest in Lyotard's concept of the differend, extensively discussed in her work, is apparent in this passage. Walker 1998 offers an assessment of Irigaray in terms of the Lyotardian differend.

3. There is a difference between the themes of the *"entre deux"* and the *"être deux."* We have seen Irigaray's argument that in order to have a strong relation to the other as an "I-you" relationship, fields of mediation are necessary, such as those of law, language, religion, and one's own relation to one's sexuate genre. Thus the "two" needs to be sustained by these institutional forms of mediation that lie between the two. Another way of putting this is that Irigaray understands vertical relations (relation to culture, law, language, religion, gender) to traverse one's horizontal relations with another subject. In this sense, the field Irigaray terms vertical would cut through and mediate or lie between the relations she terms horizontal. Irigaray's theme of the *être deux* is not exactly the same. In *Être deux*, she notes the extent to which philosophers such as Sartre assume a singular subject, rather than a double subject such as the couple, as the basis of philosophical reflection on ethics and being. Most philosophers assume us to be fundamentally "one," not "two." But we can think of many ways in which we are two: as lovers, parents, and children, for example. Irigaray notes the extent to which genealogical relations (another kind of verticality) are deemphasized in many philosophical systems. But these themes of *"être"* and *"entre"* are related: to acknowledge that a singular subject is in many ways fundamentally "two" is also, on Irigaray's model, to acknowledge that relations between subjects are always mediated, that there is always the *"entre."*

4. Here I would refer the reader again to Olkowski's very helpful discussion of mediation and the interval in Irigaray's work in *Deleuze and the Ruin of Representation* (1999).

5. Oliver's discussion of these themes in *Witnessing* (2001) is very clear.

6. See on this point Margaret Whitford's essay "Irigaray, Utopia and the Death Drive" (1994). In fact, Whitford argues that Irigaray "both does and does not recognize the death drive" (382). Whitford argues that on the one hand Irigaray's work is structured by the dichotomy between life and death, but on the other hand, Irigaray's politics are directed toward an urgent concern to intervene in the travails of the death drive: "We cannot allow the vibrations of death to continue to drown out the vibrations of life" (Irigaray with Mortley 1991, 78, cited Whitford 1994, 382).

7. It is noteworthy that Irigaray's representations of cultural difference tend to cast the net of analysis around two individual subjects, because of her interest in theorizing the *entre deux*. For example, recall Irigaray's comment that "a couple formed by a white woman and a black man can, from the fact of its being multiracial, become a site of civic education." These comments are consistent with a direction evident in much of Irigaray's recent work, which interrogates the posited experiences of the individual subject and his or her relations with a specific, sexed other. Interrogating the structural support allowed the *être deux* by the culture in which we live, Irigaray asks how rich or impoverished are the relations a sexed subject may have with another sexed subject. Of what quality are the *entre deux* relations that a subject is able to have in contemporary society? Irigaray thus tends to assess the structure and representations of race, class, and gender in terms of the projected lived experience of individual subjects.

8. Elizabeth Povinelli (1996) is among the many commentators who have noted the restrictive ways in which "imaginary 'Aboriginal traditions' serve as the measure for 'legitimate' land title claims." As she notes, why "these and not

other 'traditions,' and why 'traditions' at all and not another conception of cultural continuity and change or of cross-cultural dialogue?" She adds, "'Homosexuality,' 'miscegenation,' and 'single motherhood' . . . function as signs of decay, the loss of 'specialness' in the realm of culture, and thus the loss of any basis to claim land rights in Australia. . . . [T]he non-Aboriginal government and public have not altered their understanding of their own principles of governance: the notion that ordered familial relations serve as the basis of an ordered civil society. Loosely articulated, mobile but dense, same- and cross-sex, human-human and human-land desires and affectivities have no place in an ordered society or the law that seeks to uphold it" (83, 99).

9. This is not Irigaray's only means of questioning the status of breath, silence, embodiment, materiality in western culture. In addition to appealing to the orient, she also proposes a series of disruptive rereadings of the mythology of Christian religion, in addition to the readings of historical philosophers offered in *Speculum* and *An Ethics of Sexual Difference*.

10. "Il importe de respecter la singularité de l'autre femme, son histoire, son 'secret,' même si celui-ci n'équivaut pas au 'mystère' existant dans la relation à l'autre genre" (1996b, 199).

11. In her reading of Irigaray, Patricia Huntington (1998) sets Irigaray's claim in the context of W. E. B. Du Bois's reference to the color line as the problem of the twentieth century: "Irigaray's own dictum . . . forebodes a monism doomed to conflict with a Du Boisian centering of race as the problem facing U.S. feminist theory" (233–34).

12. I am thinking of Gayatri Spivak's politics of negotiation, represented, for example, in her maintenance of the dual positions that the subaltern other can and cannot speak (for the latter position, see Spivak 1988a, and for the former, Spivak 1994). Similar negotiations are seen in arguments that French feminism cannot be assumed to speak to multiple, transnational contexts, while it also cannot be assumed that it does not (Spivak 1988b and 1993a), and similarly, see Spivak 1983 and 1993b for a renegotiation of her response to the depiction of woman as the name of the truth that there is no truth.

References

Abraham, Nicholas, and Torok, Maria. 1984. "A Poetics of Psychoanalysis: 'The Lost Object—Me.'" *SubStance* 43:3–18.

Alcoff, Linda. 1988. "Cultural Feminism versus Post-structuralism: The Identity Crisis in Feminist Theory." *Signs* 13 (3): 405–37.

Al-Hibri, Azizah Y. 1999. "Is Western Patriarchal Feminism Good for Third World/Minority Women?" In Okin 1999, 41–46.

Armour, Ellen. 1999. *Deconstruction, Feminist Theology, and the Problem of Difference*. Chicago: University of Chicago Press.

Austin, John. 1962. *How to Do Things with Words*. Oxford: Clarendon.

Balkin, J. M. 1990. "Tradition, Betrayal, and the Politics of Deconstruction." *Cardozo Law Review* 11 (5–6) (Special Issue: Deconstruction and the Possibility of Justice): 1613–30.

Barnes, Hazel E. 2000. "Philosophy and Gender: A First-Person View." In *Resistance, Flight, Creation: Feminist Enactments of French Philosophy*, ed. Dorothea Olkowski, 25–39. Ithaca, N.Y.: Cornell University Press.

Bauer, Joanne R., and Bell, Daniel A., eds. 1999. *The East Asian Challenge for Human Rights*. Cambridge: Cambridge University Press.

Beauvoir, Simone de. 1966. "Must We Burn Sade?" Trans. Annette Michelson. In *The Marquis de Sade. An Essay by Simone de Beauvoir with Selections from His Writings*, ed. Paul Dinnage, 7–62. New York: Grove Press.

——. 1988. *The Second Sex*. Trans. H. M Parshley. London: Picador.

Bergoffen, Debra B. 1997. *The Philosophy of Simone de Beauvoir: Gendered Phenomenologies, Erotic Generosities*. Albany: State University of New York Press.

Bhabha, Homi K. 1994. *The Location of Culture*. London: Routledge.

——. 1999. "Liberalism's Sacred Cow." In Okin 1999, 79–84.

Bono, Paolo, and Sandra Kemp, eds. 1991. *Italian Feminist Thought: A Reader*. Oxford: Basil Blackwell.

Brown, Wendy. 1995. *States of Injury: Power and Freedom in Late Modernity*. Princeton: Princeton University Press.

——. 1997. "The Impossibility of Women's Studies." *differences—a journal of feminist cultural studies* 9 (3): 79–101.

Busia, Abena P. A., and Stanlie M. James, eds. 1993. *Theorizing Black Feminisms*. New York: Routledge.

Butler, Judith. 1993. *Bodies That Matter: On the Discursive Limits of "Sex."* New York: Routledge.

——. 1997. *Excitable Speech: A Politics of the Performative*. New York: Routledge.

——. 1998. "Reply to Robert Gooding-Williams." *Constellations* 5 (1): 42–47.

Butler, Judith, and Drucilla Cornell, with Pheng Cheah, and Elizabeth Grosz. 1998. "The Future of Sexual Difference: An Interview with Judith Butler and

Drucilla Cornell." *diacritics: a review of contemporary criticism* 28 (1 spring): 19–42.

Caputo, John D. 1997. *The Prayers and Tears of Jacques Derrida.* Bloomington: Indiana University Press.

———. 2000. *More Radical Hermeneutics.* Bloomington: Indiana University Press.

Chanter, Tina. 1995. *Ethics of Eros: Irigaray's Rewriting of the Philosophers.* New York: Routledge.

Cheah, Pheng, and Elizabeth Grosz. 1998. "Of Being-Two: Introduction." *diacritics: a review of contemporary criticism* 28 (1 spring): 3–18.

Chesterman, John, and Brian Galligan, eds. 1999. *Defining Australian Citizenship: Selected Documents.* Melbourne: Melbourne University Press.

Collins, Margery, and Christine Pierce. 1976. "Holes and Slime: Sexism in Sartre's Psychoanalysis." In *Women and Philosophy: Toward a Theory of Liberation,* ed. Carol C. Gould and Marx W. Wartofsky, 112–27. New York: Perigree.

Collins, Patricia Hill. 1990. *Black Feminist Thought: Knowledge, Consciousness, and the Politics of Empowerment.* New York: Routledge.

Cornell, Drucilla. 1991. *Beyond Accommodation: Ethical Feminism, Deconstruction, and the Law.* New York: Routledge.

———. 1992a. "Gender, Sex, and Equivalent Rights." In *Feminists Theorize the Political,* ed. Judith Butler and Joan W. Scott, 280–96. New York: Routledge.

———. 1992b. *The Philosophy of the Limit.* New York: Routledge.

———. 1995. *The Imaginary Domain: Abortion, Pornography, and Sexual Difference.* New York: Routledge.

———. 1998. *At the Heart of Freedom: Feminism, Sex, and Equality.* Princeton: Princeton University Press.

Derrida, Jacques. 1978a. "Cogito and the History of Madness." In *Writing and Difference,* trans. Allan Bass, 31–63. Chicago: University of Chicago Press.

———. 1978b. "Violence and Metaphysics: An Essay on the Thought of Emmanuel Lévinas." In *Writing and Difference,* trans. Allan Bass, 79–153. Chicago: University of Chicago Press.

———. 1985. *The Ear of the Other: Otobiography, Transference, Translation.* Trans. Peggy Kamuf. New York: Schocken Books.

———. 1986a. "Declarations of Independence." Trans. Tom Keenan and Tom Pepper. *New Political Science* 15 (summer): 1–15.

———. 1986b. *"Fors:* The Anglish Words of Nicolas Abraham and Maria Torok." Trans. Barbara Johnson. In *The Wolfman's Magic Word: A Cryptonomy,* xi–xlviii. Minneapolis: University of Minnesota Press.

———. 1988. "The Politics of Friendship." Trans. Gabriel Motzkin. *Journal of Philosophy* 85 (11): 632–44.

———. 1989. *Memoires for Paul de Man.* Trans. Cecile Lindsay, Jonathan Culler, Eduardo Cadava, and Peggy Kamuf. New York: Columbia University Press.

———. 1991. "'Eating Well,' or the Calculation of the Subject: An Interview with Jacques Derrida." Trans. Peter Connor and Avital Ronell. In *Who Comes after the Subject?* ed. Eduardo Cadava, Peter Connor, and Jean-Luc Nancy, 96–119. New York: Routledge.

———. 1992. "Force of Law." Trans. Mary Quaintance. In *Deconstruction and the Possibility of Justice,* ed. Drucilla Cornell, Mark Rosenfeld, and David Gray Carlson, 3–67. New York: Routledge.

———. 1994. *Specters of Marx: The State of the Debt, the Work of Mourning, and the New International.* Trans. Peggy Kamuf. New York: Routledge.

———. 1995a. "Istrice 2: Ick bünn all hier." Trans. Peggy Kamuf. In *Points . . . Interviews, 1974–1995,* ed. Elisabeth Weber, 300–326. Stanford: Stanford University Press.

———. 1995b. *On the Name.* Trans. Thomas Dutoit. Stanford: Stanford University Press.

———. 1995c. "<There is no *One* Narcissism> (Autobiophotographies)." Trans. Peggy Kamuf. In *Points . . . Interviews, 1974–1995,* ed. Elisabeth Weber, 196–215. Stanford: Stanford University Press.

———. 1997a. *Adieu: à Emmanuel Lévinas.* Paris: Galilée.

———. 1997b. *Cosmopolites de tous les pays, encore un effort!* Paris: Galilée.

———. 1997c. "Pas d'hospitalité." In *De l'hospitalité: Anne Dufourmantelle invite Jacques Derrida à répondre,* 71–137. Paris: Calmann-Lévy.

———. 1997d. *The Politics of Friendship.* Trans. George Collins. London: Verso Books.

———. 1997e. "Question d'étranger, venue de l'étranger." In *De l'hospitalité: Anne Dufourmantelle invite Jacques Derrida à répondre,* 11–69. Paris: Calmann-Lévy.

———. 1998a. "Fidelité à plus d'un." *Cahiers Intersignes* 13 (Special Issue: "Idiomes, nationalités, deconstructions"): 221–65.

———. 1998b. *Monolinguism of the Other, or The Prosthesis of Origin.* Trans. Patrick Mensah. Stanford: Stanford University Press.

———. 1999a. *Adieu to Emmanuel Lévinas.* Trans. Pascale-Anne Brault and Michael Naas. Stanford: Stanford University Press.

———. 1999b. "Une hospitalité à l'infini." In *Manifeste pour l'hospitalité,* ed. Mohammed Seffahi, 97–120. Paris: Paroles d'aube.

———. 1999c. "Responsabilité et hospitalité." In *Manifeste pour l'hospitalité,* ed. Mohammed Seffahi, 121–24. Paris: Paroles d'aube.

———. 2000. *Of Hospitality: Anne Dufourmantelle Invites Jacques Derrida to Respond.* Trans. Rachel Bowlby. Stanford: Stanford University Press.

Derrida, Jacques, and Elisabeth Roudinesco. 2001. *De quoi demain . . . Dialogue.* Paris: Fayard et Galilée.

Deutscher, Penelope. 1997. *Yielding Gender: Feminism, Deconstruction, and the History of Philosophy.* New York: Routledge.

———. 2000. "Disappropriation, or, Listening with the Fourth Ear (Sarah Kofman and Luce Irigaray)." In *Resistance, Flight, Creation: Feminist Enactments of French Philosophy,* ed. Dorothea Olkowski, 155–78. Ithaca: Cornell University Press.

Diprose, Rosalyn. 1994. *The Bodies of Women: Ethics, Embodiment, and Sexual Difference.* London: Routledge.

Doane, Mary Ann. 1987. *The Desire to Desire.* Bloomington: Indiana University Press.

Dodson, Patrick. 2000. "Lingiari: Until the Chains Are Broken." In *Essays on Australian Reconciliation,* ed. Michelle Grattan, 264–74. Melbourne: Bookman Press.

DuBois, Ellen, Mary C. Dunlap, Carol J. Gilligan, Catharine A. MacKinnon, and Carrie J. Menkel-Meadow. 1985. "Feminist Discourse, Moral Values, and the Law—A Conversation. The 1984 James McCormick Mitchell Lecture." *Buffalo Law Review* 34 (1): 11–172.

Duchen, Claire. 1986. *Feminism in France: From May '68 to Mitterand.* London: Routledge and Kegan Paul.

———, ed. 1987. *French Connections: Voices from the Women's Movement in France.* London: Hutchinson.

Duroux, Françoise. 1992. "Des passions et de la compétence politique." *Cahiers du GRIF* 46 (Provenances de la pensée—Femmes/philosophie): 103–24.

Dworkin, Anthea, and Catharine MacKinnon. 1988. *Pornography and Civil Rights: A New Day for Women's Equality.* Minneapolis: Organizing Against Pornography.

Elam, Diane. 1994. *Feminism and Deconstruction: Ms. en abyme.* London: Routledge.

Fanon, Franz. 1970. *Black Skin, White Masks.* Trans. Charles Lam Markmann. London: Paladin.

Fermon, Nicole. 1998. "Women on the Global Market: Irigaray and the Democratic State." *diacritics: a review of contemporary criticism* 28 (1 spring): 120–37.

Feuerbach, Ludwig. 1957. *The Essence of Christianity.* Trans. G. Eliot. New York: Harper and Row.

Fraser, Nancy. 1997. "From Redistribution to Recognition? Dilemmas of Justice in a 'Postsocialist' Age." In *Justice Interruptus: Critical Reflections on the "Postsocialist" Condition,* 11–40. New York: Routledge.

Freeland, Cynthia. 1998. "On Irigaray on Aristotle." In *Feminist Interpretations of Aristotle,* ed. C. Freeland, 59–92. University Park: Pennsylvania State University Press.

Freud, Sigmund. 1914. "On Narcissism: An Introduction." In *The Standard Edition of the Complete Psychological Works of Sigmund Freud,* ed. and trans. James Strachey, 14:67–102. London: Hogarth.

———. 1917. "Mourning and Melancholia." In *The Standard Edition of the Complete Psychological Works of Sigmund Freud,* ed. and trans. James Strachey, 14:237–58. London: Hogarth.

Fuss, Diana. 1989. *Essentially Speaking: Feminism, Nature, and Difference.* New York: Routledge.

Gaita, Raymond. 2000. "Guilt, Shame, and Collective Responsibility." In *Essays on Australian Reconciliation,* ed. Michelle Grattan, 275–87. Melbourne: Bookman Press.

Gallop, Jane. 1988. *Thinking through the Body.* New York: Columbia University Press.

Gatens, Moira. 1991. *Feminism and Philosophy: Perspectives on Difference and Equality.* Bloomington: Indiana University Press.

———. 1996. *Imaginary Bodies: Ethics, Power, and Corporeality.* London: Routledge.

Gilligan, Carol. 1982. *In a Different Voice: Psychological Theory and Women's Development.* Cambridge: Harvard University Press.

Gilman, Sander L. 1999. "'Barbaric' Rituals?" In Okin 1999, 53–58.

Gooding-Williams, Robert. 1998. "Race, Multiculturalism, and Democracy." *Constellations* 5 (1): 18–41.

Grosz, Elizabeth. 1986. *Irigaray and the Divine.* Sydney: Local Consumption Publications.

———. 1989. *Sexual Subversions: Three French Feminists.* Sydney: Allen and Unwin.

———. 1990. "A Note on Essentialism and Difference." In *Feminist Knowledge: Critique and Construct,* ed. Sneja Gunew, 332–44. London: Routledge.

———. 1994a. "The Hetero and the Homo: The Sexual Ethics of Luce Irigaray." In *Engaging with Irigaray: Feminist Philosophy and Modern European Thought*, ed. Carolyn Burke, Naomi Schor, and Margaret Whitford, 335–50. New York: Columbia University Press.

———. 1994b. *Volatile Bodies: Toward a Corporeal Feminism*. Sydney: Allen and Unwin.

———. 1997. "Ontology and Equivocation: Derrida's Politics of Sexual Difference." In *Feminist Interpretations of Jacques Derrida*, ed. Nancy J. Holland, 73–102. University Park: Pennsylvania State University Press.

Honig, Bonnie. 1999. "My Culture Made Me Do It." In Okin 1999, 35–40.

hooks, bell. 1990. *Yearning: Race, Gender, and Cultural Politics*. Boston: South End Press.

———. 1992. *Black Looks: Race and Representation*. Boston: South End Press.

Huffer, Lynne. 1995. "*Luce et veritas*: Toward an Ethics of Performance." *Yale French Studies* 87 (Another Look, Another Woman): 20–39.

Huntington, Patricia J. 1998. *Ecstatic Subjects, Utopia, and Recognition: Kristeva, Heidegger, Irigaray*. Albany: State University of New York Press.

Irigaray, Luce. 1973. *Le langage des déments*. The Hague: Mouton.

———. 1977. *Ce sexe qui n'est pas un*. Paris: Minuit.

———. 1981. "And the One Doesn't Stir without the Other." Trans. Hélène Vivienne Wenzel. *Signs* 7 (1): 60–67.

———. 1983. "An Interview with Luce Irigaray. Interview with Kiki Amsberg and Aafke Steenhuis." Trans. Robert van Krieken. *Hecate* 9 (1/2): 192–202.

———. 1985a. *Parler n'est jamais neutre*. Paris: Minuit.

———. 1985b. *Speculum of the Other Woman*. Trans. Gillian C. Gill. Ithaca: Cornell University Press.

———. 1985c. *This Sex Which Is Not One*. Trans. Catherine Porter. Ithaca: Cornell University Press.

———. 1989a. "Is the Subject of Science Sexed?" Trans. Carol Mastrangelo Bové. In *Feminism and Science*, ed. Nancy Tuana, 56–68. Bloomington: Indiana University Press.

———. 1989b. *Le temps de la difference: Pour une révolution pacifique*. Paris: Librairie générale française.

———. 1990. *Sexes et genres à travers les langues: Éléments de communication sexuée*. Paris: Grasset.

———. 1991a. *Marine Lover—Of Friedrich Nietzsche*. Trans. Gillian C. Gill. New York: Columbia University Press.

———. 1991b. "Questions to Emmanuel Lévinas." Trans. Margaret Whitford. In *The Irigaray Reader*, ed. Margaret Whitford, 178–97. Oxford: Basil Blackwell.

———. 1993a. *An Ethics of Sexual Difference*. Trans. Carolyn Burke and Gillian C. Gill. Ithaca: Cornell University Press.

———. 1993b. *je, tu, nous: Toward a Culture of Difference*. Trans. Alison Martin. New York: Routledge.

———. 1993c. *Sexes and Genealogies*. Trans. Gillian C. Gill. New York: Columbia University Press.

———. 1994. *Thinking the Difference—For a Peaceful Revolution*. Trans. Karin Montin. New York: Routledge; London: Athlone Press.

———. 1995. "Femmes et hommes: Une identité relationelle différente." In *La place des femmes: Les enjeux de l'identité et de l'égalité au regard des sciences sociales*, ed.

220   *References*

Ephesia (Conseil scientifique: Mission de coordination de la 4ième conférence mondiale sur les femmes, septembre 1995), 137–42. Paris: La Découverte.

———. 1996a. *I Love to You: Sketch of a Possible Felicity in History*. Trans. Alison Martin. New York: Routledge.

———, ed. 1996b. *Le souffle des femmes*. Paris: Action catholique générale féminine.

———. 1997. *Être deux*. Paris: Grasset.

———. 1999. *Entre orient et occident*. Paris: Grasset.

———. 2000. *The Forgetting of Air*. Trans. Mary Beth Mader. Austin: University of Texas Press.

———. 2001. *To Be Two*. Trans. Monique M. Rhodes and Marco F. Cocito-Monoc. New York: Routledge.

———. 2002. *Between East and West: From Singularity to Community*. Trans. Stephen Pluhacek. New York: Columbia University Press.

Irigaray, Luce, et al., eds. 1987. *Le sexe linguistique, Langages 85*. Paris: Larousse.

Irigaray, Luce, with Elizabeth Hirsch, and Gary A. Olson. 1995. "Je—Luce Irigaray": A Meeting with Luce Irigaray." *Hypatia* 10 (2): 93–114.

Irigaray, Luce, with Raoul Mortley. 1991. "Luce Irigaray." In *French Philosophers in Conversation*, ed. Raoul Mortley, 63–78. London: Routledge.

Ivekovič, Rada. 1992. *Orients: Critique de la raison post-moderne*. Paris: Noël Blandin.

Jagose, Annamarie. 1994. *Lesbian Utopics*. New York: Routledge.

Joy, Morny. 1990. "Equality or Divinity—A False Dichotomy?" *Journal of Feminist Studies in Religion* 6 (1): 9–24.

Kirby, Vicki. 1997. *Telling Flesh: The Substance of the Corporeal*. New York: Routledge.

Kofman, Sarah. 1978. *Aberrations: Le devenir-femme d'Auguste Comte*. Paris: Aubier-Flammarion.

———. 1982. *Le respect des femmes*. Paris: Galilée.

———. 1985. *The Enigma of Woman: Woman in Freud's Writings*. Trans. Catherine Porter. Ithaca: Cornell University Press.

Krell, David Farrell. 1990. "Response to the Panel on Deconstruction, Ethics, and the Law." *Cardozo Law Review* 11 (5–6) (Special Issue: Deconstruction and the Possibility of Justice): 1723–26.

Kymlicka, Will. 1999. "Liberal Complacencies." In Okin 1999, 31–34.

Lacan, Jacques. 1949. "Cure psychanalytique à l'aide de la poupée fleur." *Revue française de la psychanalyse* 4.

———. 1953. "Some Reflections on the Ego." *International Journal of Psychoanalysis* 34:11–16.

———. 1977. *Ecrits—A Selection*. Trans. Alan Sheridan. London: Tavistock.

———. 1988. *The Seminar of Jacques Lacan Book 1: Freud's Papers on Technique*. Cambridge: Cambridge University Press.

Lacey, Nicola. 1996. "Normative Reconstruction in Socio-Legal Theory." *Social and Legal Studies* 5:131–57.

———. 1998. *Unspeakable Subjects: Feminist Essays in Legal and Social Theory*. Oxford: Hart.

Langlois, Anthony J. 1999. "Who Defines Justice? The Philosophical Issues Raised by Asian Interpretations of Human Rights." Ph.D. diss., Department of International Relations, Research School of Social Sciences, Australian National University, Canberra.

Langton, Rae. 1993. "Speech Acts and Unspeakable Acts." *Philosophy and Public Affairs* 22 (4): 293–330.

Le Doeuff, Michèle. 1979. "Operative Philosophy: Simone de Beauvoir and Existentialism." *Ideology and Consciousness* 6 (autumn): 47–58.

——. 1991. *Hipparchia's Choice: An Essay concerning Women, Philosophy, etc.* Trans. Trista Selous. Oxford: Blackwell.

——. 1992. "Gens de science: essai sur le déni de mixité." *Nouvelles questions féministes* 13 (1): 5–37.

——. 1993a. "Le chromosome du crime: à propos de XY." In *Féminismes au présent (Futur antérieur supplément),* ed. M. Riot-Sarcey, 173–83. Paris: L'Harmattan.

——. 1993b. "Harsh Times." *New Left Review* 199 (May–June): 127–39.

——. 1995. Problèmes d'investiture (De la parité etc). *Nouvelles questions féministes* 16 (2): 5–80.

——. 1998. *Le sexe du savoir.* Paris: Aubier.

——. 2000a. "Feminism Is Back in France—Or Is It?" *Hypatia: A Journal of Feminist Philosophy* 15 (4): 243–55.

——. 2000b. "Interview." *Hypatia: A Journal of Feminist Philosophy* 15 (4): 236–42.

Lévinas, Emmanuel. 1969. *Totality and Infinity: An Essay on Exteriority.* Trans. Alphonso Lingis. Pittsburgh: Duquesne University Press.

——. 1987. *Time and the Other and Additional Essays.* Trans. Richard A. Cohen. Pittsburgh: Duquesne University Press.

Lingis, Alphonso. 1985. *Libido: The French Existential Theories.* Bloomington: Indiana University Press.

Littleton, Christine. 1991. "Reconstructing Sexual Equality." In *Feminist Legal Theory,* ed. R. Kennedy and K. T. Bartlett, 35–56. Boulder, Colo.: Westview.

Lloyd, Genevieve. 1984. *The Man of Reason: "Male" and "Female" in Western Philosophy.* London: Methuen.

——. 2000. "No-One's Land: Australia and the Philosophical Imagination." *Hypatia* 15 (2): 26–39.

Lorraine, Tamsin. 1999. *Irigaray and Deleuze: Experiments in Visceral Philosophy.* Ithaca: Cornell University Press.

Lugones, Maria C., and Elizabeth V. Spelman. 1990. "Have We Got a Theory for You: Feminist Theory, Cultural Imperialism, and the Demand for the Women's Voice." In *Hypatia Reborn: Essays in Feminist Philosophy,* ed. A. Y. Al-Hibri and E. V. Spelman, 18–31. Bloomington: Indiana University Press.

Lundgren-Gothlin, Eva. 1996. *Sex and Existence: Simone de Beauvoir's The Second Sex.* London: Athlone.

Mackenzie, Catriona. 1986. "Simone de Beauvoir: Philosophy and/or the Female Body." In *Feminist Challenges: Social and Political Theory,* ed. C. Pateman and E. Gross, 144–56. Sydney: Allen and Unwin.

Marks, Elaine, and Isabelle de Courtivron, eds. 1981. *New French Feminisms.* Brighton: Harvester.

Merleau-Ponty, Maurice. 1962. *Phenomenology of Perception.* Trans. Colin Smith. London: Routledge and Kegan Paul.

——. 1964. *The Primacy of Perception.* Trans. James M. Edie, John Wild, William Cobb, Carleton Dallery, Nancy Metzel, and John Flodstrom. Evanston: Northwestern University Press.

Milan Women's Bookstore Collective. 1990. *Sexual Difference: A Theory of Social-Symbolic Practice.* Bloomington: Indiana University Press.

Mills, Charles. 1997. *The Racial Contract.* Ithaca: Cornell University Press.

Mohamad, Mahathir. 1970. *The Malay Dilemma*. Singapore: Donald Moore for Asia Pacific Press.

Mohanty, Chandra Talpade, ed. 1991. *Third World Women and the Politics of Feminism*. Bloomington: Indiana University Press.

Montaigne, Michel de. 1958. "On Friendship." In *Essays*, trans. John Michael Cohen, 91–105. Harmondsworth: Penguin.

Mortensen, Ellen. 1994. *The Feminine and Nihilism: Luce Irigaray, Nietzsche, and Heidegger*. Oslo: Scandinavian University Press.

Newspoll; Saulwick, Irving; Muller, Denis; and Mackay, Hugh. 2000. "Public Opinion on Reconciliation: Snap Shot, Close Focus, Long Lens." In *Essays on Australian Reconciliation*, ed. M. Grattan, 33–52. Melbourne: Bookman Press.

Niedzwiecki, Patricia. 1994. *Au féminin! Code de féminisation à l'usage de la francophonie*. Paris: Nizet.

Offen, Karen. 2000. *European Feminisms, 1700–1950: A Political History*. Stanford: Stanford University Press.

Okin, Susan Moller, with respondents. 1999. *Is Multiculturalism Bad for Women?* Princeton: Princeton University Press.

Oliver, Kelly. 1995. *Womanizing Nietzsche: Philosophy's Relation to "the Feminine."* New York: Routledge.

——. 2001. *Witnessing: Beyond Recognition*. Minneapolis: University of Minnesota Press.

Olkowski, Dorothea. 1999. *Gilles Deleuze and the Ruin of Representation*. Berkeley: University of California Press.

Pagels, Elaine. 1988. *Adam, Eve, and the Serpent*. New York: Vintage.

Parekh, Bhikhu. 1999. "A Varied Moral World." In Okin 1999, 69–78.

Pateman, Carole. 1988. *The Sexual Contract*. Cambridge: Polity Press.

Phelan, Peggy. 1993. *Unmarked: The Politics of Performance*. New York: Routledge.

Povinelli, Elizabeth. 1996. "Of Pleasure and Property: Sexuality and Sovereignty in Aboriginal Australia." In *Thinking through the Body of the Law*, ed. Pheng Cheah, David Fraser, and Judith Grbich, 80–101. Sydney: Allen and Unwin.

Reconciliation Sheet 10 (Native Title) at *www.austlii.edu.au/au/special/rsjproject/rsjlibrary/car/infosheets/Inf_sht10.html*

Rose, Jacqueline. 1986. *Sexuality in the Field of Vision*. London: Verso.

Sandford, Stella. 1998. "Writing as a Man: *Lévinas* and the Phenomenology of Eros." *Radical Philosophy* 87 (Jan./Feb.): 6–17.

Sartre, Jean-Paul. 1958. *Being and Nothingness: A Phenomenological Essay of Ontology*. Trans. Hazel E. Barnes. London: Methuen.

Schor, Naomi. 1994. "This Essentialism Which Is Not One: Coming to Grips with Irigaray." In *Engaging with Irigaray: Feminist Philosophy and Modern European Thought*, ed. Carolyn Burke, Naomi Schor, and Margaret Whitford, 57–78. New York: Columbia University Press.

Schultz, Vicki. 1992. "Women 'before' the Law: Judicial Stories about Women, Work, and Sex Segregation on the Job." In *Feminists Theorize the Political*, ed. Judith Butler and Joan W. Scott, 297–340. New York: Routledge.

Schwab, Gail. 1996. "Women and the Law in Irigarayan Theory." *Metaphilosophy* 27 (Jan./April): 146–77.

——. 1998. "The French Connection: Luce Irigaray and International Research on Language and Gender." In *Untying the Tongue*, ed. L. Longmire and L. Merrill, 13–24. Westport, Conn.: Greenwood.

Schwartzer, Alice. 1984. *Simone de Beauvoir Today: Conversations, 1972–1982.* London: Chatto.

Scott, Joan W. 1996. *Only Paradoxes to Offer: French Feminists and the Rights of Man.* Cambridge: Harvard University Press.

Spelman, Elizabeth. 1988. *Inessential Woman: Problems of Exclusion in Feminist Thought.* Boston: Beacon Press.

Spivak, Gayatri Chakravorty. 1983. "Displacement and the Discourse of Woman." In *Displacement: Derrida and After,* ed. Mark Krupnick, 169–95. Bloomington: Indiana University Press.

———. 1988a. "Can the Subaltern Speak?" In *Marxism and the Interpretation of Culture,* ed. Cary Nelson and Larry Grossberg, 271–313. Urbana: University of Illinois Press.

———. 1988b. "French Feminism in an International Frame." In *In Other Worlds: Essays in Cultural Politics,* 134–53. New York: Routledge.

———. 1993a. "Feminism and Deconstruction, Again: Negotiations." In *Outside in the Teaching Machine,* 121–40. New York: Routledge.

———. 1993b. "French Feminism Revisited." In *Outside in the Teaching Machine,* 141–72. New York: Routledge.

———. 1994. "Responsibility." *boundary 2* 21 (3): 19–64.

———. 1999. *A Critique of Postcolonial Reason: Toward a History of the Vanishing Present.* Cambridge: Harvard University Press.

Tamir, Yael. 1999. "Siding with the Underdogs." In Okin 1999, 47–52.

Taylor, Charles. 1975. *Hegel.* Cambridge: Cambridge University Press.

———, with respondents. 1991. *The Ethics of Authenticity,* ed. Amy Gutmann. Cambridge: Harvard University Press.

———. 1994. "The Politics of Recognition." In *Multiculturalism: Examining the Politics of Recognition,* by Charles Taylor, ed. Amy Gutmann, 75–85. Princeton: Princeton University Press.

Teik, Khoo Boo. 1995. *Paradoxes of Mahathirism: Intellectual Biography of Mahathir Mohamad.* Kuala Lumpur: Oxford University Press.

Tully, James. 1995. *Strange Multiplicities: Constitutionalism in an Age of Diversity.* Cambridge: Cambridge University Press.

Vasseleu, Cathryn. 1991. "The Face before the Mirror Phase." *Hypatia: A Journal of Feminist Philosophy* 6 (3): 140–55.

———. 1998. *Textures of Light: Vision and Touch in Irigaray, Lévinas, and Merleau-Ponty.* London: Routledge.

Walker, Michelle Boulous. 1998. *Philosophy and the Maternal Body: Reading Silence.* London: Routledge.

Webber, Jeremy. 2000. "Beyond Regret: Mabo's Implication for Australian Constitutionalism." In *Political Theory and the Rights of Indigenous Peoples,* ed. Duncan Ivison, Paul Patton, and Will Sanders, 60–88. Cambridge: Cambridge University Press.

Weinbaum, Alys Eve. 1994. "Marx, Irigaray, and the Politics of Representation." *differences—a journal of feminist cultural studies* 6 (1): 98–128.

Weiss, Gail. 1999. *Body Images: Embodiment as Intercorporeality.* New York: Routledge.

Whitford, Margaret. 1982. *Merleau-Ponty's Critique of Sartre's Philosophy.* Lexington, Ky.: French Forum.

———. 1991a. Introduction. In *The Irigaray Reader,* ed. Margaret Whitford, 1–15. Oxford: Basil Blackwell.

———. 1991b. *Luce Irigaray—Philosophy in the Feminine.* London: Routledge.

———. 1994. "Irigaray, Utopia, and the Death Drive." In *Engaging with Irigaray: Feminist Philosophy and Modern European Thought,* ed. Carolyn Burke, Naomi Schor, and Margaret Whitford, 379–400. New York: Columbia University Press.

Wolf, Susan. 1994. "Comment." In *Multiculturalism: Examining the Politics of Recognition,* by Charles Taylor, ed. Amy Gutmann, 75–85. Princeton: Princeton University Press.

Young, Iris Marion. 1990. *Throwing like a Girl and Other Essays in Feminist Philosophy and Social Theory.* Bloomington: Indiana University Press.

———. 2000. *Inclusion and Democracy.* Oxford: Oxford University Press.

Ziarek, Ewa Płonowska. 2001. *An Ethics of Dissensus: Postmodernity, Feminism, and the Politics of Radical Democracy.* Stanford: Stanford University Press.

Index

226   *Index*